W9-BNE-061

SAY IT RIGHT!

*the text of this book is printed
on 100% recycled paper*

ABOUT THE AUTHOR

Harry Shaw is well known as an editor, writer, lecturer, and teacher. For a number of years he was director of the Workshops in Composition at New York University and teacher of classes in advanced writing at Columbia, at both of which institutions he has done graduate work. He has worked with large groups of writers in the Washington Square Writing Center at NYU and has been a lecturer in writers' conferences at Indiana University and the University of Utah and lecturer in, and director of, the Writers' Conference in the Rocky Mountains sponsored by the University of Colorado. In 1969, Mr. Shaw was awarded the honorary degree of Doctor of Letters by Davidson College, his alma mater.

He has been managing editor and editorial director of *Look*, editor at Harper and Brothers, senior editor and vice-president of E. P. Dutton and Co., editor-in-chief of Henry Holt & Co., and director of publications for Barnes & Noble, Inc.; he is now an editor at W. W. Norton & Co., Inc. He has contributed widely to many popular and scholarly national magazines and is the author or co-author of a number of books in the fields of English composition and literature, among them *Spell It Right!* and *Punctuate It Right!*, Barnes & Noble publications.

EVERYDAY HANDBOOKS

Say It Right!

Harry Shaw

BARNES & NOBLE BOOKS

A DIVISION OF HARPER & ROW, PUBLISHERS

New York, Evanston, San Francisco, London

SAY IT RIGHT! Copyright © 1972 by Harry Shaw. All rights reserved. Printed in the United States of America. No part of this book may be used or reproduced in any manner without written permission except in the case of brief quotations embodied in critical articles and reviews. For information address Harper & Row, Publishers, Inc., 10 East 53rd Street, New York, N.Y. 10022. Published simultaneously in Canada by Fitzhenry & Whiteside Limited, Toronto.

First BARNES & NOBLE BOOKS edition published 1972.

LIBRARY OF CONGRESS CATALOG CARD NUMBER: 79–160788

STANDARD BOOK NUMBER: 06–463317–9

CONTENTS

FOREWORD

The way you talk tells more about you than any other activity of your life. What you say — and how you say it — are more revealing of your intelligence, personality, and character than the ways you dress, eat, walk, read, or make your living. Knowing how to read and write are significant accomplishments for everyone, but neither is an *essential* part of anyone's actual existence. Communicating with others through some sort of speech signals *is* essential.

Everyone reading this book presumably can write, obviously can read, and certainly can communicate with others. Most people spend many school years learning to read and write, but few of us have ever paid much attention to learning how to talk. In infancy we learned to speak, have talked ever since, and now assume that talking is as "simple" and as "natural" as breathing. It isn't.

More time, opportunities, money, and friendships are lost through careless, slovenly, inaccurate speech than through any other activity of people's lives. Because no one can speak perfectly (any more than he can read or write perfectly), this condition will persist. And yet everyone can learn to speak with greater confidence, fewer errors, and more genuine communication if he will only study his speech habits and give the problem of talking with others the attention it fully deserves.

This book is designed to help you get rid of the faulty speech habits you may have and to confirm and strengthen you in the good ones. Improving talk is a lifetime occupation, but here are "ten commandments" that will serve as constant, never failing guides in learning to "say it right."

1. *Pronounce words carefully.*
   More errors, inaccuracies, and misunderstandings are caused by carelessness and haste than by ignorance or

inadequate vocabulary. Give speech the care and attention it deserves. Words are priceless; treat them that way.

2. *Speak to be heard.*

   If something is worth saying, it deserves to be heard. Don't shout, but don't mumble. Say, don't slur.

3. *Look alive.*

   If you show interest in what you're saying and talk in lively, vigorous tones, animation will invigorate your talk and stimulate your hearers.

4. *Take your time.*

   Your tongue is slower than your mind, but it's quicker than your listener's ear. Nearly everyone speaks rapidly, drops syllables, slurs words, and runs thoughts together in headlong haste. Slow down.

5. *Learn to listen.*

   Talk should be a two-way street. It is not only courteous to listen to others; learning to listen is the most effective means known to man for gathering facts, acquiring ideas — and improving speech. How did you learn to talk in the first place? Put your ears on stems.

6. *Vary your approach.*

   The sole requirement of effective speech is that it should communicate. The tone of your voice and your choice and use of words should vary from situation to situation, from person to person. At times, your speech should be racy and pungent; at other times, deliberate and formal. Talk should be appropriate. Shift gears.

7. *Be concise.*

   Most statements of any kind are wordy. All of us repeat an idea in identical or similar words — and then say it again. Talk should not be cryptic and mysteriously abrupt, but it should be economical. Make it snappy!

8. *Be specific.*

   Much of our speech is indefinite, not clearly expressed, uncertain in meaning. Even when we have a fairly good idea of what we wish to say, we don't seek out those exact and concrete words that would convey what we have in mind. Try to use words that have precise meaning. Don't be vague.

9. *Be original.*

It's impossible for anyone to conceive of a wholly new idea or to express an old one in fresh, original diction. And yet the greatest single error in "saying it right" is the use of trite, wornout expressions that have lost their first vigor, picturesqueness, and appeal. Avoid clichés. Don't be a rubber stamp.

10. *Have something to say.*

With rare exceptions, people tend to talk more—and say less—than they should. After all, speech is only the faculty or power of speaking. The ability to talk is one thing; thoughts and emotions are another. Spinoza once wrote that mankind would be happier if the power in men to be silent were the same as that to speak; that "men govern nothing with more difficulty than their tongues." It was a wise person who remarked at a meeting that it was better for him to remain silent and be thought a fool than to speak and remove all possible doubt. Think first, talk second.

This book will teach you how to keep these "ten commandments." They are all within the capacity of anyone free from major speech defects. If you can keep any one of these "commandments," you have taken a long step toward improvement. If you can keep any five of them, you are an above-average speaker. But few can keep them all—people have difficulty following even *the* Ten Commandments.

PART ONE
YOU AND THE WAY YOU TALK

A word is the skin of a living thought.
Oliver Wendell Holmes

Good nature is more agreeable in conversation than wit and gives a certain air to the countenance which is more amiable than beauty.
Joseph Addison

The greatest thing a human soul ever does in this world is to see something and tell what it saw in a plain way. Hundreds of people can talk for one who can think.
John Ruskin

1 THE IMPORTANCE OF SPEECH

> Speech is civilization itself. The word,
> even the most contradictory word, pre-
> serves contact — it is silence which iso-
> lates.
>
> *Thomas Mann*

Many changes are going on in American society that tend
to make the life of each of us more and more impersonal.
Computers and other machines now perform work that once
was done by people. From birth to death, we are assigned
numbers that try to transform us into cogs in a machine.
Throughout the country, television and radio use the same
programs and commercial messages. People tend to dress
alike, eat alike, often even think alike. But in one activity, at
least, people differ: they rarely *speak* alike.

Millions of other people may share our ideas, but the words
we use and the way we say them differ in many ways. The
speech habits of everyone have been formed by individual
influences: family, locale, friends, acquaintances, schooling,
travel, housing, and occupation. As will be pointed out later
in this book, each of us has his own dialect: the choice, use,
and pronunciation of words called an *idiolect*. Individuality in
speech has been preserved more than in any other activity of
our lives solely because speech is a more integral and more

individual aspect of our outward personalities than any other.

Many scholars have argued that speech is the characteristic of man that most clearly and powerfully distinguishes him from other animals. Other scholars feel that not speech alone but language in general (which includes writing) should bear this distinction. Still others have insisted that the ability to communicate, rather than solely language or speech, is man's most distinguishing characteristic.

A good case can be made for speech, however, as man's clearest distinction among hominids and all mammals. Actually, both people and animals can and do communicate in nonverbal ways. Apparently, animals issue and receive messages: bees send instructions for locating nectar, dogs bark differently at friends and strangers, birds emit warnings when a cat or other marauder appears. With people, gestures and facial expressions communicate ideas and states of mind even when no words are spoken. Music can also communicate feelings and emotions without words. Even smoke signals convey thoughts.

Almost everyone would agree, however, that nonverbal methods of communication are inadequate makeshifts in comparison with language itself.

Further, although the power of the written word cannot be denied, it should be noted that speech began thousands of years before the invention of writing. Even after the introduction of writing into the life of man — an event that occurred some 3,000 years before the Christian era — many of the world's most influential thinkers, prophets, and soldiers continued to use speech, and only speech, for expressing their ideas. The teachings of Buddha (ca. 566 – 480 B.C.) became the basis of a major religion, although the founder himself presumably wrote not a word. A century or so after Buddha, Socrates became one of the world's greatest philosophers, entirely through conversation. The personality and ideas of Jesus Christ have shaped the Western world for 2,000 years, but so far as is known he left no written word.

The speeches and conversations of other individuals have affected history as much as — or more than — their writings. Here is a brief list of notable speakers who in one way or another have affected the tides of history: Aristotle, Edmund

Burke, John Calvin, Sir Winston Churchill, Cicero, Henry Clay, Confucius, Demosthenes, Lloyd George, Alexander Hamilton, Patrick Henry, Adolf Hitler, Thomas Jefferson, Abraham Lincoln, Martin Luther, Benito Mussolini, Thomas Paine, Franklin D. Roosevelt, Theodore Roosevelt, Daniel Webster, and Woodrow Wilson. Speech has made history and presumably will continue to do so.

Well and good, you say. But what has great speech to do with me? Simply this: the destiny of the human family will depend on the ability of each of us to speak well: to communicate with all the people with whom we come in contact. The great problems of the world will continue to be confronted by the speech of individuals: war and peace, international understanding, poverty, pollution, racism, population, individual freedom, and many others. We may think that we are remote from such matters, but we are not. As John Donne wrote:

> No man is an island, entire of itself; every man is a piece of the continent, a part of the main. If a clod be washed away by the sea, Europe is the less, as well as if a promontory were, as well as if a manor of thy friends or of thine own were. Any man's death diminishes me, because I am involved in mankind; and therefore never send to know for whom the bell tolls. It tolls for thee.

In *The Miracle Worker*, a play based on the life of Helen Keller, the little blind and deaf girl's mother asks the child's teacher what is to be taught first. "Language, I hope," replies the teacher. "Language is to the mind more than light is to the eye. She has to learn that everything has its name, that words can be her eyes to everything in the world outside her. What is she without words? With them she can think, have ideas, speak, be reached. There is not a thought or a fact in the world that can't be hers." Later in the play, the teacher remarks that, without language, Helen remains in a dungeon. "With it," she says, "we are all kinfolk; at least we can *talk*." Helen Keller did indeed discover language; her speech, impeded as it was, made a glorious contribution to world history.

What we say or how we say that something is not likely to affect so profoundly the lives of others as did the talks and conversation of Miss Keller, but our speech is important for many reasons.

Many of the encounters in our lives that really matter are person-to-person, often face-to-face. To others, your speech is *you;* what you say and how you say it sometimes represents all they know about you. Your thoughts may be exciting and unusual, but if you mumble or ramble or use substandard words and expressions you may fail to impress your listeners. Conversely, many a person has gotten away with thin and unimaginative talk because he has learned to speak with vitality, clarity, and conciseness. Your friendliness and warmth may be undetected by your hearer if you speak self-consciously, ungrammatically, or wordily: "As a man speaks, so is he" is a saying containing much truth.

The person who speaks at a public meeting sometimes depends for success less upon his or her ideas than upon the personal impression created on an audience. The salesman who comes to your door depends at least as much upon his speech as his wares. Few applicants for jobs are hired or rejected until they have had a personal interview, during which their speech plays an important role.

Better speech results in increased ability to make friends.

Better speech enables you to take a place of leadership in your office, your home, your club, your community.

Better speech is essential for newscasters, announcers, actors, politicians, clergymen, teachers, salesmen, and lawyers; and for everyone's own self-expression and personal growth.

One of the most severe of all prison punishments is solitary confinement.

2 SPEECH AND WRITING

"You should say what you mean," said
the March Hare to Alice in Wonderland.

"I do," Alice hastily replied; *"at least—I
mean what I say—that's the same thing,
you know."*

"Not the same thing a bit!" said the Mad
Hatter. *"Why, you might just as well say
'I see what I eat' is the same thing as 'I
eat what I see!'"*

Lewis Carroll

Speaking and writing share a common goal, *communication*. The same principles apply whether we are engaged in conversation, making a short speech to a group, writing a letter to a newspaper editor, or preparing a report for a club committee.

Like effective writing, effective speech has *organization* of some sort. Both speaker and writer must provide a clear sense of direction. Like effective writing, effective speaking must have a central *purpose*. Aimless writing and speaking are alike boring, time-consuming, and wasteful. Like effective writing, effective speech has *focus*. Both forms of communication should take clear aim on a central issue and not scatter their shots. An effective speaker, like an effective writer, knows how to *use* language; he can express himself interestingly and correctly. Both can sum up an important idea in a memorable sentence. Both can nurse and nudge an abstract idea into a specific image.

Despite these parallels, speaking and writing differ in several respects. A speech has been called "an essay on its hind legs," but effective speaking is far more than a live oral rendering of a written composition. Brief discussion of a few of the differences between speaking and writing should be helpful in learning to "say it right."

We are normally more relaxed in talking than writing, less worried about errors and rules. But that speaking is more spontaneous than writing, that it comes more easily and naturally, does not mean that speech has no requirements, no aims, no goals. Actually, the circumstances of speaking impose conditions that for some people are more difficult than those of writing.

As a speaker, your sentences are shorter—or should be—than many of those you might construct in writing. Language is normally more direct and much simpler in speech than in writing, a requirement that helps more persons than it hinders.

A reader and writer are usually separated, but in most instances a speaker and listener are thrown into close association. Face-to-face confrontation helps some speakers to be more natural and relaxed, whereas it makes others nervous and self-conscious. What is your situation? Do you feel more at home when talking with someone in person or over the telephone? Does the physical presence of another person, or other persons, aid or hinder you?

A reader is usually alone or in a quiet room free from distractions. A listener, conversely, is normally surrounded by others and is sometimes distracted by them. Even when a listener is at home, following a speech over TV or radio, his mind tends to wander, and he cannot recapture what he has missed in the way that he can by rereading something written. Most people are more eye-minded than ear-minded. Something written can be read and then reread many times. A spoken message usually has only one hearing. The conversationalist (or speaker) who does not immediately gain the attention and interest of his listener has lost him forever. Also, a hearer cannot usually meditate upon something a speaker has said, because if he does he is certain to miss what follows.

Again, a speaker's voice, gestures, and use of his body are important considerations which affect oral communication but have no exact counterparts in writing. Such considerations can improve or impede oral communication and thus play a substantial role in all speaking situations.

A final critical difference between speaking and writing should be mentioned. You can revise and rewrite endlessly until your thoughts are clear, purposeful, well-organized, and effective. But you can't talk endlessly!

For most persons talking is more habitual, natural, informal, and relaxed than is most writing.

For almost everyone, speaking offers an excellent, almost ideal, opportunity for relaxation and self-expression.

But speaking of any kind has its requirements, which are no less real than those of writing.

Finding out what these requirements are and helping one to do something constructive about them is the sole purpose of this book.

3 THE ART OF CONVERSATION

Do you know that conversation is one of the greatest pleasures in life?

Somerset Maugham

The most universal kind of social activity, as well as the most important way of communicating with others, is conversation. A good conversationalist, one who has something interesting to say and who listens courteously and attentively, is welcome anywhere at any time. Lack of opportunity for exchange of talk with others can produce irritation, boredom, or even serious mental disorders. One of man's fundamental needs is to express himself to others.

If people are more frustrated today than ever before, if conversation is indeed a lost art, perhaps the reasons are that people are too hurried to talk *with* others and too often are engaged in the more passive pursuits of watching TV or listening to the radio. True conversation is a two-way street that cannot be passed through hurriedly and thoughtlessly.

A good and rewarding conversation—a genuine meeting of minds—has little or nothing to do with talkativeness. Chatter about such a subject as the weather is rarely good conversation, no matter how cleverly even well-chosen words may fly. Conversation becomes worthwhile, a stimulating pastime, when it represents an open, honest, thoughtful exchange of facts and opinions dealing with more than superficial subjects. Glibness may save one the trouble of clarifying or defending his position in a conversation, but it actually wastes the time of both speaker and listener.

Conversing with others comes naturally to some people, regardless of their formal education, fund of knowledge, or position in life. Such persons just naturally seem to like others, to be interested in them as people, and to be willing to listen to their points of view. These attitudes and abilities of born conversationalists provide clues for anyone wishing to become a better talker *with* (not *to*) others. Here are a few suggestions.

1. *Many a person has acquired a reputation as an excellent conversationalist primarily because he is a good listener.* Within the grasp of even the most unsure and unskilled speaker is this first requisite of a good conversationalist: he can be, or appear to be, truly interested in his partner and in what he is saying. In fact, the expression on one's face may show interest and anticipation (or the reverse) even before a conversation begins. The good conversationalist may or may not agree with what is being said, but he does not gaze away from his partner; he shows by attention and brief comments or questions that he is reacting in some way to what he is hearing. Additional comment on the invaluable techniques of listening is provided in the next chapter.

2. *Try to be straightforward and sincere but also courteous, tactful, and friendly.* A spirited discussion may be argumentative and even heated—a group of people will seldom wholly agree about any topic of real consequence—but one can state his opinion frankly and firmly without being rude and without hurting the feelings of others. Your partner's feelings can be as easily hurt as yours. If he starts a joke you have already heard, you can listen quietly or can tactfully sidetrack him; you don't have to say, "That's an old one. It stinks." If your partner makes a

misstatement, you can courteously point this out when
he finishes his statement; you don't have to interrupt
with "Can't you ever get your facts straight?" or "You've
got it all wrong" or "That's a lie" or "Only a fool believes
that." The most exciting and rewarding conversations
are those in which people express opposing points of
view, but talk can be even-tempered even when it is
argumentative.

3. *The best conversations are give-and-take affairs.*

Being a good listener is fundamental, but one should
also have something to say himself. An effective conversation resembles a game of tennis in that action
shifts from person to person. Two persons cannot play
the game of either tennis or conversation if one holds
the ball continuously. Be careful to do some attentive
listening *and* some thoughtful talking in every conversation. When one person does all the talking, what en-
sues is a *monologue* (even if this person is you). A genuine conversation is a *dialogue*, an exchange between
two or more persons.

4. *If your conversational partner is not an intimate friend
or member of your family, try to find out as much as you
tactfully can about him or her in the course of the conversation.*

For example, if you are left with a stranger at a party,
the guest of honor at a reception, or a visitor to your
office, try drawing him out rather than talking about
yourself. You probably will learn some highly interesting facts. Even if you don't, your companion will be
flattered by your interest (even if it is partly assumed)
and will remember you as a superb conversationalist.

5. *Try to keep informed about subjects of timely interest:
political affairs, current events, personalities in the news,
fashion trends, sports, art, music, and literature.*

Read as much as you can: a daily newspaper, books,
worthwhile magazines. Try to remember good stories
you hear or read, amusing or interesting incidents that
happen to you or your friends, funny or significant
events you see or read about. People who assume a

know-it-all attitude make poor conversationalists, but
so do emptyheaded ones who can talk about only what
they had for dinner.

6. *Study every conversation you have an opportunity to hear
or engage in.*

Analysis of conversations will indicate that the best
talkers are those with the largest fund of interesting
experiences and observations, or, better yet, the greatest
familiarity with subjects of most absorbing interest to
the people in the circle. You will also observe that the
most capable conversationalists do not talk constantly
but are capable of attentive listening.

7. *Practice conversation.*

Join in good talk whenever you can. Listen in on conversations when you have an opportunity to do so without being a pest or an eavesdropper. After listening to
a conversation on TV or radio, practice to yourself or
with a friend your own responses to questions raised on
topics developed.

8. *Even in informal conversations try to speak as clearly
and as effectively as you can.*

Try to avoid the major flaws in diction and pronunciation
treated in Parts Two and Three of this book. We owe it
to our conversational partners to be as alert, as informed, and as communicative as we possibly can.
Avoiding the pitfalls in choosing, using, and pronouncing words is much more than a negative effort toward
effective conversation.

4 LEARNING TO LISTEN WHILE LISTENING TO LEARN

It takes two to speak truth — one to speak and another to hear.

Henry David Thoreau

An adult spends at least half of his communication time in listening. That poor listeners are expensive and expendable employees is increasingly recognized in the business world. Indeed, many of our most important affairs depend on listening. What does a jury do? It listens — sometimes to millions of words of testimony — and then makes up its mind about the case on trial. The way one votes in an election depends to a large extent upon his ability (or inability) to listen. Listening situations and opportunities confront each of us many times every day. What else can and should one expect in a nation that has millions of television sets, more radios than bathtubs, and several million *new* telephone installations every year?

What has all this to do with learning to "say it right"? Simply this: profiting from listening opportunities and situations can rapidly and effectively increase one's speaking abilities.

For example, compared to reading, listening is often a faster and more efficient means of gathering information. If you need to learn something about a subject quickly, you can usually find an authority who will speak in terms you can understand. Further, if you don't understand something he says, you can ask a question and get immediate clarification, thus entering into the conversation and gaining added experience in both listening and speaking.

Again, writing that may seem difficult can often be understood and appreciated when it is spoken aloud. Much great literature — the plays of Shakespeare, for example — were written only to be heard. Reading aloud and listening to yourself will increase your ability to shape and pronounce words and to improve the quality of your speaking voice. Nearly everyone can find a friend to join in reading aloud. If you have access to a record player or other instrument that will reproduce the sounds of language, borrow or buy records and tapes that will bring alive our literary heritage. Matching your own delivery in speech with that of an accomplished actor or speaker can assist enormously in your efforts to improve speaking ability.

Good listening is one of the best of all ways for improving facility in language. This fact probably stems from childhood, when we learned to talk by listening to and imitating our elders. The principle remains, regardless of how old we are or how accomplished as speakers. We can and should learn to speak better by listening to speakers of all sorts — in face-to-face conversations, over the telephone, on television and radio, and in movies.

Unfortunately, most people have acquired harmful listening habits that thwart attempts in learning to listen while listening to learn. Honestly consider the following faulty listening habits. Do you recognize any of them in yourself? If you do, by trying to replace a bad habit with a good one you can improve your ability to speak more effectively.

1. *Premature dismissal of a subject as dull and uninteresting.*

   If a conversationalist's (or other speaker's) material seems boring, some of us use that impression as rationalization for not listening. We assume that if a speaker's material is not stimulating, he must have nothing to say that is worth hearing. Before we "tune out" we should recall that there are no uninteresting subjects, only uninterested persons. When one forms the habit of listening attentively, many previously dull subjects appear to take on new life. Have you never become friends with, or even fallen in love with, someone you once considered dull and uninteresting? Also, if a speaker and his material *are* unappealing, analyzing the reasons for this condition can help you to avoid them in your own speaking situations.

2. *Supersensitive listening.*

Some of us find it difficult to listen to anything that does not coincide with our own personal, private thoughts. Hearing statements that we do not like, we start planning a rebuttal and stop listening to what the speaker is saying. It's better to hear the speaker out and to make final judgments only when he has finished. One is not listening to a lecture when he is planning his counter-attack; one is not engaging in conversation when he has "tuned out" the speaker and "tuned in" his personal train of thought.

3. *Avoiding difficult explanations.*

Many listeners give up quickly when something is difficult to understand. They blame the speaker for not making his points clearer and simpler. The remedy: go out of your way to hear those speaking on topics that are hard to grasp and stick with the subject from beginning to end. Listening requires practice. In addition, it is possible that the experience of listening to difficult material will provide ideas and suggest methods for making your own talk more interesting and understandable.

4. *Finding fault with a speaker's appearance or delivery.*

Sometimes we do not concentrate on what a speaker is saying because we become deeply involved in his delivery or appearance. If his manner of speaking or the way he looks creates an unfavorable impression, we quickly lose interest. Conversely, a speaker's looks or manner may cause romantic or other favorable images that are equally distracting. The most important task in listening is to learn what the speaker says, not how he says it and how he looks when saying it. Nevertheless, for our own benefit in learning to "say it right," we should notice carefully the mannerisms of speech and behavior that add to or detract from the effectiveness of what is being said. Trying to avoid or to imitate such characteristics will help to improve our own speaking ability.

5 TALKING IN GROUPS

> *Men are never so likely to settle a question rightly as when they discuss it freely.*
>
> *Thomas Babington Macaulay*

The majority of conversations consist of two people talking with each other, and therefore the primary purpose of this book is to help you in improving one-to-one speech. However, there are growing chances that you will be called upon to engage in one or more of several types of group discussion in general use today. In recent decades, millions of people have had opportunities to speak in public through discussion groups; tens of millions have heard group discussions on TV or radio programs.

All types of discussion have basically the same purpose: to pool the information and ideas of a group of speakers and attempt to find a satisfactory approach and possible solution to the problem under discussion. Your role as a speaker in group discussion is similar to that in talking with an individual: you need to speak clearly, forcefully, grammatically, and appropriately. True, your audience is larger, but it is composed of individuals. The most effective speakers to groups are able to talk as though they were conducting private conversations with each person present.

Among the numerous situations involving group discussion, three are outstandingly popular and one is occasionally employed. Familiarizing yourself with these types will enable you to "say it right" when you become engaged in one or the other of them.

1. *The single-leader type.*

   This kind of program often follows a speech—a formal talk by one person—and provides an open-forum period during which members of the audience may address remarks and questions to the speaker. The speaker may preside, or a chairman, acting as moderator, may address questions on certain topics to the speaker. When no formal speech is involved, a leader may recognize speakers from the audience, guide the discussion, and summarize remarks at the conclusion of the session. Most assemblies and parliamentary bodies—including PTA meetings, club and union sessions, church groups, political organizations, and the like—follow this system and usually are governed by rules of conduct and order to fit the individual needs of a particular body.

2. *The panel, or round-table, type.*

   A group of experts, would-be experts, or simply well-informed people, either literally sitting around a table or placed as though they were, discusses various aspects of a selected topic. The discussion, usually quite informal, closely resembles a spirited conversation. The function of the leader, or chairman, is to keep the talk going, to sift out and clarify arguments and agreements, and at the end to summarize opposing points of view for the audience. Such panel discussions occur more and more frequently as talk situations on television and radio. They provide opportunities for listening, for studying the speech styles of different individuals, and, occasionally, for active speech participation.

3. *The town-meeting type.*

   A group of selected, knowledgeable persons, usually four, discusses opposing attitudes toward some important public question. Each speaker has at least one opportunity to reply to another's argument. The audience is provided chances to enter the discussion and to ask questions of one or more of the speakers. In this kind of speech situation, a moderator presides, introduces the speakers, and directs and controls audience participation.

4. *The debate.*

This form of intellectual sport is much less popular now than in previous years, but it continues to crop up, especially in local, state, or national political campaigns. Formal debate has characteristics in common with all types of more informal discussion, including personal conversation, but it is usually controlled by specific rules of conduct and presentation. Opposing members, if there are more than two speakers, are organized into teams, each with its captain. Every speaker is normally allowed to speak twice in a prescribed order, subject to a rigidly imposed time limit. In formal debating exercises, a judge, or board of judges, awards a decision to the team which has played this intellectual game more tellingly and skillfully.

In all formal debates, whether the speakers number two, four, or more, the proposition to be argued is carefully formulated so as to avoid ambiguity and to insure direct clash of opinion. In recent years, the tendency of debate has been to allow two speakers to oppose each other on a variety of discussion topics, rather than merely one. Whatever its form, debate is but one kind of lively conversation engaged in for the benefit of ten or ten million listeners. Engaging in debates, listening to them, and evaluating the performance of speakers can play an important role in your own speech improvement.

6 PREPARING AND DELIVERING A PLATFORM SPEECH

Put your discourse into some frame.
William Shakespeare

Possibly not more than ten out of a thousand persons who read this book will ever be called on to make what is loosely called a "public" or "platform" speech. (*Public* and *platform* are inexact words when applied to speaking: conversation in even small groups is more public than private, and one can address remarks to a group without standing on raised flooring, a stage, dais, rostrum, or pulpit.) However, although the requirements of effective speech are basically the same whether you are talking to one person or a thousand, a few additional considerations concerning a speech addressed to a large audience should be mentioned.

The success of all oral communication depends upon what a speaker has to say and how he says that something. In addressing a large audience, however, additional personal resources play an important role. Among these are *voice, physical bearing*, and *attaining rapport* with the audience.

No surer index of personality exists than the human voice. Five minutes' conversation with you will reveal to an observant stranger an astonishing amount of information about your background and personality. Oliver Wendell Holmes, himself an accomplished talker, once said, "All of a man's antecedents and possibilities are summed up in a single utterance, which gives at once the gauge of his education and his mental organization." This statement may be an exaggeration, but one's voice can characterize him or her as conceited, dull, bored, disagreeable, careless, and even physically weak. Or it can show him to be pleasant, alert, attractive, poised, gracious, reasonable, and careful.

If your voice is really poor—thin or harsh or nasal—you may wish to take a course in voice training. However, the first requirement for self-improvement is learning to hear how you sound. Many people are merely careless or thoughtless in using their voices and could rapidly improve with conscientious effort, if they had an idea of what their task was. What should be your goals in voice improvement?

In every speaking situation, regardless of the size of your audience, your voice should be *audible*. Whether you are speaking to the person seated next to you or to ten thousand people in an auditorium, your voice should be capable of being heard distinctly. No one wishes to strain his ears; no one likes speakers who mumble, swallow words, or avert their heads. You can adapt your voice to the size of your audience just as you instinctively do in ordinary conversation when you wish to include someone on the other side of a room.

Your voice should be *animated*. Whether you are talking to one person or a large group, animation is a matter of the vigor with which you speak, the energy that you put into your voice and body. Without vigor, any speaker becomes wooden, and his audience of whatever size immediately loses interest. Being lively does not involve gesticulations or loudness, but it does involve not droning away in listless, spiritless, indifferent, and languid fashion.

Your voice should be *well-pitched*. Every voice has a normal key, a base line from which it moves up and down in either steps or glides. If your voice is high-pitched, make a conscious effort to lower it. A pleasant voice covers a range in pitch; a monotonous voice stays largely on one pitch level. A flexible voice, one capable of expressing shades of feeling and degrees of emphasis, is an asset for any speaker, especially one talking to a group of people.

A speaker's *physical bearing* has much to do with the *rapport* he achieves (or fails to achieve) with an audience. The essential quality of good delivery is close contact with your audience: one should talk *with* one's listeners, not *at* them. The most effective speakers appear to look directly at audiences, not above their heads, at the ceiling, or out of a window. Really superb speakers seem so aware of their audiences that they give to every person present the feeling of being directly spoken to. Manner is important, because audiences are quick to sense whether a speaker is trying to be friendly, animated, and eager to interest them.

Posture aids or handicaps every speaker. The trick is to appear relaxed without being sloppy, alert without being tense. If a stand or table is present, don't lean on it, or at least don't do so often. Don't stand on one foot and then the other. An easy position is one in which one foot is a little ahead of the other, with one's weight centered on the ball of the forward foot. Keep your head and your torso up — not like a pouter pigeon, but enough to convey a feeling of confidence. Keep your arms at your side, unless using them for gestures that seem to grow out of what is being said. Relaxed arms and hands are never distracting, but movement of any kind attracts notice. If your hands are twisting in your pockets, tying themselves in knots behind your back, toying with a coat button, keys, a ring, or a pencil, they will divert attention from what you are saying and may even add to your own nervousness.

On the other hand, it isn't necessary to stand immobile, especially if you are speaking for more than four or five minutes. No movement at all may be as defeating as constant movement. A *change in position* of body, arms, and hands may help you keep contact with an audience when making a transition from one point to another.

Above all, *don't hurry.* Your speech should be carefully timed to meet the limits provided, but don't speed up even if you feel you are not going to finish on schedule. (Leave out something instead.) Many speeches excellent in content have been wasted because speakers have gone too rapidly, covered too much ground, run their words together, and altogether have forgotten that the ear-mind combination is often slower than the voice.

Numerous phases of platform speaking are too involved to be covered here. Selecting a topic, gathering material, and organizing a speech are topics better approached through a course in public speaking or by reading a book devoted solely to the subject.

In general, learning to "say it right" differs little from one speaking situation to another. What is really important is stocking your mind with something to say and speaking animatedly with as few errors as possible in diction and pronunciation. These two significant problems of word choice and word sounds provide important subject matter for the remainder of this book.

PART TWO
USAGE AND PRONUNCIATION

Speech is a mirror of the soul; as a man speaks, so is he.

Publilius Syrus

Speech finely framed delighteth the ears.

The Apocrypha

The right rule is to speak as our neighbors do, not better.

H. W. Fowler

1 LEVELS OF DICTION

Every prescription and rule concerning word usage must conform to considerations of place, occasion, time, and circumstances. No standards of diction are absolute; none can arbitrarily be called always good or unfailingly correct.

The words we use in talking with the person working at the desk next to us may not be appropriate when we are conversing with a member of our family, with a company official, or with a minister, rabbi, or priest. A word or phrase in correct or suitable usage a decade ago may now be outmoded. An expression appropriate in one section of the country may be unclear and therefore ineffective in another locality. Technical expressions used before a specialized group of listeners may be inappropriate in general conversation.

The best course to follow is to try to choose and use words and expressions that are normally employed by reputable speakers in all sections of the country at the present time. That is, diction is effective and appropriate when it is in *national, present*, and *reputable* use. Most people habitually use words that violate one or more of these principles. We should weed out such expressions from our vocabularies or, at least, should be on guard when we deliberately use them. Remember: any word or expression is correct if it meets these three standards; it may also be effective (appropriate although not "correct") if it does not meet these standards but is used for a particular purpose in a particular situation.

2 NATIONAL USE

Many of us are unaware that words and expressions familiar and clear to us may sound strange to the ears of persons who live elsewhere. When an Englishman announces "I was mad about my flat," he probably means "I really liked my apartment." If an American said the same thing, he would mean, "I was angry because I had a punctured (or blownout) tire." Would every American understand this notice tacked onto a door in Pennsylvania Dutch country: "Button don't bell. Bump."? To those who can translate the message as "Please knock because the bell is out of order," the expression is quaint and vivid. To others, the sign would be meaningless.

A word or phrase used and understood only in a particular region is called a *localism*. It may also be called a *regionalism* or *provincialism* (because, formerly, English used in London was "good English," whereas English spoken outside London in "the provinces" was not good English but "provincial"). One should not avoid all localisms (some are vivid and appealing) but should employ only those that effectively convey meaning and are not likely to be misunderstood.

The Western, Southwestern, Southern, and Northeastern areas of the United States are rich in localisms that add flavor to speech but that may be misunderstood. For a person living in one of those areas, such expressions are hard to detect, because as a speaker or listener he accepts them as reputable and casually assumes that they are universally understood since he himself has heard and used them from childhood. Words and combinations of words used locally are labeled by dictionaries according to the geographical area where they are most common.

The media of mass communication — television, radio, films, books, magazines, newspapers — are helping to make all American English *national*, but it is well to avoid using such expressions as these if you wish every listener from another section of the country to understand:

31

Western: *coulee* (narrow valley); *dogie, dogy* (motherless calf); *mesquite* (spiny shrub); *grubstake* (funds, supplies).

Southwestern: *mesa* (rocky hill); *longhorn* (formerly a kind of cattle); *rustler* (cattle thief); *mustang* (half-wild horse).

Southern: *butternuts* (brown overalls); *lightwood* (pitchy pine); *hoecake* (cake of Indian meal); *corn pone* (corn bread).

Northeastern: *selectman* (town official); *moosewood* (striped maple); *down-Easter* (native New Englander, especially one from Maine); *skunk cabbage* (skunkweed).

Localisms can also include *dialect:* expressions used in a limited geographical area, by a particular social group, or even on an extensive scale (Scottish dialect, Appalachian dialect). Each of us knows and on occasion uses dialect expressions, but if we wish to be understood on a national scale we should avoid such words and phrases as, for instance, *any more* ("I get sick any more"), *fress, crick, a scrounge, nibby, spritz,* and scores of similar localisms.

3 CURRENT USE

Language is constantly changing. Words go out of use or are employed less often; new words and phrases take the place of old.

Effective usage requires that words be understandable to hearers of the present time.

Except for somewhat doubtful purposes of humor, guard against expressions that are too old or too new to be intelligible to present-day listeners. Good advice to follow is that expressed by Alexander Pope:

> Be not the first by whom the new are tried,
> Nor yet the last to lay the old aside.

An *obsolete* word is one that has passed out of general use either in form or in one or more of its meanings. Because the status of such words is difficult to determine, makers of dictionaries vary in the use of labels applying to them: "rare," "archaic," "obsolete," etc. Only a few such words may occur to you, but some may persist in your vocabulary because you have learned them from books written generations or centuries ago:

In form: *egal* (for equal); *gaol* (for jail); *infortune* (for misfortune); *enwheel, mammer, ronyon.*

In meaning: *anon* (for coming); *garb* (for personal bearing); *prevent* (for precede); *permit* (for commit).

An *archaic* word is old-fashioned, a word or expression that was once common in speech but that now is retained largely in biblical or legal contexts. (Like obsolete words, many archaic words are old-fashioned in one or two meanings but in currect use in others.) Examples: *enow* (for enough); *eftsoons* (for again); *gramercy* (for thank you); *jape* (for jest); *whilom* (for formerly); *wot* (for know); *y-clept* (for named).

Poetic words, sometimes so designated in dictionaries, are

33

archaic (or obsolete) words found in poetry written in, or intended to recreate the spirit of, a somewhat remote past. Examples are certain contractions such as *'tis, 'twas;* the use of *-st, -est, -th,* and *-eth* endings for verbs *(dost, hearest, doth, leadeth);* and words such as *glebe, ope,* and *oft.*

One can also err by using *neologisms,* recently coined words that have not yet been sanctioned by a substantial number of responsible speakers. Many such coinages are fresh and clever and may become established, given time to prove their worth; but many quietly disappear and are heard no more. Obviously, fresh words connected with discoveries and new inventions are essential, but they should be used sparingly or not at all if they cause misunderstanding or confusion.

Neologisms are concocted in several ways. Some are adaptations of familiar words: *millionheiress, bookwise, avoirduprose.* The so-called "portmanteau" words are combinations: *brunch* (breakfast and lunch), *smog* (smoke and fog), *cheeseburger, transistor, witticism, chortle* (chuckle and snort). Some neologisms (known as acronyms) are derived from the initial letters of words: *loran* (long range navigation) and *radar* (radio detecting and ranging). Among "new" words in science, technology, business, and occupations may be cited *astronautics, countdown, computerize, rhombatron,* and *beautician.* In a related category are such registered tradenames and trademarks as *Dacron, Kodak, simonize,* and *technicolor.* Certain major events (such as war) help to create new words like *foxhole, jeep, blitz, bazooka, quisling,* and *genocide.*

If you use neologisms in speaking — and some are necessary, on occasion — make certain that they are appropriate to your listener and your message. Newly coined words which appear in dictionaries may carry no label or may be called "slang" or "informal" or "colloquial." Finally, some neologisms, such as *motel,* achieve permanent status and become common "correct" words.

4 REPUTABLE USE

Standard, or "reputable," English is used by those persons who carry on the important affairs of English-speaking people. Reputable English is acceptable in various situations and on various occasions merely because it is the usage of social, professional, educational, and business leaders: writers, editors, publishers, lawyers, ministers, judges, teachers, company officials, college professors, and the like.

The choice and use of English words and expressions can be divided into three broad groups: *formal standard, informal standard,* and *substandard.*

Formal standard English is that used for "proper" occasions in which dignity and seriousness are involved: writing designed as permanent literature; carefully edited books and magazines; lectures and addresses; sermons; minutes of meetings; and scientific and technical papers. Few words in your dictionary carry the label "formal," but those appearing with no restrictive label normally are considered appropriate in formal standard English.

Informal standard English is sometimes labeled in dictionaries as "colloquial," sometimes as "informal." It is the English used in everyday conversation, in friendly letters, in many business letters, in notes and memoranda, and in oral reports designed to be informative but not formal in structure or tone.

Informal is a broad term: its range is from language just above illiteracies and slang to language just below formal. It is filled with *colloquialisms* — words and phrases used in conversation and indispensable to an easy, informal style of speaking and writing. Remember that a colloquialism is never a localism and that no stigma attaches to any expression labeled colloquial. Informal standard English is relaxed, but it is not vulgar, incorrect, illiterate, or substandard. Both formal standard English and informal standard English can appropriately be used by the same speaker on different occasions.

Substandard English is the language of the careless or uneducated speaker, of persons who have neither the ability nor desire to speak formal standard or informal standard English. Substandard English may consist of improprieties, ungrammatical expressions, profanity, slang, mispronunciations, and unidiomatic phrases.

These three kinds of usage overlap, but the following sentences reveal the levels as they are generally understood:

Formal standard: I shall not speak.
                    I will not speak.
Informal standard: I'll not speak.
                    I'm not going to speak.
                    I won't speak.
Substandard: I ain't gonna speak.
                    I ain't gonna say nothing.

Eight terms, or classifications of kinds of speech, deserve brief comment. Each involves some aspect of reputable usage. An understanding of each of these terms will enable you to speak with confidence and assurance and will permit you to evaluate the language you use and hear with greater awareness of its particular level of usage and appropriateness. You will need to understand the discussion that follows in order to interpret the list of expressions beginning on p. 78.

ILLITERACIES

An *illiteracy* is a word or phrase not acceptable in either colloquial (informal) or formal speech. Illiteracies are also referred to as *vulgarisms* (the language of the uneducated) or *barbarisms.* The latter word, from a Greek term once assigned to foreigners not sharing in Greek civilization, suggests that a barbarism, or illiteracy, is a word or phrase not included in the language.

Labeling of such terms in dictionaries varies widely. An expression called *illiterate* in one dictionary may be called *substandard, dialectal, informal,* or even *colloquial* in another.

Because illiteracies really do not belong in the language, many of them are not included in dictionaries at all.

All illiteracies should be avoided in speech except as quotations from uneducated people you are describing or, rarely, for purposes of humor. Although a few illiteracies are effective (some poorly educated but deeply intelligent and sincere persons have produced eloquent speech and writing), you would be well advised not to use such expressions as these:

acrossed, ain't, afeard, anywheres, borned, boughten, brung, disremember, drownded, hisself, I been, I done, irregardless, kepted, losted, mistakened, nohow, ourn, youse.

IMPROPRIETIES

Unlike illiteracies, *improprieties* are recognized, standard words that are misused in function or meaning.

A word identified as more than one part of speech may be so employed without question, but a speaker should not create for a given word a new part of speech until this new use — known as *functional shift* — is sanctioned and is recorded in a reliable dictionary. Here are a few substandard examples of improprieties in function:

Verbs used as nouns: an *invite*, a *sell*, an *advise*, a *repeat*, a *think*, *eats*.

Nouns used as verbs: *birthing* an idea, *grassing* a lawn, *ambitioned*, *passengered*, *heired*, to *host*, to *party*.

Adjectives used as adverbs: dances *good*, *awful* short, talks *rapid*, *strong* made.

Verb forms: *seen* for *saw*, *come* for *came*, *done* for *did*, *laying* for *lying*, *set* for *sit*, *of* for *have*.

Other combinations: *this here*, *them kind*, *being as how*, *except as*.

A second group of improprieties consists of words similar to other words and used inaccurately in their place. Such words include:

1. *Homophones* — two or more words that have about the same pronunciation but are different in spelling, meaning, and origin. (In speaking, such words and phrases cause no difficulty because pronunciation is not involved. Watch out for them, however, when you are writing.) Some examples of homophones are:

bough, bow	principal, principle
capital, capitol	read, reed
fort, forte	real, reel
heir, air	row, roe
hour, our	so, sew, sow
made, maid	stationery, stationary
marshal, martial	sum, some
pale, pail	threw, through
passed, past	to, too, two

In speaking, be careful in using such near-homophones as *later, latter; midst, mist; medal, metal; accept, except; formally, formerly; allude, elude; confidently, confidentially; expect, suspect; official, officious;* and *than, then.*

2. *Homographs* — two or more words that have the same spelling but are different in meaning and origin. Some homographs cause no difficulty in speaking because no pronunciation problem is involved: *air* (melody) and *air* (atmosphere). Be on guard, however, when using *bow* (bend forward), *bow* (used to play a violin), *bow* (the forward end of a ship); *row* (propel a boat), *row* (a dispute); *wind* (air current), *wind* (to coil).

PRINCIPAL PARTS OF VERBS

Insufficient knowledge of the principal parts of verbs causes many errors in speaking.

An English verb has three principal parts: *present tense* (or *present infinitive*), *past tense*, and *past participle*. A good way to recall the principal parts of a verb is to substitute those of any verb for the following:

I *run* today. (present tense)
I *ran* yesterday. (past tense)

I *have run* every day this week. (past participle)

The past tense and part participle of many verbs are formed by adding *-d* or *-ed* or *-t* to the present tense:

save   saved   saved
dream   dreamt (or dreamed)   dreamt (or dreamed)

Such verbs are called regular, or weak, verbs.

Other verbs do not follow this pattern. Called *irregular*, or *strong*, verbs, they form the past tense and past participle in several ways. One group has a vowel change in the past tense, and in some instances in the past participle as well:

cling   clung   clung
fight   fought   fought

Some verbs in this group, in addition to the vowel change, add *-n* for the past participle:

wear   wore   worn
swear   swore   sworn

Another group changes in form completely in the past tense and past participle:

bind   bound   bound
shrink   shrank   shrunk

A few verbs change the last consonant, but not the vowel:
have   had   had

Several verbs have the same form for all three principal parts:

quit   quit   quit
spread   spread   spread

Following is a list of one hundred troublesome verbs that illustrate each of the methods of formation just mentioned. Study them carefully so as to avoid errors in speaking.

Troublesome Verbs

PRESENT TENSE	PAST TENSE	PAST PARTICIPLE
arise	arose	arisen
ask	asked	asked

PRESENT TENSE	PAST TENSE	PAST PARTICIPLE
attack	attacked	attacked
bear	bore	borne (passive: born, given birth to)
beat	beat	beaten
become	became	become
begin	began	begun
bid (auction)	bid	bid
bid (command)	bade, bid	bidden, bid
blow	blew	blown
break	broke	broken
bring	brought	brought
broadcast	broadcast, broadcasted	broadcast, broadcasted
build	built	built
burn	burned, burnt	burned, burnt
burst	burst	burst
buy	bought	bought
cast	cast	cast
catch	caught	caught
choose	chose	chosen
come	came	come
cut	cut	cut
deal	dealt	dealt
do	did	done
draw	drew	drawn
dream	dreamed, dreamt	dreamed, dreamt
dress	dressed, drest	dressed, drest
drink	drank	drunk, drunken (rare, except as adjective)
drive	drove	driven
dwell	dwelt, dwelled	dwelt, dwelled
eat	ate	eaten
fall	fell	fallen
feel	felt	felt
find	found	found
flow	flowed	flowed
fly	flew	flown

PRESENT TENSE	PAST TENSE	PAST PARTICIPLE
fly (baseball)	flied	flied
forbid	forbade	forbidden
forget	forgot	forgotten, forgot
freeze	froze	frozen
get	got	got, gotten
give	gave	given
go	went	gone
grow	grew	grown
happen	happened	happened
hear	heard	heard
help	helped	helped
hit	hit	hit
hurt	hurt	hurt
keep	kept	kept
know	knew	known
lay	laid	laid
lead	led	led
learn	learned, learnt	learned, learnt
leave	left	left
lend	lent	lent
let	let	let
lie (tell a false-hood)	lied	lied
lie (recline)	lay	lain
loose	loosed	loosed
lose	lost	lost
make	made	made
mean	meant	meant
pass	passed	passed, past
prejudice	prejudiced	prejudiced
prove	proved	proved, proven
put	put	put
raise	raised	raised
read	read	read
ride	rode	ridden
rise	rose	risen
run	ran	run
see	saw	seen
set	set	set

PRESENT TENSE	PAST TENSE	PAST PARTICIPLE
shake	shook	shaken
shine	shone	shone
show	showed	shown, showed
sing	sang	sung
sink	sank	sunk
sit	sat	sat
smell	smelled, smelt	smelled, smelt
speak	spoke	spoken
spell	spelled, spelt	spelled, spelt
spoil	spoiled, spoilt	spoiled, spoilt
spring	sprang, sprung	sprung
stand	stood	stood
steal	stole	stolen
strike	struck	struck, stricken
strive	strove, strived	striven, strived
suppose	supposed	supposed
swim	swam	swum
take	took	taken
teach	taught	taught
tell	told	told
think	thought	thought
throw	threw	thrown
use	used	used
wake	waked, woke	waked, woken
work	worked, wrought	worked, wrought
write	wrote	written

SLANG

Slang is a label for a particular kind of word usage that ranges from illiteracies to colloquialisms (informal standard English). Slang terms usually involve exaggerated or forced humor, fantastic or flippant novelty, and clipped or shortened forms of words. Much slang is colorful, fresh, and pungent and provides effective shortcuts in expression. Some slang appeals to such widespread popular fancy that it survives and is eventually labeled in dictionaries as informal or colloquial speech.

It is useless to suggest that no one should employ slang in

speaking, but three good reasons exist for using it sparingly and cautiously:

1. Using slang expressions prevents a speaker from searching for the exact words needed to convey meaning. Many slang expressions are only rubber stamps. To call someone a "swell guy" or a "lemon" or a "square" hardly expresses exactly or fully any real critical judgment or intelligent description. Instead, such words are more likely to convey the speaker's own laziness, careless thinking, and poverty of vocabulary. Slang may be colorful and humorous, but few slang expressions by themselves serve the primary purpose of conveying a clear and accurate message from speaker to listener.

2. Slang may be all right in its place, but it is frequently not in keeping with the context — what precedes and follows.

3. Most slang words last for a brief time only and then pass out of use, becoming unintelligible to hearers.

Slang appears in numerous forms.

Many *neologisms* are slang: *hornswoggle, scrumptious, wacky, beatnik, sockdologer, ixnay, scram, payola, teenybopper, pizzaz, grandiferous.*

Some slang words are formed from other words by abbreviation or by adding new endings to change the part of speech: *legit, phony, VIP, psych out, snafu, C-note, groovy, nervy, mod.*

Sometimes words in acceptable use are given extended meanings: *smack, buck, chicken, mainline, bean, dish, sack, grease, tough, snow, cat, acid, trip.*

Some slang is formed by compounding or bringing together two or more words: *egghead, hepcat, stash* (store and cache), *sweedle* (swindle and wheedle), *slanguage* (slang and language), *gogo-girl, fly-boy.*

Slang often consists of one or more coined words combined with one or more standard terms: *blow one's top, shoot the bull, live it up, get in orbit, off one's rocker, jam session, shoot the works.*

Here is a list of 150 expressions that illustrate the various methods by which slang is formed. If you do not recognize every item (or all of the slang terms just mentioned) remember that your inability to do so constitutes two good reasons why you should use little slang in speaking: it is not always understandable; it is often short-lived.

Slang Words

all-fired
attaboy (attagirl)
babe
back number
baloney
bamboozle
barf
barge in
bats
beanery
beef
big shot
bigwig
blind date
bloke
blow your stack
bolix (or bollicks)
booboo
brass hat
bread
bushed
buzz off
chump
clip joint
conk (conk out)
cornball
crackpot
cut the mustard
dame
deadbeat
dimwit
double dome
elbow grease
eyewash
fishy

flack
flatfoot
flivver
floozy
flossy
fork over
four-flusher
gatecrasher
geezer
get lost
get one's goat
get with it
girlie
gogetter
goldbrick
gold digger
goon
goner
goo
gooey
goof (and goof off)
goofy
gook
grub
gung ho
gunk
guy
gyp
halfbaked
halfcocked
hick
high-hat
hightail
hogwash
hooey

hunkydory
jeez
jerk
jinx
jughead
kibosh
kick around
kickback
kick in
kick the bucket
kid
lemon
long green
lulu
lummox
meathead
moniker
mooch
moola
moxie
natch
nix
nut
nuts
nutty
on the ball
on the beam
on the level
on the loose
on the make
on the wagon
oodles
pad
pantywaist
party pooper
peach
phiz
piker
poop
pork barrel

pusher
ratfink
rat race
raunchy
razz
razzberry
razzledazzle
razzmatazz
rhubarb
ritzy
sad sack
sawbuck
scads
screw
screwball
screw loose
screw out of
screwy
shakes
shebang
shenanigans
shiv
shyster
simoleon
slaphappy
sound off
stool pigeon
sucker
swing
tizzy
turn off
turn on
weirdie
weirdo
wheelerdealer
wise guy
wise up
wisenheimer
yak (yack, yuk)
yap

IDIOMATIC USAGE

If you are a native-born speaker of American English, idiomatic usage is likely to cause little trouble. Most of the idiomatic expressions we use and hear are familiar, deep-rooted, widely employed, and readily understandable.

The words *idiom* and *idiomatic* come from Greek terms the key meaning of which is "peculiar," or "individual." Idiomatic expressions conform to no basic principles in their formation and are indeed laws unto themselves. Every language has its peculiarities. For example, Spanish people say (in translation), "Here one speaks Spanish"; the English equivalent is "Spanish is spoken here." The French say, "We have come from eating," but our equivalent would be "We have just eaten."

As speakers of American English, we might tell foreigners not to say "many boy is," "a pupils," and "ten foot." We would utterly confuse them with such entirely acceptable idiomatic usage as "many *a* boy is," "a *few* pupils," and "a ten-foot *pole*." Much correct idiomatic usage is indeed illogical or a violation of grammatical principles.

One generalized statement about English idioms is that several words combined often lose their literal (exact) meaning and express something only remotely suggested by any one word: *bed of roses, birds of a feather, black list, dark horse, get even with, open house, read between the lines, toe the line.*

Another comment is that parts of the human body and words indicating activity have suggested hundreds of idiomatic expressions: *burn one's fingers, all thumbs, rub elbows with, step on someone's toes, take to heart, make believe, do oneself well, ride it out.*

A third generalization is that many hundreds of idiomatic phrases contain prepositions or adverbs along with other parts of speech. No prescription governs their use, yet certain combinations are acceptable idioms and others are not. Here are some examples: *make off, make out, make-ready, make up, make merry, walk off, walkover, walk-up.* Some other examples are

accompanied   *by* others
               with grief

affinity	*of* persons or things
	between two persons or things
	with another person or thing
agree	*on* a plan
	with a person
analogous	*in* a quality
	to or *with* others
concerned	*for* someone or something
	in an undertaking
	with or *about* a subject or topic
contend	*for* a principle
	with an individual
	against an obstacle
differ	*with* a person
	from something else
	on, over, or *about* a question
impatient	*at* someone's conduct
	with someone else
	for something desired
	of restraint
rewarded	*with* a gift
	by a person
	for something done

Your speech should conform to the idiomatic word combinations generally acceptable. Reliable dictionaries contain many explanations of idiomatic usage following words that require such detail.

Here is a list of twenty idiomatic and unidiomatic expressions. Study them as representative of many expressions about which you should consult your dictionary if you are in trouble.

Idiomatic and Unidiomatic Expressions

IDIOMATIC	UNIDIOMATIC
accord with	accord to
according to	according with

Idiomatic	Unidiomatic
acquaint with	acquaint to
adverse to	adverse against
aim to prove	aim at proving
among themselves	among one another
angry with (a person)	angry at (a person)
as regards	as regards to
authority on	authority about
cannot help talking	cannot help but talk
comply with	comply to
conform to, with	conform in
correspond to (a thing)	correspond with (a thing)
desirous of	desirous to
identical with	identical to
in accordance with	in accordance to
prefer (one) to (another)	prefer (one) over (another)
prior to	prior than
superior to	superior than
unequal to	unequal for

SHOPTALK

Shoptalk is vocabulary having to do with a field of work or activity ("He knows a lot of rocketry shoptalk"). The term also refers to conversation about one's occupation — one's vocation or avocation. Everyone should be careful not to bore others with excessive talk about his own activities, but, of course, some conversation of this kind is necessary, useful, and informative. Two suggestions about shoptalk may be helpful: (1) never engage in shoptalk with other than fellow-workers unless your conversational companion wishes you to; (2) when you do use shoptalk, make certain that your listeners understand the meanings of whatever words you use.

A specialist speaking to other specialists may properly use many difficult technical or specialized terms mutually known and accepted. If he talks with others who have only a general knowledge of the field concerned, he appropriately uses fewer and less difficult-to-understand expressions. If he is talking with someone who knows little or nothing of the field being discussed, he should avoid all specialized terms unless he explains them. .

The word *technical* means "peculiar to or characteristic of a particular art, science, trade, or profession." *Technical words* have special meanings for people in particular professions, fields, recreations, occupations, sports, or the like. To such words, ranging alphabetically from *Aeronautics* to *Zoology*, some forty or fifty "special subject" labels are attached in dictionaries. In the last few decades, new words have poured into dictionaries from such fields as science and technology, the social sciences and humanities, advertising, sports, fashion, and several dozen other fields and areas of human activity, supply, and thinking.

When technical words become widely used or extend their meanings, their subject labels in dictionaries are dropped: *broadcast* (from radio); *telescope* (from astronomy); *daub* (from painting); *virtuoso* (from art and music); *analog computer* (from electronics).

No matter how well known they are to you, avoid such words as the following unless you are talking with people especially well-informed in a given field: *cuprous* (chemistry), *lepidopterous* (zoology), and *sidereal* (astronomy).

To make this recommendation clear and firm, let's assume that you are a lover of sports. You engage in, read about, or witness many sports activities. Do you know of anyone who can define each of the following technical terms in sports? Do you understand every one of them yourself? Here's the list; see what you can do with it:

break, bull's-eye, ace, chucker, bank shot, broad reach, feather, royal coachman, clay pigeon, Texas leaguer, crawl, rabbit punch, fall, T.K.O., love, red dog, birdie, baby split, grand slam, javelin, set point, deuce, frame, double fault, mouse trap, goalie, vulnerable, split end, jibe, foul, gate, flutter kick, palming, double dribble, fast break, key, flanker, half gainer, let.

WORDINESS

Nearly every speaker uses more words than he needs to. In rapid-fire talk, in the give-and-take of conversation, each of us is likely to repeat himself and to use words that are meaningless or superfluous. (When writing, we have a chance to go over our work and remove the verbiage.) Truly effective speech is economical, but using enough words to cover the subject and not too many is a standard of perfection unattainable by ordinary mortals. But if we can grasp and keep in mind a few suggestions, our speech will become more concise and consequently more interesting and appealing.

In Shakespeare's *Hamlet*, old Polonius says:

> Therefore, since brevity is the soul of wit,
> And tediousness the limbs and outward flourishes,
> I will be brief.

In this context, *wit* means "understanding" or "wisdom." Actually, Polonius was a garrulous, tiresome bore, but what he said is that being brief and to the point is the best way to convey real thought. Conciseness alone does not guarantee good speaking, but it is difficult for someone to speak forcefully and entertainingly when he is using four words where one would be sufficient. The Golden Rule contains eleven words. The Ten Commandments are expressed in seventy-five words. Lincoln's Gettysburg Address consists of two hundred and sixty-seven words.

Three suggestions may be helpful:

First, do not use two or more words where one will serve. It is better to refer to "the chance of war" than to say "in the regrettable eventuality of a failure of the deterrence policy." A speaker was once asked whether certain rules should be observed. Instead of replying yes, he remarked, "The implementation of sanctions will inevitably eventuate in repercussions." A foreman suggested that an assistant give instructions to workers "very precisely and carefully." He might better have said, "Give precise instructions."

Here is a brief list of expressions for your consideration:

Eliminating Wordiness

REDUCE THESE	TO THESE
a certain length of time	a certain time
am (is, are) going to	shall, will
are (am) of the opinion	believe
as a result of	because
at the present time	now
before long	soon
by the time	when
due to the fact that	due to, since

REDUCE THESE	TO THESE
during the time that	while
for the amount of	for
in accordance with	by
inasmuch as	since
in case	if
in lieu of	instead
in regard to	about
insofar as	because, since, as
in the event that	if
in the month of May	in May
in this day and age	today
in view of the fact that	since
it has come to our attention that	(begin with the word following *that*)
it is interesting to note that	begin with the word following *that*)
I would appreciate it if	please
on condition that	if
one of the purposes (reasons)	one purpose (reason)
prior to	before
provided that	if
the length of five yards	five yards (or five yards long)
under date of July 5	of July 5
with the exception of	except

Second, avoid overusing "there is," "there are," etc. Usually, "there" beginnings are superfluous words, adding nothing. The words "there are" can be removed from the following sentence with no loss in meaning or force: "In this building there are five elevators awaiting inspection." Better: "In this building five elevators await inspection."

Third, avoid adding words to an idea already expressed. When meaning is expressed or implied in a particular word or phrase, repeating the idea in additional words adds nothing but verbiage. Common examples of this fault are using *again* with verbs beginning *re;* using *more* or *most* with adjectives and adverbs ending in *er* and *est;* using *more* or *most* with such absolute-meaning adjectives as *unique, round, square,* and *equal.*

Here is a list of sixty wordy expressions designed to make

you aware that everyone habitually uses more words than necessary.

Wordy Expressions

absolutely essential
around about that time
audible to the ear
back up
bisect in two
call up on the 'phone
choose up
Christmas Eve evening
combine together
complete monopoly
completely unanimous
connect up with
consensus of opinion
cooperate together
cover over
descend down
each and everyone
endorse on the back
entirely eliminated
extreme prime importance
few (many) in number
final end (outcome)
first beginnings
four-cornered square
from whence
important essentials
individual person
join together
long length
loquacious talker

many in number
meet up with
more angrier
more better
more older
more paramount
more perfect
more perpendicular
most unique
most unkindest
necessary essential
necessary need
old adage
personal friend
recur again
reduce down
repeat again
resume again
return back
revert back to
rise up
round in form
separate out
(a) short half-hour
small in size
sunset in the west
talented genius
this afternoon at 4 P.M.
this morning at 8 A.M.
visible to the eye

TRITENESS

Triteness, sometimes referred to as the use of hackneyed language or clichés, applies to words and expressions that are worn out from overuse.

The words *triteness, hackneyed language,* and *cliché* have origins that explain their meaning: *triteness* comes from the Latin word *tritus,* the past participle of a verb meaning "to rub, to wear out." *Hackneyed* is derived from the idea of a horse, or carriage (hackney coach), let out for hire, devoted to common use, and consequently exhausted in service. *Cliché* comes from the French word *clicher,* meaning "to stereotype," "to cast from a mold."

Trite expressions resemble slang in that both are stereotyped manners of thought and expression. Clichés may be stampings from common speech, outworn phrases, or overworked quotations. Usually they express sound ideas (or ideas widely considered sound) and are always couched in memorable phrasing. (If they were not sensible and stylistically appealing, they would never have been used so much as to become stale.) The problem with clichés is not that they are inexpressive but that they have been overused and misused to the point of weariness and ineffectiveness.

People with whom we often talk may bore us precisely because we know in advance what they are going to say and even the words and phrases they are going to use. In short, both what they say and how they say that something have become "molds" of thought and expression, constantly repeated. It should be kept in mind, too, that expressions which seem fresh and original to us may be clichés to those who have read and listened more than we have.

In daily speech, everyone is likely to use some clichés, but study of this list of 300 trite expressions will help anyone to avoid hackneyed language and perhaps to strive for freshness and originality in diction.

Trite Expressions

absence makes the heart
  grow fonder
acid test
add insult to injury
age before beauty
all in a lifetime
all in all
all is not gold that glitters
all sorts and conditions . . .
all things being equal
all wool and a yard wide
all work and no play
apple of one's eye
apple-pie order
arms of Morpheus
as luck would have it

at one fell swoop
bark up the wrong tree
bated breath
bathed in tears
battle of life
beard the lion in his den
beat a hasty retreat
beggars description
best bib and tucker
best foot forward
best-laid plans of mice and men
better late than never
better to have loved and lost
beyond the pale
bitter end
blood is thicker than water
blow off steam
blow one's horn
blushing bride
blush of shame
bolt from the blue
born with a silver spoon
bosom of the family
brave as a lion
brawny arms
breathe a sigh of relief
bright and early
bright future
bright young countenance
bring home the bacon
briny deep
brown as a berry
budding genius
busy as a bee (beaver)
butterflies in (my) stomach
caught red-handed
checkered career
cheer to the echo
cherchez la femme
chip off the old block

clear as mud
coals to Newcastle
cock and bull story
cold as ice
cold feet
cold sweat
cool as a cucumber
common, or garden, variety
conspicuous by his (her)
    absence
consummation devoutly to be
    wished
cradle of the deep
crow to pick
cut a long story short
cynosure of all eyes
dainty repast
dead as a doornail
dead giveaway
deaf as a post
depths of despair
die is cast
distance lends enchantment
dog days
doomed to disappointment
down my alley
downy couch
draw the line
dreamy expression
drown one's sorrows
drunk as a skunk
duck (fish) out of water
dull thud
each and every
ear to the ground
eat, drink, and be merry
eat one's hat
epoch-making
et tu, Brute
exception proves the rule

eyes like stars
eyes of the world
face the music
fair sex
far cry
fast and loose
fat as a pig
fat's in the fire
favor with a selection
fearfully and wonderfully
  made
feather in his (her) cap
feathered choir
feel one's oats
festive board
few and far between
few well-chosen words
fight like a tiger
fill the bill
filthy lucre
fine and dandy
first and foremost
flash in the pan
flat as a pancake
flesh and blood
fly off the handle
fond farewell
(a) fool and his money
fools rush in . . .
free as the air
fresh as a daisy
garden (common) variety
gentle as a lamb
get one's number
get the sack
get the upper hand
get up on the wrong side . . .
get what I mean?
gild the lily
give hostages to fortune

glass of fashion
God's country
golden mean
(a) good time was had by all
goose hangs high
grand and glorious
grain of salt
graphic account (description)
greatness thrust upon . . .
green as grass
green with envy
Grim Reaper
grin like a Cheshire cat
hale and hearty
hail fellow well met
hand-to-mouth
hapless victim
happy as a lark
happy pair
hard row to hoe
haughty stare
haul over the coals
head over heels
heart of gold
heartless wretch
hew to the line
high on the hog
hornet's nest (stir up)
hot as a pistol
hungry as a bear
if the truth be told
inspiring sight
interesting to note
intestinal fortitude
in the last (final) analysis
in the long run
irons in the fire
irony of fate
it goes without saying
it stands to reason

jig is up
land-office business
last but not least
last straw
law unto himself (herself)
lead to the altar
lean and hungry look
lean over backward
leave in the lurch
left-handed compliment
let one's hair down
let the cat out of the bag
lick into shape
like a newborn babe
limp as a rag
little did I think
lock, stock, and barrel
mad as a wet hen
mad dash
make a clean breast of
make ends meet
make hay while the sun
    shines
make night hideous
make no bones
make things hum
mantle of snow
meets the eye
method in his madness
mind your *p*'s and *q*'s
missing the boat
monarch of all he (she)
    surveys
moot question
more easily said than done
Mother Nature
motley crew (crowd)
naked truth
neat as a bandbox
necessary evil

needs no introduction
never a dull moment
nipped in the bud
not to be sneezed at
not worth a Continental
number is up
of a high order
Old Sol
on the ball (stick)
open and shut
opportunity knocks but . . .
out of sight, out of mind
over a barrel
ox in the ditch
parental rooftree
pay the piper (fiddler)
penny for your thoughts
pillar of society
pillar to post
play fast and loose
play second fiddle
play up to
point with pride
poor but honest
pretty as a picture
pretty kettle of fish
pretty penny
psychological moment
pull one's leg
pull the wool over . . .
pull up stakes
pure as the driven snow
put a bug (flea) in one's ear
put on the dog
rack one's brains
raining cats and dogs
read the riot act
reckon without one's host
red as a beet
rendered a selection

ring true
rub the wrong way
sad to relate
sadder but wiser
sail under false colors
save for a rainy day
seal one's fate
seething mass
self-made man
sell like hot cakes
set one's cap for
set up shop
seventh heaven
show the white feather
shuffle off this mortal coil
sick and tired
sight to behold
sing like a bird
sleep the sleep of the just
snare and a delusion
sow wild oats
start the ball rolling
steal one's thunder
stick in the craw
strong as an ox

stubborn as a mule
stuffed shirt
take it easy
teach the young idea
tell it to the Marines
tenterhooks, be on
terra firma
that is to say
throw in the sponge
throw the book at
time hangs heavy
tired as a dog
tit for tat
too funny for words
too many irons in the fire
truth to tell
turn over a new leaf
view with alarm
wee small hours
wet to the skin
where ignorance is bliss
wide open spaces
wolf in sheep's clothing
you can say that again
your guess is as good as mine

SUMMARY — USAGE

In every speaking situation, one's aim should be to use only words and phrases that are appropriate, fit, suitable, proper. The appropriateness of language is determined by the subject being discussed, the place where talk is taking place, and the identity and relationship of speaker and listener. Each of us employs a different level of usage depending upon whether we are speaking or writing, upon our audience or readers, and upon the kind of occasion involved.

Among *cultural* levels of speech may be included illiteracies, narrowly local dialects, ungrammatical speech, slovenly vocabulary and construction, and an excessive resort to slang, shoptalk, and even profanity and obscenity. On a higher level is the language spoken by cultured people over wide areas; such speech is clear, relatively concise, and grammatically correct. In general, these two levels may be referred to as *substandard* and *standard*, with the latter category divided into *informal standard* and *formal standard*.

Functional varieties of speech may loosely be grouped in two classes: *familiar* and *formal*. Included in *functional varieties* of speech independent of cultural levels are colloquialisms. Such expressions exist in varying degrees of formality: familiar conversation, private correspondence, formal conversation, public worship, platform speech, etc.

For every occasion when one needs to speak formally there will be a hundred or a thousand situations involving informal speech. Here the aim should be to speak naturally and easily, with as much interest and animation as one can summon up. No matter how important what one has to say is, and no matter how interested one is in saying that something, he should try to choose his words to fit the occasion. In doing so, he should strive as hard as he can to avoid such roadblocks to effective speech as illiteracies, improprieties, grammatical errors, excessive slang, unidiomatic expressions, shoptalk, wordiness, and triteness.

5. WHAT PRONUNCIATION IS AND DOES

For each of us, words actually live in oral rather than in printed or handwritten form. It is a rare person indeed who does not speak a hundred or a thousand times more often than he writes, who does not listen more than he reads. Consequently, pronunciation, which is the act of making the sounds of speech, is the direct, immediate, and constant concern of everyone who wishes to "say it right."

Although people spend more time in speaking and listening than in any other pursuit of their lives (breathing and possibly sleeping excepted), the way they pronounce words is not so critical and important as choosing and using words themselves. How can this be? An answer will be provided later in this section, but first let's free the widespread everyday activity of pronunciation from some of the false ideas that have grown up about it.

EVERYONE SPEAKS HIS OWN LANGUAGE

Even if one wished to, it would be impossible for him to speak *the* English language or even "American English." Everyone makes speech sounds with characteristics related to a specific locality, individual background, and particular social group. Everyone learns and usually hangs on to certain speech patterns that are uniquely his own, patterns derived from the members of his family, the locality or localities in which he grew up, the schools he attended, his acquaintances, his occupation, his hobbies and recreations. That is, no such thing as total conformity in pronunciation is possible because every speaker of a language (English, American, Italian, German, French, Spanish, Russian, or whatnot) employs his own dialect. Every pronouncer of words in no matter what language has a speech pattern peculiar to him at a specific period of his life. One's individual speech pattern is known as his *idiolect*, his unique way of forming the sounds of speech. To the expert, the speech sounds of no two persons are, or ever can be, identical.

NO SINGLE PRONUNCIATION STANDARD EXISTS

With many millions of idiolects for the English language (or any other language) in daily use, no way of sounding a given word can be said to be its *only correct* pronunciation. True, nearly everyone pronounces more than 90 percent of all words in general use in about the same way, so nearly the same that for all practical purposes the pronunciation could be called identical. And yet a trained ear would detect differences. Also, even if pronunciations of individual words seem identical, they would change and shift as they appeared in connected speech (talk, that is) because people speak at different rates and with differing emphasis on specific words.

The distinctive speech patterns of sections of the United States involve flavor and color more than substance, so that communication between speakers in different areas creates no real problem. But individual systems of pronunciation can and do exist throughout the country, no one of which can flatly be called "standard" or "universal" or "correct."

WHAT IS CORRECT PRONUNCIATION?

The only accurate answer to this question is that the pronunciation of any word or phrase is correct if it is one used by a majority of educated, cultivated speakers under similar sets of circumstances in a particular major speech area. This definition suggests that *more than one* "correct" pronunciation exists for the majority of words. Such an answer lacks final authority, but it is the only honest, informed answer that is possible. It is a basic principle of all experts on pronunciation, including the makers of dictionaries, that the one and only test for correctness is *usage*. Of no significance in determining "correct" or "good" pronunciations are rules, tradition, spelling, or word derivation.

ISN'T A DICTIONARY AN AUTHORITY?

No reliable dictionary published within recent decades attempts to dictate what "correct" pronunciation is or should be. Only to the extent that the compilers of a dictionary are acknowledged as accurate and objective recorders and interpreters of usage can their work be considered authoritative. A good dictionary tries to provide an authentic and unbiased description of pronunciation usage; it will *never* flatly state that such-and-such a pronunciation is "right" or "wrong."

The attitude of competent dictionary-makers is expressed in this statement by Dr. Daniel Jones, author of *The Pronunciation of English* and an eminent former professor of phonetics (the study of speech sounds and their production, transmission, and reception):

> It is useful that descriptions of existing pronunciation should be recorded, but I no longer feel disposed to recommend any particular forms of pronunciation . . . or to condemn others. It must, in my view, be left to individual English-speaking persons to decide whether they should speak in the manner that comes to them naturally or whether they should alter their speech in any way.

We should learn, and never forget, that the so-called authority of a dictionary derives from the speech and writing of a community of what has been termed "effective" citizens. As Professor Cabell Greet, a recognized authority and a former consultant on pronunciation to a large radio and television network, has said:

> Without seeking to impair any citizen's right to be his own professor of English, we [the makers of dictionaries] look for what is national, contemporary, and reputable. This is our standard of correctness.

WHY, THEN, STUDY PRONUNCIATION AT ALL?

Every speaker has his own idiolect and cannot attain an unvarying standard of pronunciation even if he tries. Furthermore, no rigid standard exists. Finally, not even the dictionary, any dictionary, either is, or claims to be, a final authority. So why bother about pronunciation? What's all the fuss about? Why shouldn't everyone pronounce words in whatever way comes naturally?

The statements made and questions raised in the preceding paragraph lead us back to the remark made earlier that the speaker of English should not be so much concerned about his pronunciation as about his choice and use of words. The reason is simple: diction involves hundreds of knotty problems for every one caused by pronunciation. That is, choosing and using the words of everyday speech is often difficult; pronouncing these same words is relatively simple.

We use remarkably few different words in ordinary speech, and the overwhelming majority of them cause no pronunciation problems whatever. It may be both startling and reassuring to learn that only twelve simple words account for about 25 percent of everything spoken and written in English. The dozen most used words in English are *a, and, he, I, in, it, is, of, that, the, to*, and *was*. These twelve and thirty-eight more (a total of fifty words) make up half of the running total in all English speech and writing. If you increase the number to the thousand most common words in English, you will account for 80 percent of all words everyone uses in speaking and writing and comes across in reading.

You may be inclined to doubt these statements, but they are substantiated by the word count contained in *The Teacher's Word Book of 30,000 Words*, prepared under the direction of two outstanding scholars, Edward L. Thorndike and Irving Lorge (New York: Teachers, 1944). Other experts unhesitatingly accept the findings of Thorndike and Lorge.

If only one thousand different words appear in some 80 percent of all the expressions that one says, hears, writes, and reads, it follows that the task of learning to pronounce that small number should be simple. And yet the problem is even more elementary: almost none of the thousand words creates any pronunciation difficulty whatever for the ordinary speaker.

In a running count of many millions of words used by speakers and writers of English, the words *a, and, of, the*, and *to* will appear more than a hundred thousand times; *he, I, in, it, is, that*, and *was* will appear more than fifty thousand times. None of these words is a pronunciation demon, nor indeed are many of the 620 words appearing more than one thousand times in the same word count. For proof of this statement, note the thirty-nine most often used words beginning with the letter *a:*

A

a	am
about	American
according	among
across	an
act	and
action	another
add	answer
after	any
afternoon	anything
again	appear
against	are
age	arm
ago	army
all	around
almost	art
alone	as
along	ask
already	at
also	away
always	

Do you find any hard-to-pronounce words in this list? Perhaps someone may say *acrost* (acrossed) instead of "uh KRAWS" or "uh KROS"; in careless or rapid speech, some might drop the final "g" in *according*. The entire list, however, is so simple that no ordinary speaker need waste time in thoughts about pronunciation.

Just so you will not think that the list is "rigged" with words starting with *a*, see whether the following *b, n,* and *u* words are any more difficult.

B

baby	better
back	between
bad	big
bank	bill
battle	black
be	body
became	book
because	both
become	boy
bed	bring
beer	British
before	brought
began	brown
begin	building
behind	built
being	business
believe	but
best	by

N

name	next
nation	night
national	no
nature	nor
near	north
necessary	not
need	note
never	nothing
new	now
news	number
New York	

U

uncle	up
under	upon
understand	us
United States	use
until	

That only one thousand words comprise 80 percent of all the words used in speaking of course does not mean that in any particular conversation (or piece of writing) those words would appear in exactly that percentage. Nor does this basic fact have any bearing upon two other considerations: (1) some of the remaining 20 percent do involve problems in pronunciation; (2) the actual words comprising this remaining 20 percent vary widely with individual users. And yet it should be reassuring to know that, roughly speaking, 80 percent of all so-called problems in pronunciation are nonexistent, or nearly so.

Your best plan of attack on the problem of pronunciation is to concentrate only on those words in the remaining 20 percent that you do use and that do cause trouble.

6 TACKLING THE PROBLEM OF PRONUNCIATION

If you have a good ear and spend considerable time listening to speakers in person and on radio and television, you can learn the pronunciation' of many troublesome words. This method of learning by ear has several flaws, however, among which two may be mentioned: (1) not every effective speaker (including broadcasters and telecasters) is infallible in pronunciation; (2) in any particular conversation, speech, or broadcast, you may not hear the words you wish and need to learn to pronounce.

The surest, most economical way to learn to "pronounce it right" is to consult your dictionary *when the need arises.* Remember: Do not worry about the pronunciation of any word until you read it, hear it, or anticipate the need for it in your own speech.

What such words will be must vary from person to person. No two people have the same vocabulary, just as no two people have the same fingerprints. No two people make the same demands on language because no two can have the same audience or identical things to say. As a conscientious student of pronunciation, you will make your own lists of trouble spots. Looking up words as you need to and entering them after a period of time in your own wordbook in alphabetical order (or some other order that appeals to you) is the most efficient way to improve your pronunciation.

Here, for instance, is the record of a careful student of pronunciation who in one month found that he had encountered in hearing or reading the following words beginning with *d*, about the pronunciation of which he was doubtful:

D

dais	debris
data	decorous

deign	diffuse
demesne	diocese
deprecatory	diphtheria
dereliction	disparate
descant	divan
despicable	draught
detour	duress
diapason	dysentery

Any list of *d* words you would make would differ from this one for several reasons: you would not encounter the same words in reading or listening; you would have no problem with the pronunciation of some of them; you would run across other words that would raise problems; not all the words on this list would be those that you presently need or foresee a use for. The point is that you should note the words you do need, study them carefully in your dictionary, and record them in a notebook with their correct spelling, varied meanings, and standard pronunciation(s).

HOW SHOULD I USE MY DICTIONARY IN LEARNING PRONUNCIATION?

Every modern American dictionary presents its own system of recording pronunciation. Your first move should be to familiarize yourself with that system. Read the essay on pronunciation included in the front matter of your dictionary; every reliable dictionary contains such an article. Study the full pronunciation key provided on the inside of the front or back covers of your book, or in both places. Examine the abbreviated pronunciation key appearing at the bottom of each page, or each alternate page, of your dictionary. Only after you have taken these steps are you in a position intelligently to use your dictionary as a guide in pronunciation.

Pronunciation, as you already know and as your dictionary will again inform you, depends upon the *sound* given to alphabetical letters or letter combinations and upon *accent* of emphasized syllables.

Dictionary-makers have had to concoct systems for representing sounds because only twenty-six letters must be used in some 250 common spellings of sounds. The best-known set of symbols for providing a consistent system for transcribing the sounds of language is the International Phonetic Alphabet (IPA). This alphabet, applicable to all languages, including English, is highly accurate, but it is likely that the ordinary speaker will find it somewhat cumbersome and involved.

Your most sensible approach will be to study the "pronunciation word" that appears in parentheses immediately after an entry word. It is a respelling of the word, giving the sounds of vowels and consonants by syllables, according to the pronunciation key that the dictionary has adopted. (Every dictionary compiler has chosen anywhere from forty to sixty symbols that he judges adequate to explain all practical problems in pronunciation.) Study the key in your dictionary to find out the various sounds of vowels, consonants, and letter combinations as indicated in illustrative sample words.

As an indication of the kinds of information provided about pronunciation in your dictionary, see how it represents the varied sounds of, say, the letter *o*. You will find that the sounds of *o* are indicated by some or all of these symbols:

o — as in *odd, hot, lot, ox*
ō — as in *go, open, over, no*
ô — as in *order, horn, ought*
o͝o — as in *took, book, look, poor*
o͞o — as in *pool, ooze, boot, too*

Each of the signs (symbols) appearing with words in a pronunciation key is a kind of diacritical mark. (The word *diacritical* comes from a Greek term meaning "capable of distinguishing," "distinctive.") Still other signs, or points, are occasionally added to letters to indicate a particular sound value. Among these are the *circumflex* (raison d'être); the *tilde* (cañon); *umlaut* (schön), and the *cedilla* (façade). Some dictionaries supply these and other diacritical marks with individual entries; other dictionaries provide a separate "foreign sounds" key. All diacritical marks are somewhat inexact in suggesting the reproduction of sounds, but their use is one further example of the pains dictionary makers have taken in trying to provide a faithful record of the sounds of language.

The matter of stress, or accent, is much less involved than

the pronunciation of sounds. But it is important. Examine the method your dictionary employs for indicating where accents fall in given entries. Some dictionaries provide both accent marks and syllabication periods (dots) in the entry word. Others use only dots to indicate syllabication in the entry word and insert accent marks in the "pronunciation word." Learn the methods your dictionary has provided for indicating heavy (primary) stress and less heavy (secondary) stress. Whatever devices your dictionary uses are made fully clear in an article at the front of the book.

When two or more pronunciations of an entry are provided—that is, when sounds or accents are indicated differently—the pronunciation more generally used may or may not be given first. One reliable current dictionary shows first the pronunciation its compilers consider the one most widespread in "general American" usage. Another equally reliable dictionary lists first the pronunciation most prevalent in Eastern speech (along the North Atlantic seaboard). Any pronunciation shown is "standard," although some dictionaries do make a distinction by preceding a given pronunciation with the word "also." You should additionally note that pronunciations are sometimes labeled *British*, or *chiefly British*, or give some other indication of regional usage.

Pronunciation, or what may be called the sound system of language, is important, although relatively less so for the average speaker than diction or what is broadly called grammar. And yet phonology, the sound system of language, really *is* "the grammar of speech." Although the problem of pronunciation is not acute for most speakers in their daily use of language, it should not be minimized. Every user of language will find gaps in his knowledge when he encounters certain words and will be doubtful about pronunciation. When this situation occurs, he should pull out his dictionary.

Nor should it be overlooked that phonology is a science that has been deeply studied. Someone interested in more than cursory fashion in pronunciation should read such a learned and helpful article as "Guide to Pronunciation" in *Webster's Third New International Dictionary*. If he has a deep and abiding interest in pronunciation, he might also dig into such authoritative (and relatively difficult) works as these:

American Pronunciation, by John S. Kenyon (Ann Arbor: Wahr, 1962)

A Pronouncing Dictionary of American English, by John S. Kenyon and Thomas A. Knott (Springfield: Merriam, 1953)

English Pronunciation, by Robert Lado and Charles C. Fries (Ann Arbor: University of Michigan, 1954)

The Pronunciation of English, by Daniel Jones (New York: Cambridge University, 1956)

Comfort yourself with the realization, however, that the one thousand words appearing most often in your speaking, hearing, writing, and reading—the words that comprise 80 percent of all the words encountered—present few problems in pronunciation. Further simplifying pronunciation is that only nine thousand additional words (the next most frequently occurring ones) account for 18 percent of *all* words spoken, heard, written, or read. That is, only ten thousand words comprise 98 percent of all expressions regularly used. After the first ten thousand, pronunciation demons *do* appear more often. However, words in the 10,001–20,000 frequency group appear less than one-twelfth as often as those in the first ten thousand. Those in the 20,001–30,000 frequency group appear on an average only one two-hundredths as often as words in the most common ten thousand. In short, errors in pronunciation do occur, but they appear infrequently because of rare use and because comparatively few words are involved.

WHAT IS MY PARTICULAR PROBLEM WITH PRONUNCIATION?

Assuming that you have no serious impediment in speech or hearing, whatever difficulties you encounter with pronunciation probably arise from two causes: (1) you do not systematically and carefully study in your dictionary the pronunciation of words you need in your vocabulary; (2) you speak in a careless, slovenly manner.

Hopefully, enough has been already said about dictionary study to set you on the right path. Remember, however, that you should not "swallow the dictionary" but should carefully study only those words that you need, or feel that you may need, in your own speech activities. If you are a public speaker by profession, a minister or trial lawyer or broadcaster or tour guide or teacher, you will need to consult your dictionary often. If you are an "average" citizen, the problem is rather simple.

No matter how cultivated and knowledgeable you are as a user of language, it is likely that on occasion you pronounce words in a hurried, careless, and slovenly fashion. No one is always on his best behavior in pronunciation any more than he is in any other activity of his life. Each of us pronounces many words in one way when we are listening to what we are saying *and* when we say the words alone. We may sound quite differently when we use these same words in ordinary conversation.

Now, few people are so prim and precise as to wish always to speak in a formal way. Nearly everyone will agree that stilted conversation is less agreeable, less desirable, than the informal give-and-take of friendly communication. The danger is always present, however, that if we engage too often in glovenly, slurred, and imprecise pronunciation, we may find it difficult to pronounce in standard fashion when the need arises for us to do so.

In the speech of even educated, careful speakers, vowels in unaccented syllables tend to become indistinct. Cultivated speakers whose pronunciation is normally standard often slur certain consonants and occasionally drop out entire syllables. We are all aware that in speech words often flow together without the pauses which, in writing, are shown by spaces. The "sound boundary" of a word or phrase—known to linguists as *juncture*—is nowhere indicated in any dictionary and is often blurred in speech.

Such speech habits are not necessarily faulty; so long as one's hearers understand without difficulty what is being communicated, no "error" occurs. In saying "boys and girls" or "bread and butter," for example, one can accent each word, but in formal and informal and standard and nonstandard speech, the phrases sound more like "boys 'n girls" or "boysandgirls," "bread 'n butter" or "breadnbutter." In everyday speech, even educated and cultivated talkers may pronounce "it's all right" as "sawright."

Check your own speech habits for the following pronunciations. If many of them appear, possibly you should be more careful. If you feel that they occur because of ignorance rather than informality, you should be doubly careful. We should not be stiff or formal in making speech sounds, but perhaps we do owe our listeners pronunciation that is clear, pleasing, and widely accepted.

Careless Pronunciation

accep (for *accept*)
accidently (for *accidentally*)
arncha (for *aren't you*)
asprin (for *aspirin*)
carmel (for *caramel*)
cartoon (for *carton*)
colyum (for column)
congradulate (for
   congratulate)
defnite (for *definite*)
dintcha (for *didn't you*)
disasterous (for *disastrous*)
doncha (for *don't you*)
envirament (for *environment*)
famly (for *family*)
finely (for *finally*)
gennelman (for *gentleman*)
gonna (for *going to*)
havncha (for *haven't you*)
hinderance (for *hindrance*)
histry (for *history*)
hundered (for *hundred*)
innerference (for *interference*)
inny (for *any*)
izda (for *is the*)
jester (for *gesture*)
kep (for *kept*)
kintergarden (for
   kindergarten)

liberry (for *library*)
partener (for *partner*)
perfessor (for *professor*)
porpose (for *propose*)
preform (for *perform*)
probly (for *probably*)
progidy (for *prodigy*)
rememberance (for
   remembrance)
represenative (for
   representative)
shudder (for *shutter*)
similiar (for *similar*)
smothertam (for *some other
   time*)
tempature (for *temperature*)
tempermental (for
   temperamental)
umberella (for *umbrella*)
victry (for *victory*)
wanna (for *want to*)
wozzat (for *what's that*)
whachusay (for *what you say*)
whosit (for *who is it*)
willya (for *will you*)
wunnerful (for *wonderful*)
y'noh (for *you know*)

SUMMARY – PRONUNCIATION

The grammar of speech – phonology, pronunciation – should be a concern of everyone during nearly every waking hour of every day. (We can ignore the pronunciation problems that arise when we talk in our sleep.) The most systematic and reliable way to tackle a study of pronunciation is through consistent and informed use of a dictionary. Two other suggestions, however, may be helpful.

First, you can try to form the habit of listening carefully to the speech you hear in person and over the air. When you hear an unfamiliar word that interests you, when you hear a pronunciation different from your own, when you hear what you think is an "error" in pronunciation – you should promptly haul out a dictionary. It is possible greatly to improve pronunciation by tuning the ear, especially when one is listening to cultured, educated, and truly informed speakers.

Second, try experimenting with listening to yourself. Many of us never *really* hear what we say. If one makes a conscious effort, he can hear the sounds of his own voice and can form some judgment of its quality. It is not difficult to hear one's own production of sounds and to question accent, vowel formation, articulation, and inflection. If careful listening to your voice inhibits you from speaking at all (everyone becomes self-conscious at times), try "taping" your voice. Home recorders are easy to use. If you do not have access to such a machine, investigate the possibility of using someone's Dictaphone or of having a few minutes of your talk (or reading aloud) recorded by a commercial firm. The cost will be minimal; what you learn may be significant.

Above all, become aware of your pronunciation without becoming frightened or overly self-conscious at your method of speaking. Remember that your primary aim should be "to speak as your neighbors do, not better." Make friends with your dictionary. Finally, try to avoid the careless, slovenly, and sometimes uninformed habits of pronunciation that do make nearly everyone seem less intelligent and less socially aware than he really is.

PART THREE
COMMON ERRORS IN CHOOSING
AND PRONOUNCING WORDS

To be sure, the English language is a changing and growing thing. All its users have, of course, a perceptible effect upon it. But in changing and growing it needs no contrived help from chitchat columnists or advertising writers and comic strip artists or television speakers. It will evolve nicely by itself. If anything, it requires protection from influences that try to push it too fast. There is need, not for those who would halt its progress altogether, but for those who can keep a gentle foot on the brake and a guiding hand on the steering wheel.

Theodore M. Bernstein

The following list contains words and expressions often misused, confused, or mispronounced. It is a shortcut discussion of some of the more common problems of diction and pronunciation, not a complete inventory of all the problems encountered when one wishes to "say it right." Learning what follows, however, will constitute a major attack upon difficulties facing every speaker of the English language.

In studying this glossary, remember that usage is constantly changing and that words and expressions now restricted in some way may later be considered standard. You should also remember that no dictionary and no author is a final authority. Because American English is a changing, growing language, however, authorities are less conservative than once they were; they tend to be less dogmatic, more liberal, more tolerant, more permissive. Currently acceptable language includes optional and allowable choices, even replacements. The statements that follow may certainly, in time, be altered. For now, this list is offered as a handy guide for everyday speakers who wish to improve their choice, use, and pronunciation of language.

a, an. Correct choice of *a* and *an* depends on the initial sound of the word which follows. *A* should be used before all words beginning with any consonant except silent *h* (an *honor*) and even before words beginning with vowels that represent combined consonant and vowel sounds (*eunuch, unit*). *An* should be used before all vowel sounds.

a boy	an envelope
a European	an *f*
a *g*	an hour
a picture	an orange
a store	an unknown

With the words *history* and *historian*, a preceding *a* is more often used today than *an*. In *history*, the *h* is always pronounced; the *h* in words such as *historian* and *historical* was formerly not pronounced, but it frequently is in contemporary usage. Always say "*a* history book," but refer to *an* or *a* "historian" or *an* or *a* "historical novel" as you please. Both are standard usage.

Neither *a* nor *an* is really needed in such expressions as *no such (a) thing, no greater (an) honor.*

a-. (*Aloud, aboard, abed, arise, athirst.*) This is a prefix with many meanings: "in," "on," "at," "up," "not," etc.

This prefix also appears in highly colloquial or provincial speech (but not in standard use) in such expressions as *a-fishing, a-hunting, a-laughing,* and *a-talking* (usually with the final *g* omitted). Except when you are quoting someone or trying to be humorous, don't use this hesitant *uh* sound in expressions such as those cited.

ability, capacity. *Ability* means the physical, mental, financial, or legal power to do something (*ability* to walk, to read, to pay a bill, to assess property). *Capacity* is the ability to hold, absorb, or contain (a bucket with a *capacity* of one gallon, a motel filled to *capacity.*)

able to. A wordy and unidiomatic expression for "can" or "could." "This work *could* not be finished in a month" is preferable to "This word was not *able to* be finished in a month." Confine use of *able* to persons or objects which possess ability: "He was *able* in science."

about, around, round. *About* is a commonly used word with several meanings and shades of meaning, but most of them develop the idea of "circling," "on every side," or "here and there" (walk *about*, look *about*). It has also the meanings of "nearly," or "approximately" (*about* one hundred books). It is informally used in the sense of "almost" (*about* ready to go). The phrase *at about* ("at about midnight") is wordy: the *at* can be omitted unless you intend *about* to mean "approximately."

Around has many of the basic meanings of *about* ("on all sides," "here and there"), as in *walk around* and *look around*. But in such senses *around* is more informal than *about*. *Wait around, to travel around, to have been around,* and *around noon* are fully permissible in colloquial (spoken) usage.

Around is usually preferred to *round* in such expressions as *around the world* and *around the Horn*. To say "meet me *round* noon" is more informal than "meet me around noon"; preferably, say or write "meet me *about* noon."

about to. The word *about* has a meaning of readiness or willingness; the phrase *not about to* conveys an idea of unwillingness, unreadiness, or opposition of some sort. ("He was not *about to* pay the bill.") The expression is both trite and informal and usually should be avoided by careful speakers.

above. Some grammarians object to the use of *above* in the meaning of "preceding," or "previously mentioned or written" ("the examples given *above*" or "the *above* examples"). However, *above* can be an adjective as well as an adverb, so that no actual grammatical error is involved. The objection to using *above* in this sense is that the word may refer vaguely, or even loosely and incorrectly, to preceding material; overuse of it may make you sound legalistic or stilted. As a preposition, *above* presents no usage problems ("*above* the earth"). As a noun, *above* is both vague and informal. Instead of "The *above* states my position fairly," it is much better to say "This is my position," or "The preceding statements present my position fairly."

absolute. This word means "complete," "unlimited," "perfect," "unconditional." Logically, *absolute* admits neither comparison nor shading; to refer to one's *very absolute effort* or *too absolute statement* is illogical. However, if a qualifying word such as *nearly* is used, this objection is removed: *one's very nearly absolute statement.*

absolutely. This word means "positively," "definitely." All these words are overused to mean "quite," or "very," or even "yes": "She was *absolutely* lovely; he was *positively* godlike; it was *definitely* the wedding of the year; did you attend it?" can be gushily answered, "Absolutely." Suggestion: omit the italicized words in the question and supply the simple answer yes.

accept, except. These words have different pronunciations and different meanings. *Accept* means "to receive," "to agree with," "to say yes to." As a verb, *except* means "to omit," "to exempt," "to exclude"; as a preposition, *except* means "other than." It should not be used as a conjunction. "He won't go *except* I tell him to" is wrong. Some correct sentences are: "He did not *accept* the proposal." "Tod was *excepted* from the list of the invited." "Everyone *except* me knew the right answer."

access, excess. These words differ in pronunciation and

meaning. *Access* means "admittance," "way of approach." *Excess* means "surpassing limits," "over and above." "Joe has *access* to the bank vaults." "The *excess* of profits this year over last is gratifying."

accidentally. This word, meaning "happening by chance," "occurring without design," "unexpected and unforeseen," is often mispronounced and misspelled. The word has five syllables (ac·ci·den·tal·ly); omit *al* in neither spelling nor pronunciation. There is no such word as "accidently."

accidents will happen. This trite expression has been quoted so often that it has lost much of its effectiveness and seems jaded and stale. In addition, it often strikes a false note of levity and unconcern over a serious situation; more importantly, it is not wholly true: many accidents can be prevented.

accumulate. This word, meaning "to collect," "to gather," or "to amass," is often mispronounced and misspelled. It has four syllables (ac·cu·mu·late). The first *a* and the second *u* have approximately the sound of the first and third *a* in *banana* and should not be omitted in pronouncing the word.

accurate. Meaning "precise," "without error," "conforming to truth or to a standard," this word is occasionally misspelled and mispronounced. It has three syllables (ac·cu·rate), each of which should be pronounced (ak·yer·it). Do not say "ak·rit."

acme, climax. *Acme* means "summit," "highest point." *Climax* implies a scale of increasing, ascending values and is applied to the highest point in interest, force, or intensity. "His performance was the *acme* of professional skill." "The *climax* of the indoor games was the mile run."

acoustics. This word can be used with either singular or plural verbs, depending upon what you mean. When you refer to that branch of physics dealing with the laws of sound, use a singular verb after *acoustics*. When discussing the sound-producing qualities of a room, use a plural verb. ("*Acoustics is* a branch of physics." "The *acoustics* of this theater *are* superb.")

acquiesce in, to. Formerly used with *to, acquiesce* is now correctly and idiomatically used with *in* to mean "consent," "concur," "comply": "The salesmen *acquiesced in* the plans of company management."

acquitted of, from. The correct idiomatic expression is *ac-*

quit of, not *acquit from*. ("He was *acquitted of* all blame.")
However, one can say "He was *freed from* all blame" and
"He *acquitted* himself *like* a brave man."

across, acrost. Only *across* is acceptable in pronunciation
and spelling. *Acrost* is substandard, either dialectal or illiterate.

act, action. An *act* is a deed, a thing done. *Action* is closely
related in meaning but more precisely suggests the *doing* of
something, of being in operation or motion. ("That was an
act of kindness." "Your *action* was unselfish.")

actual, real, virtual. *Actual* and *real* are closely related in
meaning—"existing in fact," "not imaginary"—but they may
be distinguished. *Actual* places emphasis upon "*coming*
into a sphere of action or fact"; *real* expresses objective or
material *existence*. *Virtual* means having the effect but
not the form of what is specified. ("Is this an *actual* assignment or only something to keep me busy?" "Is this *real*
money or counterfeit?" "After the president resigned, the
vice-president was the *virtual* head of the firm.")

actually, really. Each of these adverbs is used, often overused, to suggest doubt or disbelief: "Did you *actually* tell
him that?" "Did you *really* buy the car?" See also *real, really*.

ad. This is a clipped form of *advertisement*. It is informal
(colloquial) and should appear rarely, if at all, in strictly
formal writing. But the use of *ad* in everyday speech is both
widespread and justified. Also, one could hardly play tennis
without using *ad*, an abbreviation for *advantage*.

adapt, adept, adopt. To *adapt* is "to adjust," "to make suitable." Note the second syllable (*dapt*) which resembles *apt*,
meaning "fit" or "suited to the purpose." *Adept* has something of the meaning of *apt* ("skilled," "proficient"): one can
say, "Bob was *apt* in science," or "Bob was *adept* in science."
Adopt means "to accept" or "to take as one's own." One refers to *adopted* children and *adoptive* parents. ("You must
adapt yourself to this situation." "He is *adept* in dancing
the latest steps." "I shall *adopt* your proposal." "This milli-
ner is *adept* in *adapting* styles from abroad and finds that
women here *adopt* them eagerly.")

addicted, devoted. The former has an unfavorable or undesirable sense of "given to a practice or habit." *Devoted* also

suggests habitual action or attachment but only to matters which the speaker or writer considers good, beneficial, or favorable: "He was *addicted* to narcotics (or lying or thievery or alcohol)." "Jim was *devoted* to his mother (or his country or good literature)."

additionally. In speaking, this word is often slurred. It has five syllables, each of which should be pronounced: ad·DI·tion·al·ly.

addled. An *addled* egg is spoiled, rotten. To call someone an *addlehead* or an *addlebrain* is therefore to imply that he is not just giddy or confused but also "stinking." File this word in your vocabulary among those terms to be used carefully and rarely.

address. Perhaps the preferred pronunciation of this word as both verb and noun is *a·dress*. The initial *a* should be sounded like the first *a* in *banana*, not like the *a* in *day*. Including the sound of *d* in the first syllable (ad·dress) is permissible but not usually recommended as standard.

ad hoc. Pronounced *ad·hok*, this Latin phrase means "toward this." In English, its meaning is "for a specific purpose" and is overused in reference to *ad hoc* committees, *ad hoc* plans, etc.

ad lib. This verb, meaning "to improvise," "to deliver spontaneously," is derived from Latin *ad libitum*, meaning "at pleasure." It can correctly be used to mean "freely" but is often overused. *Ad lib* is now a trite expression when used to mean adding words or gestures hastily improvised, or concocted, that are not in the script or not intended to be expressed by word or action.

admission, admittance. The former means "allowing to enter" or "permitted entrance," and applies to acceptance that carries certain rights and privileges. *Admittance* means "physical entry" without reference to rights or membership privileges. ("He sought *admission* to the party." "*Admittance* is by invitation only.")

adult. This common word, meaning "grown-up" or "mature" or "fully developed," may be pronounced either a·DULT or AD·ult. The former pronunciation, with *a* sounded like *a* in "above," is considered preferable by educated and *adult* speakers.

advance planning. This phrase is a classic example of our general tendency to use more words than necessary. *Planning* itself involves the idea of "looking ahead," of "devising a program for future action," a "method of carrying out a design." The word *advance* is here a useless and wordy appendage.

adverse, averse. The former means "opposed," "contrary," "hostile." *Averse* means "reluctant" and "unwilling" and implies a holding back because of distaste or dislike. ("The employees had an *adverse* opinion of the company plan." "The company treasurer is *averse* to lending money to anyone.")

advise. This word, with a basic meaning of "to counsel," "to give advice to," can also mean "tell" or "inform." It is overused in all its meanings in business letters and other forms of commercial communication. Say "I wish to *tell* you (not *advise*) that your order has been received." *Advise* is always and only a verb; *advice*, a noun spelled and pronounced differently, means "an opinion" or "recommendation." A noun formed from *advise* is spelled *advisor* or *adviser*.

affect, effect. These words have slightly different pronunciations and quite different meanings. *Affect* is always a verb (except for one use as a noun in psychology) and means "to influence," "to cause a response." ("This article will *affect* my thinking.") *Affect* also means "to assume," to "be given to" or "pretend." ("She *affected* a silly manner of speaking.") As a noun, *effect* means "result," "accomplishment." ("What was the *effect* of this appeal for money?") As a verb, *effect* means "to cause," "to bring about." ("The new manager will *effect* major changes in our sales methods.") In plural form, *effects* can mean "goods," "property." ("The deceased man's *effects* were willed to charity.")

aficionado. This term, an overused word from Spanish, means "an enthusiastic admirer," "a devotee." It is pronounced a·fee·see·a·NAH·dough.

afraid. This word, meaning "filled with fear, apprehension, concern, or regret," is overused in everyday conversation as a loose and inaccurate synonym for "think," "feel," "believe." Avoid such statements as "I'm *afraid* you're wrong" and "I'm *afraid* not," unless your concern, regret, or worry is strong and intense.

afternoons, mornings. These words are now considered adverbs, meaning, respectively, "on any afternoon," "in the mornings repeatedly." You may correctly say or write, "The office is closed *in the afternoon* during July" or "The office is closed *afternoons* in July." *Mornings* may be used in the same idiomatically correct manner. So, too, may be used such words as *Mondays* ("He always goes fishing *Mondays*"). The construction with *of* ("of a Monday") is dialectal and should not be used except regionally.

afterward, afterwards. Both *afterward* and *afterwards*, meaning "at a late or succeeding time," are correct. Studies reveal that *afterward* is more often used than *afterwards* by precise and unusually careful speakers and writers.

again. This word means "another time" or "in return" and always suggests the idea of "in addition." Therefore, it is superfluous in such expressions as *repeat again* because the prefix *re* has the meaning of *again*. Say "*Tell* your story *again*" or "Retell your story," not "*Retell* your story *again*"; "*Repeat* that, please" not "*Repeat* that *again*, please."

agenda. This word is a plural form of *agendum*, a word derived from Latin, meaning "program" or "list of items or things." The word *agendum* (plural form also *agendums*), meaning only one in a complete list of topics or matters to be considered, is rarely used today. In contemporary use, *agenda* (strictly a plural) is regarded as singular: ("*An agenda* was prepared." "The *agenda* was adopted.") Formal and precise usage distinguishes between these words: ("A firm *agendum* was drawn up," "There were three *agenda* prepared for consideration."), but standard usage permits the use of *agenda* with either a singular or plural verb.

aggravate. *Aggravate* is derived from a Latin word meaning "to make heavy" and, in English, means "to make worse," "to increase something unpleasant," "to intensify." *Aggravate* is often used informally to mean "annoy" or "provoke" or "irritate." (Sneezing *aggravated* his nasal passages. The buzzing fly annoyed, or irritated — not *aggravated* — me.)

agnostic, atheist. The former comes from a Greek word meaning "unknown and probably unknowable"; an *agnostic* is one who withholds belief because he is unwilling or unready to accept the evidence and spiritual experience acknowledged by others. An *atheist* is one who denies the existence of God and rejects religious faith and practice of all kinds. The *atheist* says, "I flatly deny"; the *agnostic* says, "I don't know." These two attitudes are considerably different.

agony, agonize. These two powerful words are overused. *Agony* means "intense pain," "suffering," "anguish"; *agonize* means to writhe or be contorted with intense pain of body or mind. "Jim was in *agony* because his new jacket didn't fit" or "Judy *agonized* over spilling the milk" are overstatements. Jim was merely *uncomfortable*; Judy may have been *embarrassed* or *mildly upset*. *Agony* and *agonize* are among the strongest words in the English language. Use them carefully and sparingly.

agree to, with, on. Each of these three prepositions may be correctly used with *agree*. If the *-ing* form of a verb (a gerund) follows *agree,* use *on:* "We *agreed on* paying the bill." Otherwise, say "We *agreed to* pay the bill," or "We *agreed that* we would pay the bill." See page 47.

a half. *Half,* meaning either of two equal parts, does not always require the use of *a.* Omit *a* in such wordy expressions as "I want *a half* of that" and "*A half* of the town is flooded."

a hold of. This is a dialectal and substandard expression. To *get hold of* something is itself a wordy, informal way to express *grasp* or *seize* or *understand* but is preferable to saying "get *a* hold of."

aim at, aim to. *At* is used with *aim* only in the sense of pointing or directing a weapon, act, or remark toward some person or object. ("Don't *aim* the gun *at* me." "He *aimed* his comments *at* those seated in the last row.") *Aim to* in the sense of "intend" or "propose" is idiomatically correct: I *aim to* please all my customers." Using *intend* or *propose* or *wish* or *hope* could substitute one word for two (always desirable in both speaking and writing) and will not seem so formal as to be stuffy.

ain't. In nonstandard and substandard speech, *ain't* is widely used as a contraction of *am not, is not, are not,* and occasionally *has not* and *have not.* However, most careful speakers avoid using *ain't* except in informal talk or when they are attempting to be humorous or achieve a "plain folks" ("I'm one of you") approach. *Ain't* rarely appears in writing except when used to characterize the speech of someone considered uneducated, illiterate, or self-made. Although widely used orally, *ain't* has not been accepted as have other contractions: *isn't* (is not); *aren't* (are not); *weren't* (were not); *hasn't* (has not); *haven't* (have not).

Although *ain't* is generally considered dialectal or illiterate, our language does need an acceptable contraction for *am not*. *Amn't* is not in favor, and *aren't I* is both ungrammatical and illogical. Until an acceptable contraction is available, it is better to say *I am not* and *am I not*.

à la. This is a French phrase meaning "in the manner of," "after the style of." Actually *à la* (ah·lah) is a shortened form of the French phrase *à la mode* ("according to the fashion"), but *à la mode* in our language usually means "topped with ice cream," as in *apple pie à la mode*. The first syllable of *à la*, when written, sometimes carries a grave accent and is usually pronounced like the *a* in "cart" or the *a* in "add." Here is a list of expressions often appearing in cookbooks and on restaurant menus: *à la carte* (in accordance with the bill of fare; each item separately priced); *à la française* (in the French style); *à la king* (cooked in a cream sauce, usually with mushrooms, green peppers, or pimentos); *à la mode* (served with ice cream; in style, fashionable; braised with vegetables and served in gravy); *à la Newburg* (cooked with a sauce made of cream, sherry, butter, and egg yolks); *à l'anglaise* (in the English style).

The phrase *à la* (with or without the grave accent) is sometimes used to describe or indicate a manner or source: an artist "à la Michelangelo"; "à la the Atlantic Monthly."

alibi. This word means "a plea or fact of having been elsewhere when an offense (crime) was committed." It is, however, now widely used to mean "an excuse," "any kind of defense," and, as a verb, "to offer an excuse or defense." Two good reasons for avoiding the overuse of *alibi* to mean "excuse": (1) it is now a trite and jaded term; (2) it suggests a tinge of cunning and dishonesty or improbability which may not be warranted.

all. This common word is primarily an adjective but it is also a noun, pronoun, and adverb. Since it is a short and useful word fulfilling many functions, it is overused by many speakers. *All but,* for example, is a wordy substitute for "almost" in "We are *all but* ready to leave." In "We are *all* ready to leave," *all* is ambiguous, since it may mean either *everyone, each of us, very much, quite, fully.* It is wordy (superfluous) in a statement such as "*all during* the game" and can be omitted without loss. *All* is slangy and trite in *all-fired,* which presumably means "completely": "He was *all-fired* sure of himself." *All in,* meaning "tired," "exhausted," is considered both informal and slangy; *all in all* is a trite and rather meaningless expression meaning "taken as a whole." *All things considered* is a vague and loose expression which should be made more specific. The *of* should be omitted in such an expression as "Not *all of* the women were married." *All out,* meaning "entirely" or "wholly," is somewhat informal: "The team went *all out* for a score." *All over* is informal when used to mean "in every way": "That's Fred *all over.*" Such expressions as *all the farther* and *all the faster* are nonstandard when used to mean "as far as" and "as fast as." *All to the good* is a trite phrase with little specific meaning. In summary, use *all* due caution when using *all.* See *first.*

allow, calculate, guess, reckon. Each of these words has distinct meanings, but each also has regional meanings of "think," "suppose," or "expect." Depending upon where you live in the United States, you may *allow* or *reckon* or *guess* or *calculate* that, for example, it will rain. In standard, nationally approved speech you would *think* or *suppose* or *expect* it to rain. Specifically, *allow* means "to permit," "to let": "*Allow* me to write to you." *Calculate* means "to determine," "to ascertain": "Please *calculate* the capacity of this truck." *Guess* means "to form an opinion or judgment on the basis of incomplete or uncertain knowledge or evidence": "I *guess* I shall have enough money for the trip." *Reckon,* like *calculate,* usually applies to mathematical determination but is normally applied to simple types of counting or mental arithmetic: "It is time to *reckon* your grocery bill."

all right. This term is considered slang when used to mean "dependable," "honorable" (an *all-right* man). *All righty* is a coy, overworked slang expression.

allude, elude. The former means "to make reference to," "to refer to casually or indirectly." ("The mailman *alluded* to the cold weather.") *Elude* means "to escape," "to evade." ("The culprit *eluded* the police for several hours.") Be careful to pronounce these words differently.

allude, refer. For the meaning of *allude*, see above. To *refer* is "to direct specific attention to." For example, one *alludes* to the work of Shakespeare (makes a casual or general comment) but *refers* definitely to a specific play or act or scene.

allusion, delusion, elusion, illusion. Watch carefully the different pronunciations of these words. *Allusion* means "a reference to," "incidental mention": "The manager made an *allusion* to another salesman." A *delusion* is a belief contrary to fact or reality, whereas an *illusion* means "a deceptive appearance." A *delusion* differs from an *illusion* in that it is accepted; a *delusion* may result from mental illness (the *delusion* that he was the son of George Washington). An *illusion* is a belief that something is real or true which only seems so (a mirage is an *illusion*). *Elusion* means "escape," "avoidance of something," "evasion."

almighty. This word, formerly often used as an intensive (*almighty* quick to find fault, *almighty* clever), has not been heard so often in recent years. Perhaps it has fallen into disuse (has become an archaic or obsolete word) because people who used *almighty* may have thought it referred to God and did not wish to blaspheme. But it has tiresomely persisted in the phrase *almighty dollar*. Whether *almighty* here means "all powerful" or "ever present," the phrase has been worn out through overuse. Also, a deflated dollar is not so *almighty* as it once was.

almost, most. *Almost* is an adverb meaning "approximately" or "very nearly." ("He was *almost* ready to speak.") *Most*, an adjective, is the superlative of *many* and *much* and means "greatest in degree, amount, or quality" ("The *most* money you can make is $2.00 an hour"). In informal speech, *most* is sometimes used where standard usage calls for *almost*: "He has *almost* (preferably not *most*) completed his assignment." "*Almost* (not *most*) everybody was invited."

alongside of. This phrase is wordy. Omit *of* in a sentence such as "The small boat lay *alongside* (not *alongside of*) the large freighter."

along the line of. This phrase and others like it (*along this line*, *along these lines*) are vague, wordy, and overworked expressions for "also," "in addition," "furthermore," etc. We should stop using a phrase which is vague, wordy, and trite—the unholy trinity of poor diction. *Be along* is highly informal when used to mean "come" ("The bus will *be along* soon"). *Right along* is substandard when used to mean "without interruption" ("The work is progressing *right along*").

alongst, amidst, amongst. Each of these words was formerly used in both speech and writing. But for more than a century *along* has generally replaced *alongst*, and *amidst* and *amongst* are obsolescent, being replaced by *amid* (*midst*) and *among*. These dying words sound all right in certain kinds of poetry but seem old-fashioned in contemporary speech.

aloud, out loud. *Aloud* is standard English, whereas *out loud* is considered informal or unidiomatic. It can hardly be both, since a characteristic of colloquial (informal) speech is its genuinely idiomatic quality. Whatever the label attached to it, *out loud* has a meaning less wordily and more effectively expressed by *aloud* or *audibly* or *loudly*.

already. This word means "earlier," "previously," "before a certain time." ("They have *already* left for town.") *Already* requires a following word to complete its meaning. It is substandard usage to say "They went home *already*" or "He has stopped talking *already*."

also. An adverb meaning "in addition," "besides," "likewise," *also* is not a standard substitute for *and*. Instead of saying "I lost my watch, *also* my wallet," say "I lost my watch *and* my wallet." A slang term, hardly suitable in standard speech, is the noun *also-ran* (any unsuccessful competitor, whether a horse or a political candidate).

alternate, alternative. As an adjective (its primary and major use), *alternate* means "occurring by turns, every other one." *Alternative*, primarily a noun, means "a choice between two," one of two things or ideas which are mutually exclusive. ("We visit at the hospital on *alternate* Sundays." "The policeman had no *alternative* but to arrest Fred.") The plural of *alternative* is *alternatives*. Corresponding adverbs are *alternately* and *alternatively*.

although, though. These words may be used interchangeably in most expressions. *Although* is preferred as the first word in a clause conceding something ("*although* I was ill"); *though* is the more common term in linking single words.

alumnus, alumni, alumna, alumnae. The word *alumnus* comes from a Latin word, *alere* ("to nourish"), and originally meant a "pupil" or "foster son." (Note the connection between this meaning and that of *alma mater*, a term meaning "fostering mother" and referring to the institution of learning one attended.) *Alumnus* is used to refer to any male graduate (or even former student) of a university, college, or school. The plural of *alumnus* is *alumni* (male graduates or former students). A female graduate or former student is an *alumna* (feminine form of *alumnus*); women graduates are *alumnae* (plural). Since in English grammar (though nowhere else) men are more powerful than women, both male and female graduates can properly be referred to as *alumni*, just as both male and female degree holders are called *bachelors* of arts and science. But do not use *alumna* as a plural or *alumni* as a singular. The word *alumni* is preferably pronounced with the accent on the second syllable and with the *i* sounded as the *i* in *ice* (a·lum′·nai). The final sound of *alumnae* is that of the first *e* in *even* (a·lum·ne).

amateur. Until recent years, the pronunciation of this word was often considered a test of one's degree of culture and education. Knowledgeable people pronounced the word with accent on the first syllable and with the second syllable (*a*) pronounced like the *i* in kitten; the final syllable (*teur*) was pronounced either *choor* or *toor*. In recent years, many people have also accented the final syllable as *tur,* but the former pronunciation is still preferred.

In meaning, *amateur* is related to *dabbler*, *dilettante*, and *tyro*, but it comes from the Latin word *amator* (lover) and suggests one who engages in a sport or activity through love of it, not for monetary reward.

amaze, astonish, surprise. *Amaze* means "bewilder," "perplex," "astound," "stun"; its meaning can be recalled by thinking that to be *amazed* is to be "lost in a maze." *Astonish* means "to strike with sudden fear or wonder." To be *astonished* is to be dazed or silenced, to be "turned to stone." *Surprise* means "take unawares." We are *amazed* at what seems extremely difficult, impossible, or improbable; we are *surprised* by the merely unexpected or unanticipated; we are *astonished* when our "surprise" is so great as to silence or daze us. Paralyzing (numbing) shock is implied by *astound* and its colloquial equivalent, *flabbergast*. A story is told of Dr. Samuel Johnson (1709–1784), English author and lexicographer: his wife unexpectedly came upon the author kissing a household maid and said, "I am surprised." Dr. Johnson reportedly replied, "No, Madam; *I* am *surprised; you* are *astonished.*"

amenable. This word, meaning "capable of being persuaded," "tractable," may be pronounced with the *e* sounded as the *e* in *even* or with the entire second syllable pronounced men, (ah·meen·uh·b'l or ah·men·uh·b'l). The former pronunciation is generally considered preferable.

amend, emend. *Amend* means "to put right," "to change for the better." We *amend* by adding or altering, as the noun *amendment* suggests. *Emend*, once merely another spelling of *amend*, has a similar meaning but is properly used to refer only to corrections or changes made in a literary or scholarly work; the corresponding noun is *emendation*. Both *amend* and *emend* are verbs; *amend* in plural form *(amends)* becomes a noun meaning "recompense" or "compensation": "He made *amends* for his careless driving."

am I not: See *ain't*. There is no accepted contraction for *am I not, amn't* and *aren't* being rejected as affected, awkward-sounding, or illogical. Until a shortened form becomes acceptable, continue to say "am I not?" even though it may sound stilted.

among, between. Standard usage requires that *among* be used to show the relationship of more than two objects or persons and that *between* be used to refer to only two objects or, occasionally, to more than two when each object is considered in relation to others. This distinction probably traces from the fact that the "tween" in *between* comes from the Old English word for *two*. The majority of careful speakers observe this distinction, but remember that *between* can correctly refer to more than two objects in certain instances. We speak of "a trade agreement *between* England, France, and the United States" because each country has an individual obligation to each of the others. And we do not say that a triangle is the space *among* three points or that the water-level route runs *among* New York, Albany, Cleveland, and Chicago. Keep these examples in mind: "We distributed the toys *among* Jill, Gray, and Effie." "We distributed the toys *between* Jill and Gray." "Understanding *between* nations is desirable."

amoral, immoral, unmoral. *Amoral* means "not concerned with moral standards," "not to be judged by the criteria or standards of morality." Animals and morons may be considered *amoral*. *Immoral* means "wicked," "depraved," "contrary to accepted principles of right and wrong." The acts of thieves, rapists, and murderers are *immoral*. *Unmoral* means "having no morality," "unable to distinguish right from wrong." Thus, an infant or a mentally retarded person may be considered *unmoral*. *Amoral*, *unmoral*, and the less-used *nonmoral* are virtual synonyms.

amount, number. *Amount* is used of things involving a unified mass — bulk, weight, or sums. In accounting, it has the same meaning as *total;* generally, it is safe to use *amount* to refer to anything which can be measured. *Number* is correctly used to refer to items which can be counted in individual units. "What is the *amount* of the bill?" "He has left only a small *amount* of food." "Joe has a *number* of old suits for sale."

ample, enough. *Ample* means "more than enough," "more than adequate in size, capacity, or scope." *Enough* means "sufficient," "in or to a degree or quantity that satisfies." Since *ample* means what it does, it is silly to attempt to qualify it; "*barely* ample" and "*scarcely* ample" are illogical. Adequate synonyms: "abundance" for *ample*, "sufficient" or "adequate" for *enough*.

an, a. See *a*.

analogy between, to, with. *Analogy* means "similarity," "agreement," "resemblance." The corresponding adjective is *analogous.* Idiomatically, one refers to "an *analogy to* or *with* something else" and to "an *analogy between* or *of* things."

analysis, synthesis. Meaning "separation of a whole into its parts or elements," *analysis* is the antonym (opposite) of *synthesis* ("putting together"). Both *analysis* and *synthesis* are tiresomely and inexactly overused for the words "study," "examination," "consideration." Only a few persons other than laboratory scientists normally engage in analysis or synthesis. Corresponding verbs are *analyze* and *synthesize,* also often misused. Noun plurals are *analyses* and *syntheses,* with the last *e* in each having the sound of *e* in *easy.*

and. This useful conjunction, which connects words and groups of words, is the most used word in our language. In fact, it is greatly overused. Repeatedly connecting sentences and clauses with *and* creates a childish or careless effect ("I opened the door *and* I saw Bill *and* then I saw the revolver *and* the body on the floor"). Using *and* for *to* in such expressions as *try and do this, come and see me, go and do what I say* is informal usage to be avoided. *And so* is overused by careless speakers and writers and by children and other immature persons. However, there is nothing ungrammatical or incorrect about starting a sentence with *and.* Usually, a stronger (more dynamic) word should receive the beginning position; also, a group of sentences beginning with *and* is monotonous. But if the sentences themselves are powerful enough (the King James version of the Bible contains numerous sentences beginning with *and*), it doesn't make much difference what the initial word is.

and all. A vague, loose expression. See *all, still and all.*

and etc. This phrase is a combination of *and* and an abbreviation of the Latin *et cetera,* meaning "and so forth." To say or write *and etc.* is redundant, the equivalent of saying "and and so forth," "and and odds and ends," "and and a list of additional unspecified items." Always omit the *and* in this phrase. Also, *etc.* can only be pronounced *e, t, c* or in its full Latin form *(et cetera).*

and how! This is a slang expression indicating explosively strong feeling or agreement. It should be avoided in stand-

ard speech and writing because it is (1) exaggerated and
overly energetic and (2) worn out and tiresome through
overuse.

and/or. This expression, formerly used exclusively in legal
documents and business communications, has become acceptable English primarily because it is a convenient time-
and word-saver. It means about the same as *each and every*
and is often equivalent to the simple word *or*. You can say
"boots and/or shoes." You can also say "boots or shoes or
both." Purists object to *and/or* as being awkward and un-
sightly, but it is fully permissible in all save fastidious
usage.

and which, and who. Correct sentence structure provides
that these phrases should appear in clauses only if preceded
by clauses also containing *which* and *who*. This rule, which
also applies to *but which* and *but who* clauses, is a matter of
parallel construction. Do not say "He is a man of intelligence, *and who* is an industrious worker." You can omit
and or add a *who* clause: "He is a man *who* is intelligent
and who is an industrious worker." Better still eliminate
the verbiage and say "The man is intelligent and industrious." The best way to improve "He showed much energy at
first, *but which* soon vanished" is to omit *but*.

anent. This word, meaning "about" or "concerning," today
seems pompous and affected. If you don't mind being considered quaint and archaic, say "*Anent* your proposal. . . ." Most
good speakers and writers would use *about* or *concerning*.

angel. The use of this word to mean a backer or sponsor is
somewhat informal, but it has had a respected place in
financial circles for centuries.

angle. One of several meanings of *angle* is "point of view." It
also suggests "an aspect seen from a specific or restricted
point of view." But *angle* has been twisted and strained to
mean "analysis," "interpretation," "official position," and
"approach." The result: *angle* is tiresomely overused:
"What's his *angle*?" "He gave us the *angle* on his new sales
technique." Use the word sparingly to avoid both inexact-
ness and triteness.

angry, mad. *Angry* means "indignant," "wrathful," "in-
flamed." In idiomatic English, you may be *angry about* a

situation or event, *angry at* an animal or an inanimate object, and *angry with* — not *at* — a person. In formal English, *mad* has a suggestion of abnormality, of being "disordered in intellect, insane." A *mad* person is insane; a *mad* dog has rabies; *mad* haste is frenzied; a *mad* suggestion is unwise or senseless. The formal word for *wrathful* is *angry;* colloquially, *mad* is used for *angry,* but *mad* is used by precise speakers to convey only a sense of disorder or abnormality.

Antarctic, Arctic. The former term refers to regions surrounding the South Pole, the latter to the North Pole specifically and to polar regions in general. These words are correctly pronounced in two ways: *ARK·tik; AR·tik; ant·ARK· tik; ant·AR·tik.* The a in *Arctic* has the sound of *a* in *palm.*

anxious, eager. In precise use, *anxious* implies "anxiety," "worry," "uneasiness." ("I am *anxious* about your health.") *Eager* means "keenly desirous," "wanting to." ("I was *eager* to see my old friend.") *Eager* is rarely used where *anxious* is meant, but *anxious* is often incorrectly substituted for *eager:* "The little boy was *anxious* to go fishing." One is *anxious* about something of which he is fearful; he is *eager* concerning something looked forward to.

any. This useful word of several meanings is considered colloquial by experts when it is used as an adverb to mean "at all." ("He did not work *any* last month.") You can substitute *at all* for *any* in such a sentence. Or you can, if you wish, consider that *any* in the sentence quoted is a pronoun rather than an adverb. *Any and all* is a wordy, trite expression.

anyhow. This adverb means "in any manner whatever," "in any event." It is a standard word, but one which is overused, vague, and imprecise.

anymore. This word, preferably spelled as one word rather than two, means "now," "at present," "from now on." It is a standard word, but when it is placed at the beginning or end of a sentence, it often is meaningless or ineffective. ("*Anymore* they are coming to see us" and "They are picking apples *anymore.*") Yet when used with a negative, *anymore* (*any more*) is standard: "Susie doesn't stay there *anymore.*" Suggestion: use *anymore* only when it is accompanied by a negative — *not, doesn't, won't*, etc.

anyplace. *Anyplace* (preferably spelled as one word but often as two) is an adverb, a synonym for "anywhere." It, together with *no place, every place,* and *some place,* is informal (colloquial) and should be avoided in careful speech as a substitute for *anywhere.* As a noun, *anyplace (any place)* is standard: "You may go *anyplace* you wish to."

anyways. This is a nonstandard form of *anyway,* used principally by uneducated and illiterate speakers. In standard speech, use *anyway* or *anyhow*—but use either one sparingly.

anywheres. *Anywheres* is an expression characteristic of uneducated speakers. So are *nowheres* and *somewheres.* Omit the final *s* in each word; say "anywhere," "nowhere," "somewhere."

ape. This word is slang when used to refer to a clumsy, stupid person and in the expression *to go ape* (be enthusiastic about).

apology, excuse. An *apology* is an "admission of discourtesy or error together with an expression of regret." An *excuse* is a "statement made or reason given for being released from blame." An *apology* accepts guilt and seeks to make amends; an *excuse* seeks to shift blame, deny guilt, and avoid censure. ("Please accept my *apology* for neglecting to send you an invitation." "His *excuse* for being late is that his alarm clock failed to go off.") See *excuse me.*

apparatus. This word has two standard pronunciations: the third syllable may be pronounced *ray* or with the sound of *rat* (ap·pa·RA·tus; ap·pa·RAT·us). The plural is *apparatus* or *apparatuses,* never *apparati.*

apparent, evident. These words are closely related in meaning, but *apparent* often suggests the use of reasoning: "It is *apparent* that Jackson will win the election." *Evident* implies the existence of external signs, facts of some sort: "His sorrow was *evident.*" *Apparent* has another meaning: that of "seeming," "not necessarily real or actual": "The *apparent* unconcern of the physician did not fool Nurse Brown."

apt, liable, likely. Distinctions in the meanings of these words have broken down somewhat, but careful speakers continue to observe them. *Apt* suggests "fitness," "tendency": "Jake is *apt* in physics." *Liable* implies exposure to something unwanted, disadvantageous, burdensome: "The driver is *liable* for damages." *Likely* means "expected," "probable": "It is likely to rain today." *Likely* is the most commonly used of the three words; *apt* and *likely* are near-synonyms; use *liable* only in the sense of "responsible," "answerable."

aren't I? See *ain't. Aren't I* is ungrammatical and not entirely logical (no one would say "I are not"). The phrase, which seems pompous or affected to most users of American English, is often employed by educated Englishmen and, occasionally, by speakers along the northern Atlantic coast in the U.S.A.

around. See *about.*

as. One of the most useful and most overworked words in the language, *as* is a proper conjunction, adverb, pronoun, and preposition essential to good idiomatic English. As a conjunction, however, *as* is usually weaker (less effective) than *since, because,* and *when* — each of these being more exact: "*Since* — preferably *not* as — it was snowing, we stayed indoors." *As* is often used for a more specific *that* or *whether.* "I don't say *that* (*not* as) he was right." "I doubt *whether* (*not* as) he was correct." *As* is incorrectly used for *who* in a sentence such as "Those *as* have no tickets are out of luck" and for *whom* or *that* in "The car hit the man *as* I had just spoken to."

as . . . as. In negative comparisons, unusually careful speakers prefer *so . . . as* to *as . . . as:* "Tom is not *so* talkative *as* his sister." But *as . . . as* is in reputable use, although the term is not considered quite *so* correct *as* "so . . . as."

as a whole, on the whole. These two phrases are trite through overuse and should usually be avoided. If you do use them, note that the former applies to a group but not necessarily to individuals; *on the whole* means "for the most part," "in general." "*As a whole,* our salesmen get much credit and attention, but some salesmen are low in prestige and income." "*On the whole,* the storm did little damage."

ascared. This word appears only in illiterate or narrowly dialectal speech. Use *scared.* See *a-.*

ascend up. This is a wordy expression from which *up* should be omitted, despite its appearance in the Bible (King James version). The idea of *up* is contained in *ascend,* as *down* is in *descend.* So do not use the wordy phrase *descend down.*

as far as, insofar as. These expressions are wordy substitutes for *as for* or *concerning* or *about*. "*As for* (concerning, about) your decision, I am doubtful" is preferable to "*As far as* (insofar as) your decision is concerned, I am doubtful."

as for my part. A wordy expression; say "for my part" or "as for me." Better still, omit the idea entirely and begin with "I."

as good as. This expression properly indicates comparison ("This suit is *as good as* that one.") But it is a wordy substitute for *practically* in sentences such as "He *as good as* promised to go" and "This suit is *as good as* new." See *practically*.

ashamed of, for. Ordinarily, use *ashamed of* ("I am ashamed of myself, of them, of their deed," etc.). Use *ashamed for* only when referring to someone who should be, but isn't, *ashamed of* himself.

aside from. A wordy expression more economically expressed by *besides*.

as if, as though. Each of these expressions is permissible. *As if* is used more often in speech and in informal writing than is *as though*, which is preferred by especially careful writers. Both expressions are followed by a verb in the subjunctive mood. "He left the room *as though* (*as if*) he were angry." (In informal or substandard use, *like* — which see — sometimes substitutes for *as if* and *as though* but is never followed by the subjunctive mood.)

ask a question. The verb *ask* means "to inquire about," "to put a question to." In nearly every conceivable situation and meaning, *a question* should be omitted from this expression: *ask* implies *a question* and should stand alone.

as long as. Some experts claim that this expression is a wordy substitute for "since," "because," "inasmuch as," but its use is now standard in such a statement as "It doesn't matter *as long as* you are here."

aspect. This word of several meanings is most often used to refer to the appearance of an idea, problem, or situation. It is overused; also, the idea it conveys may be expressed more exactly by *phase*, *stage*, *angle*, or *facet*, although each of these words is also becoming trite through overuse.

as per. *Per* means "according to," "by." *As per* is a wordy phrase, since *per* can convey the intended idea by itself. ("Take medicine *per* directions.")

as such. A usually meaningless phrase, rarely needed.

as the crow flies. A battered figure of speech. Say "by air" or "in a straight line."

as the result of. An overworked phrase often used inexactly for "*a* result of" or "*one* result of."

as to. Are these words necessary? Usually, a more precise single word will serve better. "Eleanor was in doubt *as to* his meaning" is better expressed "Eleanor was in doubt *about* his meaning." *As to whether* is even more useless and wordy. Instead of saying "Sandy expressed concern *as to whether* it would snow," say "Sandy expressed concern *that* it would snow." *As to where* can usually be shortened to *where*.

astonish. See *amaze*.

at. This word, a preposition, requires an object. One should not ask "Where are you staying at?" but "What motel are you staying at?" or, better, "At what motel are you staying?"

   At is unnecessary in expressions such as *at about* and *at around* (see *about*). *At all*, meaning "to the slightest degree," is nonstandard when used in a statement such as "They were thoughtless *at all*." When used to mean "wholly" or "completely," *at all* should be replaced by *of all:* "Sue is the finest girl *of all*."

   Here is a short list of trite expressions beginning with *at: at loose ends, at death's door, at long last, at one's wits' end; at first blush, at the end of one's tether* (rope).

atheist. See *agnostic*.

athlete, athletics. These words are often mispronounced, with a vowel sound added. Say "ATH·leet" and "ATH·let·ics." Like many nouns ending in *-ics, athletics* may be used with a singular or plural verb. When one refers to the principles of athletic training, one should use a singular verb, "Athletics *is.* . . ." *Athletics* considered as activities takes a plural: "Athletics *are* competitive sports."

attack, attacked. Watch pronunciation. Say "uh·TAK" and "uh·TAKT." Each word is sounded with only *two* syllables.

at the present time. This is a wordy phrase, the idea of which can always be expressed by "present" or "now." Often, the entire idea can be eliminated without real loss. *At this time* is also wordy; it means "now."

au. This expression from French, meaning "to the," "at the," and "with the," appears in numerous phrases. It is pronounced like the *o* in *old* and is used in expressions such as *au beurre* (with butter); *au gratin* (with cheese) *au lait* (with milk); *au naturel* (in the natural state).

authentic. Pronounce the second *t:* aw·THEN·tik.

avenge, revenge. *Avenge* is used in the sense of achieving justice ("Jim *avenged* his mother's injury"); *revenge* stresses retaliation and usually has for its subject the person wronged ("He *revenged* himself" or "He *revenged* the injury done to him").

average, median, mean. *Average* applies to what is midway between extremes on a scale of evaluation. With a series of numbers, you find the *average* by adding them and dividing by their number. You would find the *median* by discovering which is the middle number in an arithmetically arranged series. You would find the *mean* by adding the two extreme numbers and dividing by two. Thus, with the numbers 4, 6, 8, 12, and 15, the *average* would be 9; the *median* would be 8; the *mean* would be 9½.

Average should never be used when you mean *ordinary*, *typical*, or *common*. Also, avoid such trite expressions as *on the average* and *common ordinary* when you may think you are expressing the idea of *average*.

averse. See *adverse*.

avocation, vocation. An *avocation* is a minor occupation, hobby, or interest which calls one away from his *vocation*, his ordinary business, profession, or occupation.

aware, conscious. *Aware* implies knowing something either by perception or through information: "The lecturer was *aware* that he had lost his audience." *Conscious* has much the same meaning but is more often applied to a physical situation: "The injured player was *conscious* but could not stand." In informal use, the words are employed interchangeably.

awful, awfully. The former is used, indeed greatly overused, to mean *ugly, bad, shocking, great, disagreeable*, and much else. In addition to its overuse, *awful* is a loose, inexact word in most instances of everyday employment. The same cautions apply to *awfully*. Avoid such expressions as "I was *awful* cold," "He looks *awful*," "I'm *awfully* scared," and the like. *Awful* really means "filled with awe." Exact use of *awfully* is revealed in this sentence from Stevenson's famous story, *Markheim:* "He looked about him *awfully*."

awkward. This is an *awkward* word to pronounce: say "AWK·wuhrd," being careful to sound the second *w*. If you like neither the looks nor the sound of the word, try *clumsy, bungling, ungainly, gauche, inept,* or *unwieldy.*

Babel. This term, usually signifying a confused mixture of sounds or a scene of noise and confusion, may be pronounced BAY·buhl or BAB·l. The latter pronunciation is more commonly used for a word related in meaning, *babble.*

back of, in back of. Usage of these terms to mean "behind" is divided. Each may be considered standard, but actually both are wordy, using two or three words where one will suffice. No one questions the reputability of *in front of,* which *could* be replaced by the shorter *before.*

bad, badly. *Bad* is an adjective, *badly* an adverb. Despite this clear grammatical distinction, people tend to say "I feel badly" about as often as the more correct "I feel bad." In time, distinction between the forms may break down further, but as of now *I feel bad* is preferable. When the verb is to be modified—that is, when one is referring to a sense of touch, or feel, only *badly* is accurate: the student learning Braille might say, "I feel *badly* this morning."

balance. The use of *balance* in an extended sense of "rest" or "remainder" is debatable and should be avoided in all except informal speaking situations. The central meanings of *balance* deal with weighing and bookkeeping. Say "The *remainder* (*not* balance) of the day was wasted." Also, *on balance* has become a tiresome phrase through overuse.

ball. In singular or plural form, this otherwise useful word appears in numerous slangy, trite, or vulgar expressions: *be on the ball, carry the ball, have something on the ball, a lot on the ball, keep* (or *start*) *the ball rolling, ball the jack, ball up, ball and chain* (one's spouse), *balls* (nonsense).

ballyhoo. This term, meaning "clamor," "outcry," or "noisy uproar," has ascended from the status of slang to that of informality. A picturesque word, it should be avoided in formal usage, but it seems destined to move farther up the scale of reputability.

baloney. An informal variant of *bologna* (smoked sausage), *baloney* is slang when used to mean "foolishness" or "nonsense."

bank on. An overused, informal expression when used to mean "rely," "have confidence in."

bawl out. An overworked and highly informal expression meaning "to scold," "to reprimand."

bay window. Slang for a "paunch," a "protruding belly."

beam. In radio and aeronautics, the terms *off the beam* and *on the beam* have reputable usages. When used to mean "wrong," "incorrect," and "proceeding well," these expressions are slangy and trite.

bean. In singular and plural form, this word appears in numerous slang expressions: *beans* (the slightest amount: "Joe doesn't know *beans* about anything"); *full of beans* (active, energetic); *spill the beans* (disclose a secret); *bean* (one's head); *bean* (to hit on the head with an object such as a baseball).

beat. This useful and usable word should be avoided in such informal and slangy expressions as *beat down* (lower the price); *beat it* (go away); *beat out* (defeat); *beat* (exhausted, worn out), *beat up* (thrash); *beat* (reporting a news item ahead of competitors). *Beat around the bush* is an exceptionally trite metaphor.

beatnik. This informal term for a member of the *beat generation* (itself an informal phrase) has a dubious construction — from *nudnik*, a term derived from Yiddish and Polish, meaning a pest or boring person. However, *beatnik* is widely used in formal and informal speech and writing.

because. This conjunction is definite and specific in meaning; *because* is used to express cause or reason. As a subordinating conjunction, *because* should not be used to mean *that* (a relative pronoun): Say "The reason is *that*," not "The reason is *because*." We do not say "The cause is because"; logically, we should state not the cause for the reason but the reason itself. "The reason for my absence was illness" is more concise and more logical than "The reason for my absence was because of illness" or ". . . because I was ill." Also, note that *because of the fact that* is an excessively wordy expression.

beer. This familiar word should be pronounced BIR or with the *ee* sound like that of the *e* in "equal." *Beer and skittles* is overworked slang for "an easygoing existence" or "good time," suggesting a period devoted to beer and bowling (ninepins).

before in the past. Speakers sometimes say, "As never before in the past. . . ." The expression is wordy; use *before* or *in the past*, but not both.

beg to advise. This expression is overworked, especially in business letters. No sound reason exists for its use anywhere at any time.

being as, being as how, being that. Each of these phrases borders on illiteracy; all are vague, wordy, and illogical. Say "*Because* (*not* being as, being as how, being that) I am already here, I'll help."

believe, feel. Precisely, *believe* suggests "have convictions about," "judge," "think"; *feel* indicates emotion rather than reason. In daily use, the words are interchangeable, "I *feel* — or I *believe* — that we should go." Careful distinction is shown in such a sentence as "I *feel* cheerful when I hear from you, because I *believe* you still like me."

bellyache. *Belly* is an acceptable word, usually more accurate than other terms often used. *Bellyache* is a tiresomely trite and slangy term meaning "to grumble" or "complain."

beside, besides. In reputable usage, *beside* is usually a preposition meaning "by the side of." *Besides,* also a preposition meaning "except," is more commonly used as an adverb in the sense of "moreover" and "in addition to." ("I am resting *beside* — not *besides* — the stream." "I have more work to do; *besides* — not *beside* — I am not in the mood to go.")

best, better. The former is the superlative degree of *good* and *well* and should be used to refer to more than two things: "Jack chose the *best* of three jobs." Loosely and informally, *best* is used in such an expression as "May the *best* team win." If more than two teams are involved, the expression is correct; if not, say *better*. The use of *better* in

the sense of "more" is usually considered informal or narrowly dialectal. "The distance is *better* than a mile" should
be expressed "The distance is *more* than a mile." Exact
users of the language would wish to know what could be
better or *worse* than a mile.

be sure and. Each of these three words is inoffensive, but
the idea which their combination expresses should be conveyed by "be sure *to*." In such a construction, what follows
be sure is always an infinitive, not a group of words connected by *and* ("Be sure *to*—not *and*—let me hear from
you.")

be to. An illiterate, or at least informal, phrase in a statement such as "Mother is over *to* her friends' house." *Be at* is
idiomatically correct. Only in the sense of going and returning can *be to* be used: "I've already *been to* the store."

better had. A substandard (illiterate) expression used to
mean "should," "must," or "ought to." When one is told to
do something, a non-reputable reply would be "I guess I *better had*." These two words reversed (*had better*, meaning
"safe," "wise," "to one's advantage") are also often substituted for *ought* or *should*, but inversion does not remove the
error. Also illiterate are some other forms of these expressions: *would better* and *'d better* (you'd better).

better half. A tiresomely trite term for "spouse," one's partner in marriage.

between. See *among*.

biannual, biennial. A strict distinction exists between *biannual* (twice a year, *semiannual*), and *biennial* (once in two
years or lasting two years). While the prefix *bi-* has your
attention, fix in mind that *bimonthly* means "every two
months" and that its use as "twice a month," or "semimonthly," is nonstandard. *Biweekly* means "once in two
weeks." If you remain in doubt, it's always safe to say,
somewhat wordily, "twice a month" and "twice a week."
Biyearly means "once in two years"; *semiyearly* means
"twice a year."

big. This useful word appears in numerous slangy, trite
terms that should be avoided in all but highly informal
conversation: *big on* (enthusiastic about); *talk big* (speak
boastfully); *go over big* (be successful); *big cheese* and *big*

shot (important person); *big eye* (invitation, summons); *big idea* (unsolicited or objectionable proposal or plan); *big mouth* (loud person); *big talk* (exaggeration); *big time* (enjoyable time, or high level); *big wheel* and *big wig* (influential person); *big head* (conceit, egotism); *big house* (penitentiary). It's possible that you use *big* in even more terms than those listed here. *Be big* and avoid them all.

bimonthly, biweekly. See *biannual.*

bird. This word appears in several slangy expressions to be avoided: *bird* (girl); *for the birds* (worthless); *birdbrain* (silly person); *bird colonel* (a full colonel); *bird dog* (one who seeks out something); *birdfarm* (aircraft carrier); *birdman* (aviator); *birdseed* (something of little value); *give someone the bird* (disapprove, hiss at, boo). The word also appears in such clichés as *bird in the hand, birds of a feather, eat like a bird*, and *kill two birds with one stone.*

bitch. This is a reputable word meaning "a female dog or other canine animal." The term is slang when used to refer to a mean or promiscuous woman and when used as a verb to mean "complain." *To bitch up* is a slang term meaning "to botch." *Bitchy* is a somewhat vulgar and unfair adjective meaning "bitchlike."

biweekly. See *biannual.*

biz. A slang term, a shortened and altered form of *business.* Make it your business to avoid using *biz.*

blame it on me, blame me for it. Where a preposition is needed with the verb *blame*, standard idiomatic usage requires *for*: "She *blamed* me *for* the accident" *not* "She blamed the accident *on* me." The construction *blame on* ("*Blame* this situation *on* your employee") is becoming acceptable, although formal usage would stipulate "Blame your employee for . . ." or "Place the blame on . . . ."

blast. Slang when used as a noun to mean "an elaborate or wild party" or "a telephone call" and as a verb meaning "to criticize," "to attack," and "to shoot."

blitz. A shortened form of the German *Blitzkreig* (swift and sudden warfare), *blitz* is a slang term meaning "to overcome" and "to red-dog" (a shoptalk term in football meaning to rush through a hole between two linemen).

blow. This word appears in several slang terms and clichés, all of which should be avoided: *blow* (to boast, to go away, to spend money freely, to handle clumsily and unsuccessfully); *blow hot and cold; blow off* (to give vent to emotions, feelings); *blowout* (large party), *blow one's lines, blow one's stack, blow one's top.*

blue. The following expressions have been overused until they have lost their original flavor and sparkle: *into the blue; out of the blue; once in a blue moon; blue in the face;* and *bluestocking.* These terms are shoptalk: *blue chip* (finance); *blue note* (jazz); *Blue Lodge* (freemasonry); *blue line* (ice hockey); *blue peter* (sailing); *blueprint* (construction); *blue alert* (military defense). These expressions are slangy: *bluebeard* (ladykiller); *blue devils* (delirium tremens); *blue dicks* (policemen); *bluejacks* (sailors); *bluebill* (duck); *blue Monday* (depressing workday); *blue streak* (rapid).

blurb. A twentieth-century coinage meaning a laudatory announcement, a brief advertisement. The word is standard but is fast becoming overused as both noun and verb.

bolster up. A wordy phrase; *bolster* means "to prop up with support," so that *up* is not needed.

bombed. This past participle of *bomb* is slang for "drunk," "intoxicated." *Bomb* is football slang (shoptalk) for a long forward pass; to *bomb* or *bomb out* is slang for "to fail miserably."

boner. A slang term meaning "blunder" or, in somewhat dated parlance, a "diligent student." (The origin of the expression in its first meaning lies in the game of cricket, where careless play results in kicks on the shinbone; in the second meaning, one who studies intensely is "exercising his skull.") Trite phrases to avoid: *feel in one's bones, have a bone to pick with, make no bones about.* No one reading this book would ever need to know that *bones* is a quite informal term for "dice."

boob, boo-boo, booby. *Boob* and *booby* are slang terms for a foolish or stupid person. A *boo-boo* (slang) is a thoughtless mistake or blunder. *Booby hatch* is nautical shoptalk for a raised covering over a hatchway; it is general slang for a mental hospital. *Boob tube* has become a tiresomely used phrase for a television set.

book. This word appears in these expressions that are slangy and, like all slang, trite: *one for the books, throw the book at*, and *read him like a book*. *Bookie* is a slang term for "bookmaker"; *to make book* is racetrack shoptalk for "accept bets."

booze. As noun and verb, this word is a slang term for "alcoholic drink," "a drinking spree," and "imbibing liquor."

boughten. In such expressions as *boughten bread* and *a boughten suit*, this past participle of the verb *buy* appears in certain areas of the country, but it is not accepted in standard English. Also not generally recognized in standard usage as an adjective is *bought* (a *bought* hat, a *store-bought* shirt) as distinguished from homemade articles. The safest course is never to say *boughten* and to stick to standard forms of the verb: *buy, bought, bought*.

boundary. Until recently, standard pronunciation was in three syllables; BOWN·duh·ree. Also acceptable today is BOWN·dree.

boxed in. Sound idiom, but a phrase greatly overused. Say *enclosed, surrounded, thwarted, cut off, shut in*, or *confined* occasionally, just to relieve monotony.

boy friend. This term, once considered slang, reveals how an expressive, useful term can improve its status. It is now generally considered informal and eventually may appear in dictionaries with no label whatever. *Girl friend* and *girl Friday* enjoy the same status as *boy friend*. Each of these terms is overused.

brand-new. Curiously, experts have long debated whether the first word in *brand-new* (fresh, unused) should be spelled and pronounced with or without a final *d*. Both forms are acceptable, with the full version apparently preferred; but the shortened form (*bran-new*) is more common in everyday talk.

brass. This word appears in the following expressions and uses that are slangy or trite or, as usually happens, both: *brass* (self-assurance, nerve; high-ranking officer; money; a prostitute); *brass hat* (superior officer); *brass tacks* (essentials).

bread. The following are trite expressions: *break bread with, cast one's bread upon the waters, know on which side one's bread is buttered, take the bread out of someone's mouth*.

Bread is slang for "money," *breadbasket* for "stomach," *breadboard* for "an experimental model" or "prototype."

bring, take. The former indicates movement toward a place identified with the speaker; it suggests "come here with." *Take* suggests movement away from such a place and indicates "go there with." One *takes* money to a supermarket and *brings* home groceries (and no money). In ordinary usage, these words are often interchanged, but the distinction just noted persists to a degree. You can *take* or *bring* someone to a party, *take* or *bring* someone to have lunch, but the word selected has some bearing upon the relationship to the speaker of the place involved in the action.

Both *bring* and *take* combine with many prepositions to form phrases with distinct meanings: *bring about, bring around, bring down, bring forward, bring in, bring off, bring on, bring out, bring over, bring to, bring up; take aback, take after, take apart, take back, take for, take on, take over, take to, take up,* etc. Each word also appears in many trite expressions, normally to be avoided. *Take it lying down, take it on the chin, take a back seat,* and *take five* are examples. So, too, are *bring to an end,* a wordy expression since *end* conveys the full idea — as it does in *put an end to* and *come to an end.* The cliché *bring to a head* is really an unpleasant expression, as well as being trite and wordy: it means "to cause pus to form." Why not say, instead, "precipitate" or "crystallize"? *Bring to a boil* and *bring to a climax* are less unpleasant but equally trite locutions.

broad, wide. Each of these adjectives is used to indicate horizontal extent. *Broad* is preferable when the word it modifies is a surface or expanse viewed as such (broad stream, broad field, broad shoulders). *Wide* is preferably used when the sense of space is stressed (the table is four feet wide) or when the distance across a surface is mentioned indefinitely (the lake is wide at that point). These words are often interchangeable, but idiomatic usage normally prevails: *wide* mouth, *broad* grin, etc.

Broad is slang when used to refer to a girl or woman. *Wide* is shoptalk (in the game of cricket) when it refers as a noun to a ball bowled outside of the batsman's reach.

broke. A slang term meaning "out of funds," "bankrupt."

The expression *go for broke* (attempt anything and everything) is especially trite. *Broken* is the proper past participle of *break*: "The toe is *broken*" (*not* broke).

brother. A much overused exclamation with vague meaning (*oh, brother!*) and an informal word when used in direct address to mean "friend" or "fellow."

brother's-in-law, brother-in-law's. Standard practice in indicating possession in compound nouns is to add an apostrophe and *s* to the element nearest the object possessed: "my brother-in-law's office." The same rule applies to possession with *mother-in-law, father-in-law, ex-president, fellow-citizen, somebody else, Dun and Bradstreet*, etc.

Compound nouns form their plurals by adding *s* or *es* to the most important word in the compound. Sometimes the word considered most important comes first, sometimes not. With *brother-in-law*, the plural would be *brothers-in-law*. If you have more than one brother-in-law and wished to show possession, you would say "my brothers-in-law's office."

The end element is usually pluralized if it and other elements are so closely related as to be considered a single word: *housefuls, handfuls*. Occasionally, more than one element in the same word is pluralized, but the apostrophe and *s* is always added to the last element to show possession.

Here are a few terms that illustrate the erratic principles involved. It might be a good idea to study them: *attorneys at law; attorneys general* or *attorney generals; bystanders; commanders in chief; consuls general; hangers-on; major generals; master sergeants; sons-in-law.*

brunch. This is a coined word, a combination of *breakfast* and *lunch*. It bears no restrictive label, but it is becoming trite through constant and often inexact use for *late breakfast* or *early lunch*.

brung. An illiteracy. See *bring*.

buck. The following word meanings and idiomatic phrases are both slangy and trite: *buck* (to resist strongly; to move by jerks and bounces; of the lowest rank; a dollar); *buck up* (summon one's courage); *buck for* (try determinedly); *pass the buck* (shift responsibility); *the buck stops here* (accept responsibility).

bucket. This word is slangy when used to mean a field goal (basketball); it also appears in several hackneyed expressions such as *kick the bucket* (die) and *drop in the bucket* (small amount or number). It is financial shoptalk in *bucket shop* (a fraudulent brokerage operation).

buddy. This word is tiresomely overused to mean "good friend," "comrade." It may be (and sounds like) a baby-talk variation of *brother*.

buffalo. A slang expression when used to mean "intimidate," "deceive," or "confuse."

bug. Although *bug, bugged,* and *bugging* are becoming reputable in the sense of electronic eavesdropping, *bug* is slang when used to mean "an enthusiast," "a devotee," and, as a verb, to mean "pester" or "annoy." *Bug-eyed* (agog, surprised) and *bug-house* (insane asylum) are also slangy, as is *bug off* (get going, leave).

build up. As a verb phrase, this expression is often wordy; *up* should usually be omitted. As a noun meaning "extravagant praise," *build-up* is slang.

bull. This adult male bovine mammal has had his name borrowed for slang terms meaning "a policeman or detective" and "empty, foolish talk." *To shoot the bull* is "to spend time talking aimlessly or foolishly," possibly using clichés as slangy as *shoot the bull, bull in a china shop,* or *take the bull by the horns.*

bulldoze. A slang term when used to mean "to bully," "to coerce."

bum. This is an informal word, but it becomes outright slang when used to mean "living the life of a hobo," "in a state of disorder or disrepair," "to get something for nothing," "to sponge on others," "the buttocks," or "of poor or miserable quality." The phrases *a bum steer* and *bum's rush* are hackneyed and slangy.

bump off. A slang term for "murder."

bundle. A slang term when used to mean "a sum of money" or "an attractive female."

bunk. When this shortened form of *bunkum* is used to mean "nonsense," "twaddle," "humbug," it is slangy. *Bunk into* is an illiterate substitution for *bump into* (meet by chance), itself an informal idiom.

burgle. An informal or narrowly dialectal expression meaning "to burglarize" (break into and steal).

burned, burnt. Each of these forms is correctly considered a principal part of the verb *burn: burn, burned* or *burnt* (past tense), *burned* or *burnt* (past participle). Don't worry about which form to use; use the one you prefer. However, it would be well to avoid both when you mean *disillusioned* or *cheated;* also, *to burn oneself out* is an exceptionally trite phrase, as is *burned up* (angry).

business. This term is overworked as an approximate synonym for *commerce, traffic, trade, industry, calling, vocation, company, firm, duty,* or *employment.* Expressions such as *to mean business, get down to business, mind one's own business,* and *have no business* are as trite as they are inexact. *To give one the business,* or *the works,* is slang at its best— or worst.

bust. The principal parts of *burst* are *burst-burst-burst.* As verb forms, *bust* and *busted* are illiteracies. To *get busted* (be arrested), to *go bust* (become bankrupt), to *bust up* (disagree, break up), and *a bust* (failure) are slang expressions.

but. A heavily overworked word, *but* often can effectively be replaced by such words as *still, however, yet, nevertheless.* Vary your usage to avoid monotony. *But* (or *and*) at the beginning of a sentence is an entirely sound construction; avoiding such an opening is a matter of stylistic taste only. *But what* is idiomatically less preferable than *but that:* "I do not doubt but that (*not* but what) he will agree."

but which. See *and which.*

butt. Meaning the unburned end of a cigarette, *butt* has achieved respectability. When used to mean a whole cigarette, *butt* is slang. It is also slangy when used to refer to the buttocks; *butt in* (to meddle) and *butt out* (to stop meddling) are slangy and hackneyed.

butter-and-egg man. A prosperous business man who spends money lavishly may have nothing to do with either butter or eggs. Avoid this trite slang expression.

button. Expressions such as *to have all one's buttons* (be sane), *button up* and *button one's lips* (keep quiet), *button* (chin) and *on the button* (precisely, exactly) are considered highly informal or outright slang.

buy. As a noun meaning "a bargain" ("She got a good *buy* on that dress"), *buy* is substandard. The phrase *buy in* is slang when used to mean "purchasing favor." *Buy off, buy up,* and *buy out* are informal standard idioms. In the sense of "believe" or "accept," *buy* is slang ("I don't buy that"). *Buy it* is British slang for "getting killed" ("The soldier bought it in the last World War.")

buzz. As an expression meaning "telephone call" or "making a telephone call," *buzz* is slang. It may be considered informal or slangy when used to mean "fly low over" or "mildly intoxicated."

by. This word has many reputable uses as a preposition, adjective, and noun. Such phrases as *by the same token, by and by, by the by, by the boards,* and *by and large,* are tiresomely overused; the last named is not only hackneyed but usually a meaningless conversational filler. *Bye now* and *bye-bye* are baby-talk for "good-by."

caboodle. This odd word, perhaps a combination of *kith* and *boodle,* is highly informal, if not slang. *The whole kit and caboodle* is a trite phrase.

cahoots. The phrase *in cahoots,* meaning "in a dubious partnership," is a lighthearted expression considered informal and hackneyed. *To go cahoots* and *go in cahoot with* are equally banal.

cake. To *take the cake* (surpass, excel) and *a piece of cake* (something easily done), once picturesque expressions, have lost much of their expressiveness through overuse.

calculate, reckon, guess. These words are localisms for "think," "suppose," and "expect." Each has standard and reputable meanings (for example, one can *calculate* a mathematical problem), but each should be avoided as narrowly dialectal and somewhat old-fashioned synonyms for a mental concept. See *allow.*

call. The expressions *call up* (to telephone) and *call off* (to cancel or postpone), formerly considered localisms or informalities, are now fully acceptable in ordinary speech. *Call into being* and *call into question* are standard phrases, although trite. Both *call a halt to* and *call a spade a spade* are worn and hackneyed; the latter is also illogical in that it contradicts what it advocates: it is coarser things than spades that are glossed over with inoffensive terms (euphemisms).

calliope. This term for a musical instrument fitted with steam whistles has two standard pronunciations: ka·LI·o·pee and KAL·ee·ope.

Calvary, cavalry. These words differ in spelling, pronunciation, and meaning. The latter, pronounced KAV·uhl·ree, refers to troops on horseback or, more recently, troops in armed vehicles. *Calvary*, the hill outside Jerusalem where Jesus was crucified, is pronounced KAL·ver·ee.

camp. Few words in recent years have been more overused and carelessly used than *camp*. In the general sense of either appreciation or affectation of tastes, manners, and activities considered vulgar or banal, *camp* has been loosely defined and widely exploited. Vague in both origin and meaning, *camp* in the sense of artificiality, extravagance, and inappropriateness may waste away like many other neologisms.

can. In several senses, *can* is considered slangy or vulgar: a jail or prison; to dismiss or fire; to make a recording of *(can* the song); to quit or dispense with (*can* the chatter); the buttocks; a depth charge; to throw something away; a bathroom or toilet.

candid, frank, open. Each of these words implies truthfulness in action and speech. A *candid* remark is accurate and complete. A *frank* person speaks freely and even embarrassingly. An *open* person conceals nothing. In ordinary speech, the terms are interchangeable.

candidate. This word is often misspelled and mispronounced. Say KAN·duh·dayt, KAN·di·dayt, KAN·duh·dit, or KAN·di·dit. Do not omit the first *d* in spelling or speaking.

candle. This word also contains a pronounceable *d:* KAN·duhl. *To burn one's candle at both ends* and *to hold a candle to* are idiomatically sound, but hackneyed, expressions.

can do. This is a tiresome, trite, and slangy expression meaning "surely" or "of course."

can, may, might. *Can* suggests mental or physical ability. ("Jane *can* sing beautifully when she tries.") *May* implies permission or sanction. ("Babs *may* borrow my suitcase if she wishes.") This distinction between *can* and *may* is illustrated thus: "Jim *can* swim, but his mother says that he *may* not."

May also expresses possibility and wish (desire): "It *may* snow tonight" (possibility). "*May* you have a good rest this weekend" (desire).

Might is used after a governing verb in the past tense, *may* after such a verb in the present tense: "She says that we *may* go." "She said that we *might* go."

cannot (can't) help but. In this expression, *but* should be omitted because its use results in a double negative (*cannot,* or *can't,* and *but*). Instead of saying "I *can't help but* think you are mistaken" say "I can't help thinking you are mistaken"—a more concise statement with no double negative involved.

can't hardly. Omit the *not* in the contraction so as to avoid a double negative. Prefer *can hardly* to *can't hardly* (and *can't scarcely*).

can't seem to. Is *seem to* ever needed in this expression? Doesn't *can't* express the idea by itself? What does *seem to* really add?

capable. This word means having adequate capacity to do, make, or receive an action ("Larry is a *capable* player." "This problem is *capable* of solution.") A common error arises from using *able* for *capable* in one of these senses: "This law is *capable* (not *able*) of being enacted." One should say "I am *able to* solve this problem" and "I am *capable of* solving this problem."

capacity. See *ability*.

caramel. What people say, not what people *should* say, determines usage. *Caramel* has a second syllable that careful speakers pronounce, however lightly: KAR·uh·mel. Many persons (especially those doing television and radio commercials) drop the *uh* sound, so that KAR·mel is now listed as a second pronunciation in most up-to-date dictionaries.

card. An overworked and informal term for an amusing or eccentric person, *card* also turns up in such trite expressions as *have a card up one's sleeve, lay one's cards on the table, it's in the cards,* and *play one's cards right*.

care to. In such expressions as "Do you *care to* play?" this phrase appears often. The basic meaning of *care* is "to be concerned or solicitous," "to have thought or regard." As a substitute for *prefer to* or *want to, care to* is a silly phrase.

carton, cartoon. The former is a box, especially one made of corrugated paper; a *cartoon* is a drawing. They also differ in spelling and pronunciation: KART·un, kar·TOON.

case. In origin, *case* really is two different words, one derived from a form meaning "receptacle" or "container," the other meaning "instance" or "example." In both senses, the word has been abused and overused. *Case* is slang in such expressions as *case the joint* (examine the place or premises) and Jack's *a case* (an eccentric or peculiar person). The phrase *the case of* is nearly always verbiage and adds nothing to any statement: omit it in both speaking and writing.

casual, causal. This pair of words is often mispronounced and misspelled. The former, meaning "relaxed," "unconcerned," "not planned," is pronounced KAZH·oo·uhl or KAZH·yoo·uhl; *causal* means "involving a cause" or "expressing a cause" and is pronounced KO·zel (with the *o* sounded like "aw" in "paw").

cat. This word appears in the tired, tiresome expression *let the cat out of the bag*, and it is slang in several senses: (1) any person, especially a devotee of jazz; (2) *to tomcat* (seek feminine companionship); (3) a caterpillar tractor.

catch. The following expressions involving *catch* are slangy, trite, or highly informal: *catch it* (to receive punishment or a scolding); *catch on* (to become popular); *a good catch* (a desirable person, especially a mate); *catch* (to see, especially a play or other performance; a drawback, hindrance, or liability).

catsup. This word is interchangeable with *ketchup*. The word is also spelled *catchup. Ketchup* is preferred by precise speakers, largely because this term for any of various sauces for meat and fish is derived from a Chinese word *ketsiap* (which means pickled-fish brine).

cause, cause of. *Cause* and *reason* are often confused in meaning. *Reason* is what one produces to account for, or justify, an effect; *cause* is what actually produces an effect. (His *reason* for speaking is clear. The *cause* of his leaving early is debatable.)

Cause of and *on account of* do not have the same meaning. "The *cause of* my lateness was a slow bus" is preferable to "The cause of my lateness was *on account of* my bus was slow." Both terms can usually be omitted entirely.

cavalry. See *Calvary*.

censor, censure. To *censor* is to examine carefully, to find fault or objection. To *censure* is to criticize or harshly reproach. ("The lieutenant does not like to *censor* the letters his men write." "The policeman was *censured* for making a hasty arrest.")

center around. A wordy phrase in which *around* can always be replaced by the shorter and more accurate *on*. Both *center about* and *center around* are informal ways to say "focus."

certain. This word is overused with vague and unspecified meaning: a *certain* place, a *certain* man. Why not *name* the place, the man?

certain, certainly, sure, surely. *Certain* and *sure* are adjectives; *certainly* and *surely* are adverbs. Say "I *certainly* (or *surely*) am going." "Bob is a *certain* (or *sure*) winner in that contest." *Certainly* and *surely* are rarely misused, but *sure* and *certain* constantly occur in statements requiring adverbs.

chameleon. This somewhat rare word causes pronunciation difficulty. It may be pronounced kuh·MEE·li·uhn or kuh·MEEL·yuhn.

chassis. This word may be pronounced SHAS·ee, SHAS·is, or CHAS·ee. The plural, also spelled *chassis*, is pronounced SHAS·eez or CHAS·eez.

check, check into. As a verb meaning to investigate, inquire, or verify, *check* is tiresomely overused. *Check into* is a wordy phrase from which *into* can nearly always be omitted.

cheese, cheesecake, cheesy. *Cheese* is slangy in the phrases *big cheese* (important person) and *cheese it* (get away rapidly). It is also slang when used to mean "stop" and in the word *cheesecake* (photograph of a scantily clad pretty girl). *Cheesy* is a slang term meaning "of poor quality."

Cheshire cat. A saying made popular by the grinning cat in *Alice's Adventures in Wonderland*, to grin like a Cheshire cat is trite. A possible synonym: *inscrutable smile*.

chestnut. The expression *to pull one's chestnuts out of the fire* is hackneyed. A *chestnut* is a slangy or highly informal term when used to mean a stale joke or anecdote.

chicken. The expression *to count one's chickens before they are hatched* is tiresomely trite. *Chicken* is slang when used to mean "cowardly" or "a young and inexperienced girl." *To chicken* or *to chicken out* is slang for "lose one's nerve," "become fearful." *Chicken colonel* is military slang for a full colonel as distinguished from a lieutenant colonel. *Chicken feed* is slang for a small or trifling sum of money. Both *chicken-hearted* and *chicken-livered* are informal expressions meaning "timid" or "cowardly."

childish, childlike. The suffix *-ish* often has unfavorable connotations. *Childish* refers to undesirable characteristics (childish temper, childish selfishness, etc.). The suffix *-like* frequently causes neutral or pleasing reactions (childlike innocence, childlike faith). *Childish* and *infantile* are only approximate synonyms; their antonyms are *adult* and *mature*.

chimera. This difficult-to-pronounce word with several meanings — usually that of "a creature of the imagination," "a foolish fancy" — is sounded with a *k*: ki·MEE·ruh or kai·MEE·ruh.

chip. Such phrases as *chip off the old block, a chip on one's shoulder*, and *when the chips are down* are hackneyed. *In the chips* is a slang term meaning "rich." To *chip in* is an informal expression for "contribute" and "participate."

chiropodist. Both *chiropodist* ("foot doctor") and *chiropractor* (treater of nerve functions and the spinal column) are pronounced with a *k* sound: kai·ROP·o·dist, ki·ROP·o·dist; KAI·ro·PRAK·ter.

chisel. This word is slang when used to mean "cheat" or "swindle." A *chiseler* is a slang term for one who engages in such practices.

chocolate. Formerly this word had only one reputable pronunciation: CHOK·uh·lit. Usage has resulted in respectability for both CHAWK·uh·lit and CHOC·lit.

chops. *To lick one's chops*, meaning "to await with pleasure," "to anticipate," is a slangy, trite expression. *Chops* is an informal term for jaws or cheeks. A helicopter is, in slang, a *chopper. Choppers* is slang for "teeth."

chow. A slang term for food. Since *chow* is a slang term, so is *chow line.*

Christer. A rude slang term for one who is notably moral or religious.

Christmas tree. The phrase *lit up like a Christmas tree* has been so overused that it has lost its original picturesqueness.

chuckleheaded. A slang term for "a stupid person," "a blockhead."

claim. This word is overused to mean "state," "allege," "maintain." The primary meaning of *claim* is to "demand," to "assert one's rights."

clean. This word appears in several phrases that are slangy, or trite, or both: *come clean* (tell the truth); *a clean slate* (fresh start); *clean cat* (someone not using narcotics); *with clean hands* (innocent); *clean bill of health* (found guiltless); *cleaned* (without money); *to clean house* (to remove corruption, inefficiency, etc.); *take to the cleaners* (cause to lose one's money or other property); *to hit cleanup* (to bat in the fourth position on a baseball team).

clench, clinch. As verbs, both of these words apply to the act of holding or securing. One is occasionally mispronounced for the other; also, they differ somewhat in meaning. *Clinch* only is used for the securing of an agreement, argument, or verdict and to denote "holding" in boxing. One *clenches* an object with hands, fingers, jaws, or teeth.

climactic, climatic. These words, often confused, differ in pronunciation and meaning. The former (klai·MAK·tik) refers to a climax; *climatic* (klai·MAT·ik) refers to the climate.

climax. See *acme*.

cliff-hanger. An overused and informal expression for a contest in which the outcome is not certain.

clip. This word may be considered informal or slangy when used to mean "hit with a sharp blow," "to cheat or overcharge," and "a brisk pace" (go at a good *clip*.) A *clip joint* is slang for an establishment where customers are overcharged or otherwise defrauded.

clique. Most careful speakers continue to pronounce this word KLEEK, but its pronunciation as KLIK now appears in modern dictionaries because of widespread usage.

close. As a verb, this word is pronounced KLOZ, as an adjective or adverb, KLOS. It appears much too often in such clichés as *close call* and *close shave*.

cloud nine. A slang term meaning a state of well-being or great happiness.

clue. (A variant spelling is *clew*.) This word, which suggests guiding or directing toward the solution of a problem, is hackneyed in the expression *clue me in*.

cock. Such expressions as these are slangy, trite, or both: *cockalorum* (self-important little fellow); *cock-and-bull story* (improbable or absurd tale); *cockeyed* (off-center, or ridiculous, or drunk); *cocky* (swaggering, boastful); *cock of the walk* (leader, chief); *cockadoodledoo* (rooster); *knock into a cocked hat* (to destroy, demolish); *cock a snoot* (condescend to).

cold. This useful word appears in numerous hackneyed expressions such as *in cold blood, throw cold water on, out in the cold,* and *cold feet* (failure of nerve). The word is informal or slangy when used to mean unconscious (*knocked cold* or *out cold*); completely (*cold sober*); a slight or snub (*cold shoulder*); prearranged cards (*cold deck*); a reserved or shy person (*cold fish*); and to stop short (*cold turkey*).

column. This word, pronounced in two syllables, has no *y* sound: say KOL·uhm.

combine. As a noun, this word (pronounced KOM·bine) is informally used to mean a group, or ring, of people. As a verb *combine* (kom·BINE) appears in the phrase *combine into one. Combine* means "to unite" or "join," so that *into one* should be omitted. An informal term, *combo* refers to a small jazz or dance band.

come. This verb can be combined with almost every preposition in the language to form acceptable idiomatic phrases. Among phrases that should be avoided as slang expressions, informalities, and clichés are these: *come across* (do or give what is wanted); *come again* (to repeat); *come down on* (criticize); *come off it* (stop, desist); *come over* (visit); *come through* (do as expected); *come up with* (produce, propose); *how come?* (why).

Came time (when it *came time* to . . .) is a wordy expression that usually can be omitted. *Comes a time in everyone's* . . . is both wordy and affected.

come and. The verbs *come, go,* and *try* are often followed by *and* (*come and* get your food; *go and* get your ticket; *try and* get some rest). In such expressions *and* is a substitute for *to*. These phrases are idiomatically sound but are considered informal and, although widely used, are not recommended.

comeuppance. An informal term for punishment or retribution that should be avoided in careful speech.

commentate. Since the word *commentator* has become well-known because of television and radio, people generally have felt the need for a verb to describe what a commentator does. Thus a neologism has been born. To *commentate* a game, or fashion show, or what not, is considered dubious usage by most authorities. Why not stick with *comment, comment on, describe,* or *narrate?*

common, mutual. These words are loosely interchangeable, but they do have distinct meanings. *Common* refers to something shared by two or more persons ("our *common* heritage"). *Mutual* refers to something *done* or *felt* by each of two persons toward the other ("Jack and Bill have a *mutual* dislike for each other.") Many good speakers and writers, however, do not preserve this subtle distinction.

compact. Be certain to pronounce the final *t* in this word. As a verb and adjective it is pronounced kuhm·PAKT; as a noun, KOM·pakt.

compare, contrast. These words are often confused, perhaps in part because they are vaguely related in meaning. To *compare* is to examine in order to note similarities more than differences; to *contrast* is to set in opposition in order to show differences more than similarities. Idioms are *compare to* and *compare with*. As a verb, *contrast* is usually followed by *with;* as a noun, *contrast* often takes *between*. The phrase *in contrast* may be followed by *to* or *with*.

complected. A vulgarism (barbarism) for *complexioned*. Never say *complected* unless you are quoting the talk of someone who is illiterate.

complete. As an adjective, this word is an absolute term in certain senses and therefore is incapable of qualification: something is either complete or not complete and cannot be "more" or "less" complete. However, a qualifying word such as *nearly* can remove illogicality; it is acceptable to say, for example, "The *most nearly complete* account we have. . . ."

comprehensible, comprehensive. Although these words have different spellings, pronunciations, and meanings, they are sometimes confused. The first (KOM·pre·HEN·si· bl) means "intelligible," "capable of being known or understood." *Comprehensive* (KOM·pre·HEN·siv) means "including much," "large in content or scope."

con. As a transitive verb, *con* is a slang term meaning "to swindle," "to dupe." As a noun, it is slang for "a swindle" and "a convict." *Con man* is slang for "confidence man" (one who swindles by gaining the confidence of his victim). *Con game* is a related slang term.

conditioned. An overworked term used by many psychologists and educators to mean "accustomed," "used to," or "generally." "Judy was *conditioned* to being alone" is understandable, but the italicized word can be replaced by one less jargonish.

confidant, confident. Confusion between these two similar words results in an impropriety. *Confidant* (kon·fuh·DANT) refers to one to whom secrets or other private matters are entrusted. A female confidant is a *confidante* (kon·fuh· DANT). *Confident*, an adjective meaning "assured, certain of success," is pronounced KON·fuh·duhnt or KON·fi·duhnt.

confidently, confidentially. The former means "with assurance, certainty, confidence": "Joe acted *confidently*, but his speech was halting." *Confidentially* means "in secret," "intimate," and "entrusted with confidence" ("The postman told me *confidentially* that the letter has been destroyed").

conk. A slang term for the head and the nose and for the verb "to hit." *Conk out* is a slang term meaning to fail or to tire.

connected. For some reason, this word seems to attract unnecessary prepositions. *Connected with, in connection with*, and *connect up with* are wordy phrases. Such expressions can usually be dropped in favor of "about," "before," "during," or another shorter *connection*.

conniption. This is an informal, or narrowly dialectal, expression meaning "excitement" or "anger." It should be avoided in general use, especially in the form of *conniption fits*, a wordy localism.

conscious. See *aware*.

consensus. Often misspelled and misused, *consensus* means "general agreement" or "collective opinion." The phrase *consensus of opinion* has been used so freely and widely that it is a stock expression; however, it is wordy (*of opinion* is not needed to express the thought) and is now considered a hackneyed term.

considerable. This adjective meaning "significant, important, fairly large in extent or amount" is often used where the adverb *considerably* should appear: "The foreman helped me *considerably* (*not* considerable) with the job." As an intensive, *considerable* is also an impropriety (talked *considerable* strange); say *considerably* or *very* or omit any modifier.

consist. The idiomatic phrases *consist of* and *consist in* are sometimes confused. With *consist of*, materials, ingredients, or parts are spoken of: "Water *consists of* hydrogen and oxygen." Something resembling a definition is given when *consist in* is used: "Tact *consists in* trying to avoid offending others."

contact, contacted. As a noun, *contact* denotes "a coming together" and also "a connection," "a person who might be of use." In both senses, its use is now considered reputable. As a verb meaning "get in touch with," *contact* is thought to be an informality or impropriety in all contexts. One should avoid *contacting* someone else, an unfortunate recommendation since *get in touch with* says the same thing but says it wordily. Other possibilities: *telephone, call, call upon, communicate.*

contagious, infectious. These words have precise scientific meanings, but in everyday usage they are often confused. *Contagious* emphasizes the speed with which contagion (contact, communication, medium) spreads: "*Contagious* fear ran through the audience." *Infectious* suggests the powerful or irresistible quality of the source of contagion: "Mark Twain's *infectious* humor stimulated prolonged laughter and applause."

contempt. In saying this word, don't neglect the final *t* sound: kuhn·TEMPT. (A verb, *contemn*, meaning "to treat with scorn or contempt," is properly pronounced kuhn· TEM.)

contents noted. A tiresomely overused and wordy phrase which usually can be omitted from any letter (or other communication) without loss of meaning.

continual, continuous. In some senses and uses, these words are synonymous. One distinction is that *continual* implies "a close recurrence in time, rapid succession," whereas *continuous* suggests "without interruption, constant." "The *continual* ringing of the doorbell" and "The ticking of the clock was *continuous*" illustrate this subtle distinction.

continue on. The word *continue* means "to go on," "to keep on." Therefore, *on* should be omitted from this phrase. Vary your word choice: why not try *persist* or *persevere* or *last* or *endure*?

contract. This word is pronounced KON·trakt when used as a noun, kuhn·TRAKT in other parts of speech. The final *t* should always be sounded.

contrast. See *compare*.

convey back. The word *convey* means "to carry, bring, or take from one place to another." Omit *back* from such a statement as "Please *convey* my regards (*back*) to your associates."

convince, persuade. These words are related in meaning but do have distinctly different uses. *Convince* means to satisfy the understanding of someone about the truth of a statement or situation: "Johnny *convinced* me by quoting exact figures." *Persuade* suggests winning over someone to a course of action, perhaps through an appeal to reason: "Jim *persuaded* the grocer to consult a lawyer."

cook, cookie. The following expressions are trite, slangy, or highly informal: *what's cooking?* (what's taking place, occurring?); *to cook one's goose* (to destroy one's hopes, ruin one's chances); *cook up* (contrive, concoct, lie about); and *cook the books* (falsify). *Cookie* is slang when used to refer to a person (a tough *cookie*) and informal when used to refer to one's sweetheart or friend. To *shoot one's cookies* is picturesque slang for vomiting, regurgitating. To *snap one's cookies* and *drop one's cookies* are also slang phrases.

cool. This word has several meanings and numerous applications, not all of them appropriate. *Cool* is overused to mean "calm," "controlled," "not excited." Why not occasionally say *composed* or *collected* or *nonchalant* or *imperturbable* or *unruffled* or *detached*? They are effective words, too.

Cool appears in several slang meanings and phrases: *a cool million* (entire, full); *cool it* (calm down); *cool one's heels* (to be kept waiting); *keep one's cool* (composure); *a cool job* (a superior performance); *cool cat* (a sophisticated individual).

coop. This word is slang for "jail"; *to fly the coop* (escape from prison) is both slangy and trite. Spelled with a hyphen (*co-op*), the word is pronounced in two syllables as an abbreviation for a cooperative store or other enterprise.

cooperate together. The word means "to work together," "to act in combination." Drop the *together*; all it adds is a useless word. See *mutual*.

cop. An informal term for a policeman, *cop* is slang when used to mean "steal" or "to seize or catch." *Cop out* is a slang term meaning to fail or to refuse to commit oneself. *Cop a plea* (plead guilty) is slangy.

corespondent, correspondent. These words differ in spelling, meaning, and pronunciation. It is usually safer to be a *correspondent* (KOR·i·spon·dent, meaning one who writes letters) than a *corespondent* (KO·ri·SPON·dent, one charged with adultery).

corker. A slang term, now outdated, for anything or anyone outstanding or remarkable. As an exclamation, *corking* is an informal expression meaning "excellent," "splendid."

corn. This word is informal when used to mean whiskey distilled from corn and is slang in the sense of anything dated, trite, overly dramatic, or mawkish. *Cornball* is slang for someone who acts in an unsophisticated or stupid way. *Corny* is a slangy adjective meaning banal, hackneyed, or sentimental. *Cornfed*, when used in this sense of *corny*, is also slang, but sometimes includes the idea of a healthy, strong person who is provincial and unsophisticated.

corporal, corporeal. The first of these words, pronounced KAWR·puh·ruhl, means "belonging to the body" (corporal punishment), or "personal" (corporal possessions), or a noncommissioned officer (Corporal Dugan). *Corporeal*, pronounced kawr·POH·ri·uhl or kawr·PAW·ri·uhl, means "bodily," "mortal," "tangible" (*corporeal* effects of the deceased person).

corral. Possibly because of inaccurate speech on television and in films, this word is often mispronounced. Say kuh·RAL or kuh·RAHL; accent never falls on the first syllable.

cotton. In the sense of "flatter," *cotton up to* is a trite, informal expression. *Cotton pickin'* is a slang term meaning whatever the user has in mind, if anything; usually it seems to suggest "worthless" or "no good."

cough up. A slang term meaning "to give reluctantly," "to hand over."

couldn't scarcely, couldn't hardly. See *can't hardly*. *Couldn't* is a contraction of "could not." Drop the negative part of the phrase when using it with *scarcely* or *hardly*.

could of. In normal speech, *could have* sounds like *could've*, which in turn sounds like *could of*. Not only *could of* but also *may of, might of, should of*, and *would of* are illiteracies. *Of* is not a verb.

coupe. When used to refer to a closed two-door automobile, this word may be pronounced koo·PAY or KOOP. Especially precise speakers prefer the former pronunciation, but the latter is more general.

couple. In ordinary conversation, *couple* is sometimes placed immediately before a noun (*a couple weeks, a couple dollars*). Although this usage follows that of *dozen* (*a dozen roses*), it is not standard; *couple* should be followed by *of* (*couple of months*). However, when such words as *less* and *more* appear, the *of* is dropped (*a couple more seats*).

   Couple may correctly be used with a singular or plural verb ("The couple *was* dancing" or "The couple *were* dancing").

   Couple together is a wordy phrase. *Couple* alone expresses the idea; omit *together*.

coupon. This word may be pronounced KOO·pon or KYOO·pon. Take your pick.

crab. This word is considered either informal or slang when used to mean (1) interfere with or ruin, (2) find fault with, and (3) complain.

crack. The expressions *crack a smile, crack a book*, and *cracked up to be* are idiomatically sound but trite and slangy expressions. *Crackerjack*, meaning "of excellent quality or ability," is also considered slang. *Cracky*, as in *by cracky*, is a form of *crikey*, itself an interjection formed from *Christ*; the expression is considered either rude or narrowly dialectal.

crap. In the meaning of "nonsense" or "drivel," *crap* is a slang term. As a verb, *crap* is slang in *crap around* (act in a silly or useless way).

crash. Expressions like *crash a party* and *a crash program* are hackneyed and informal.

credible, creditable, credulous. A story is *credible* if it is believable, and a character in a story (or play) is *credible* if he or she seems true to life. One is *credulous* who believes on slight evidence much of what he reads or is told. An action or person is *creditable* if it or he is worthy of praise and deserves credit or esteem.

crème de la crème. A French term meaning "cream of the cream." This phrase is tiresomely overused to express "the essence of excellence," "the very best."

crib. This term is slang when used to mean (1) a petty theft, (2) to cheat, (3) to plagiarize, and (4) a retreat for thieves or prostitutes.

crick. This word is standard when used to mean a cramp or muscle spasm, but it is an illiteracy or localism when it refers to a *creek* (small stream).

crisis. This term meaning "a turning point" or "crucial situation" has a plural form, *crises*. Never say (or try to say) "crisises." The singular is pronounced KRAI·sis, the plural KRAI·seez.

criterion. A word meaning "standard, rule, or test" for forming a judgment or decision, *criterion* (KRAI·TEER·ee·uhn) is singular in form and meaning. The plural *criteria* (KRAI·TEER·ee·uh) cannot be used for *criterion* in such expressions as *a criteria, one criteria*. *Criterions* is a less preferred but acceptable plural.

crow. *To eat crow* (be forced into a humiliating position) is an informal if not slangy expression. *As the crow flies* is a trite, wordy expression. In this jet age, why not say "by air"?

crud. A slang term, sometimes considered a vulgarity, for "worthless rubbish."

crummy. Also spelled *crumby*, this is a slang term with several meanings: *cheap, miserable, wretched, shabby.*

crush. This is a highly informal, possibly slangy, term for "infatuation" and for the object of short-lived affection or passion.

crust. A slang term for "gall," "insolence," and "audacity."

cuppa. A nonexistent term, *cuppa* in ordinary speech replaces "cup of," as in *a cuppa coffee.* No particular stigma attaches to this pronunciation, but it should appear only in informal speech.

curiously enough. A legitimate expression which, *curiously enough*, has little meaning. (Remove the phrase from the sentence you have just read and from your speech. Nothing will be lost.)

curtains. A slang term meaning "the end," "death," "utter ruin." Like all slang, the expression is hackneyed.

cuss. This is an informal, or narrowly dialectal, term for "to curse" (verb) and "a curse" (noun). It is also a slang term for "a worthless person" as in *a no-good cuss.*

cut. This useful little word appears in such overworked phrases as *cut a figure, cut and run, cut-and-dried, cut of one's jib, a cut above, cut no ice,* and *cut a rug. Cut* is either highly informal or slangy when used to mean (1) failure to attend; (2) to stop; (3) a share of profits; (4) an insult.

cute. This is an overworked word meaning about what the speaker wishes it to: *pretty, dainty, vivacious, charming, precious, delicate, cunning, tender, clever, adroit, radiant, dazzling, pert,* and so on and so on. Wouldn't one of the words listed here come closer to what you have in mind when you carelessly say "cute"?

cycle. Standing alone, this word is pronounced SAI·k'l. When it is combined with a prefix or other word element (*bi-, motor-*), it may be pronounced either SAI·k'l, or SIK'l.

daffy. An informal word, the meaning of which can usually be more clearly expressed by "silly," "foolish," or "zany."

dago. This alteration of the common Spanish name *Diego* is an offensive slang term when used to refer to an Italian, Portuguese, or Spaniard. *Dago red* is a slang expression meaning "cheap red wine."

dairy, diary. These everyday words are sometimes confused in pronunciation, spelling, and meaning. The former, pronounced DAY·ri or DEHR·i, refers to milk and milk products. *Diary*, pronounced DAI·uh·ree, is a daily record or journal.

daisy. This is a slang term when used to refer to something or someone of first-rate quality, and is informal and trite in the phrase *to push up daisies* (to be dead).

dandy. An overworked, colloquial expression meaning "of excellent quality," "outstanding."

darky. An offensive term for a black person (also spelled *darkie* and *darkey*).

data. This term, meaning "facts," "information," "statistics," and the like is really the plural of *datum*. In general use, however, *data* now appears as a singular and plural collective noun. The plural construction ("*these* data *are . . .*") is appropriate in formal usage, although "*this* data *is . . .*" is more often used.

date. As both noun and verb, *date* occurs in informal standard usage: "Joe made a *date* for dinner." "Ellen's *date* came early." "Emily is *dating* Dick." In addition to being informal in these senses, *date* is tiresomely overused; occasionally use *appointment, engagement, occasion,* or *court* and add variety to your diction.

dead. This word is overused as an informal term for "weary," "wornout," or "exhausted." It also appears in such slangy or trite word combinations as *deadbeat* (a loafer, a person who does not meet his obligations); *dead beat* (weary, tired); *deadhead* (one who uses a ticket without payment); *dead duck* (a person or thing destined for failure); *deadeye* (an expert marksman); and *deadpan* (lifeless expression or manner). To urge someone to *drop dead* is a rude and slangy invitation for him to keep quiet or leave. The phrase *dead giveaway*, meaning "complete betrayal" or "total revelation," is trite.

deal. As a noun, *deal* has a meaning of "amount" ("He talked a great *deal*"), a sense also conveyed by "lot," "lots," and "heap." *Deal* should be used before only mass amounts: Say "a great deal of lumber," but "a great many trees."

As noun and verb, *deal* appears in several trite, slangy,

or informal expressions generally to be avoided: *big deal* (important event, issue); *deal me in* (include me); *deal me out* (exclude); *raw deal* (unfair treatment); *wheeler-dealer* (a sharp or clever operator).

debunk. An informal and overused term meaning "to expose or ridicule."

debut. This importation from French is pronounced de· BYOO, DAY·boo, and DAY·byoo. As a noun, it means "first public appearance," the "beginning of a career," or "formal presentation." *Debut* is not yet established as a verb in standard usage, although it is appearing ever more frequently in both speech and print: "The actress *debuts* tonight in a new play." "The company will *debut* its new model tomorrow." Until *debut* is accepted as a transitive and intransitive verb by reliable dictionaries, continue to use the word only as a noun.

décor. This word from a French verb meaning "to decorate" is an overused noun meaning "a decorative style or scheme" and "setting" or "scenery." Its generally accepted pronunciation is DAY·kor, but di·KOR is also widely heard.

deduce, deduct, deduction, induce, induct, induction. Uses of these six words do not cause as much trouble as do those of *imply* and *infer* (which see), but they can be troublesome. *Deduce* means to "reach a conclusion by reasoning" or to "infer from a general principle." *To deduct* has the same sense as *to deduce*, in addition to its meaning of "subtracting" and "removing." *Deduction* is a noun form of the verb *deduce* in both of these meanings. *Induce* means to "influence," to "persuade," to "prevail upon," but also means to "infer by inductive reasoning." To *induct* means to "install," "to place in office," to "initiate" and has no reference to reasoning or thinking processes as such. *Induction* is a noun form with both of the general meanings of *induce* and also that of *induct*.

defective, deficient. The former applies to that which has a recognizable, discernible fault or flaw and is concerned with quality. *Deficient* refers to incompleteness and insufficiency and is primarily a quantitative, not qualitative, term. In your mind, associate *defective* with "defect" and *deficient* with "deficit."

definite, definitive. Each of these words applies to that which is clearly set forth and explained, but the latter also has a meaning of "final," "total" or "complete." ("The time of his arrival is *definite*." "This is a *definitive* life of the author.")

definitely. An overused exclamation for "surely," "without doubt," "certainly." See *absolutely*.

degree. This word, usually suggesting a series of steps, stages, or points, is overused by nearly everyone. Such expressions as *to some degree* and *by degrees* are usually only fillers and have no precise meaning or purpose. As a form of jargon, *degree* can be omitted without loss from most statements.

delivery. This word has four syllables, each of which should be pronounced: di·LIV·uhr·i. Do not omit the *uh* sound and pronounce the word di·LIV·ri (except, of course, in rapid, informal conversation).

delusion. See *allusion*.

de luxe. This word, which in French means "of luxury," may be pronounced di·LOOKS or di·LUKS. The former is more often used by careful, educated speakers. The phrase is heavily overworked; occasionally say *elegant, luxurious*, or *sumptuous*.

dentifrice. This word for powder, paste, or other preparation for cleaning teeth is often mispronounced by speakers who transpose letters. The middle syllable is *ti*, not *tri*; say DEN·tuh·fris.

deprecate, depreciate. The former means to "express disapproval of," to "plead against," to "protest." The latter means to "belittle," to "lower in value." Because the two words look somewhat similar, *deprecate* is sometimes used in the sense of "belittlement" ("Jesse *deprecated* his contribution to the cause"), but the words actually have distinct meanings and pronunciations: DEP·ri·kayt (deprecate) and di·PREE·shi·ayt (depreciate).

descend down. Omit *down*. See *ascend up*.

descent, dissent, decent. These words have distinct spellings and meanings. *Descent* (di·SENT) refers to the act, process, or fact of descending, of "leading down." *Dissent* is pronounced like *descent*, but its meaning is that of "disagreeing" or "differing." *Decent* (DEE·suhnt) means "free from indelicacy," "modest," "kind," or "acceptable." ("Before he made his *descent* from the platform, the *decent* man expressed strong *dissent*.")

desert, dessert. As a noun, *desert* differs in spelling, pronunciation, and meaning from *dessert*. The term for an arid region is pronounced DEZ·uhrt. The term for a pastry, pudding, or whatever final course of a meal is pronounced di·ZUHRT, as is the *verb* "desert."

despicable. This adjective meaning "vile" or "deserving of contempt" may be pronounced DES·pi·kuh·b'l or des·PIK·uh·b'l. The former pronunciation is considered preferable by most authorities, although the latter is often used by careful speakers when they wish to *emphasize* the idea of "contemptible," "something deserving to be despised."

despite of. A wordy phrase from which *of* should be omitted. Even more wordy is the expression *in despite of,* from which both prepositions can usually be dropped without loss. However, *in spite of* is a standard idiomatic phrase. Even so, occasionally say *notwithstanding* or *regardless* or *nevertheless,* because one word is usually preferable to three.

detour. This commonly seen and often used word may be pronounced DEE·toor or di·TOOR. The former is more often used, but careful speakers prefer the latter pronunciation.

deus ex machina. This Latin phrase ("god from a machine") is used to refer to a deity brought in by stage machinery in a play or to any unexpected, artificial device, event, or character introduced to resolve a situation or untangle a plot. The first word in the phrase may be pronounced DAY·oos or DEE·os; the second two words sound like eks·MAK·ee·nah.

device, devise. The former, a noun, refers to a machine or contrivance of some sort; it is pronounced di·VAIS. *Devise,* a verb, means to "plan, invent, or contrive." It is pronounced di·VAIZ.

devoted. See *addicted.*

diddle. This verb meaning to "waste time," or "dawdle," and to "jerk up and down" has moved from the status of slang to informal standard usage. It is, however, a vague and overused word.

didn't ought. An illiterate expression. Say "shouldn't."

didn't use to. *Didn't* is a contraction of "did not." *Use to* sometimes is employed to mean "formerly" ("*use to* they lived near here"), but the expression may be considered either illiterate or narrowly dialectal. Other nonstandard expressions to be avoided are *used to didn't be; usen't to; used to wasn't.*

dincha, didja. These expressions are hurried, conversational forms of "didn't you" and "did you." Avoid them in all except the most informal and rushed of conversations.

die of, from, with. In its customary sense of "cease living," *die* is preferably followed by *of* ("He died *of*—not *from*—a coronary attack.") *Die with* expresses an idea not related to a cause of death ("He died *with* courage.")

different. This word is an adjective, not a noun. "He doesn't know any *different*" is standard informal usage, but "He doesn't see any *different* between them" is an illiterate statement. In a remark such as "I consulted three *different* lawyers," *different* is superfluous. It is also unneeded in "I bought three *different* kinds of soap."

different from, than, to. The first two of these expressions are widely used, but *different from* is preferred by careful, educated speakers. Unfortunately, but correctly, *different from* often leads to extra words because *than* is a convenient shortcut for "from that which." Even so, say *different from* rather than *different than* until widespread usage sanctions the latter term. *Different to* appears more often in British than in American usage.

dig. This word is slang when used to mean "understand," "appreciate," or "enjoy": "I don't *dig* you." It is informal when used to mean to "work hard," to "study diligently." *Dig up* is an informal expression for "discover" or "find by chance."

dilemma. This word means a situation wherein one faces equally undesirable alternatives or choices. *Dilemma* is loosely used when the predicament does not suggest alternative courses and does not even involve an idea of choice. In most instances, *situation, problem,* or *predicament* would be a more exact and suitable word than *dilemma.* An especially trite saying is *on the horns of a dilemma.*

dilly. A slang term meaning something remarkable or startling.

dingus. A slang word for a gadget or contrivance or article of some sort, the name of which eludes the speaker or is unknown to anyone.

dirt. As an informal term for gossip or scandal, *dirt* is picturesque but trite. To *do someone dirt* is a slangy expression meaning to "cause someone to lose status" or to "to do someone an evil turn." To *eat dirt* is a slang expression meaning to "accept criticism," to "humble oneself."

disastrous. This word, meaning "unfortunate," "ruinous," and "calamitous," has only three syllables. Do not add an extra *e*; say di·ZAS·truhs or di·ZAHS·truhs.

discover, invent. The former means to "get knowledge of, to find out, to learn of something previously unknown" (*discover* America, *discover* uranium). To *invent* is to "originate," to "conceive of or devise first." (*Invent* the sewing machine.) Synonyms for *discover* — none of which apply to the basic meaning of *invent* — are *detect, discern, notice, ferret out,* and *espy.*

disgusted with, at, by. Idiom decrees that one is *disgusted with* a person or a person's actions, *disgusted at* some particular action or behavior, and *disgusted by* a personal quality or act.

dish. This word is slang when used to refer to an attractive girl or woman. It also appears in such slangy, trite expressions as *dish it out* (to deal out, distribute, or to abuse physically or with words) and *dull as dishwater* (boring).

disinterested, uninterested. *Disinterested* means "impartial," "unbiased," "not influenced by selfish motives." *Uninterested* suggests "aloofness," "indifference," "not interested." Say "The judge rendered a *disinterested* verdict" and "The judge was *uninterested* in the courtroom behavior of the accused."

dislike. One takes a *dislike to* a person and has a *dislike for* a thing.

disregardless, irregardless. Both words are illiteracies. The prefixes *ir-* and *dis-* are superfluous. Say *regardless, unmindful, heedless, anyway*, or even the wordy *in spite of everything* and thus avoid a double negative (*dis-* and *ir-* plus *-less*). See *double negative.*

disremember. This word is dialectal rather than illiterate, but good speakers prefer "forget" or "fail to remember."

dissimulate, simulate. To *dissimulate* is to conceal or hide; to *simulate* is to pretend. ("He *dissimulated* his injury by waving his arms." "She *simulated* pain by writhing on the grass.")

district. This is one of the most frequently mispronounced words in English. It ends in *t*, not *k*. Say DIS·trikt (*not* DIS·trick).

ditch. A slang term when used to mean to "throw aside, discard, desert," to "avoid, escape from," and to "bring down an aircraft on water."

dive. Principal parts of the verb *dive* are *dive*, *dived* or *dove*, *dived*. One may say, "The boy *dived* (or *dove*) into the lake." If you use *dove* as the past tense, say *dove* (with the *o* sounded like the *o* in "over"). As a noun, *dive* is slang for a "disreputable or rundown bar or club" and for "a knockout arranged in advance between prize fighters."

divvy. This is a slang term as both verb and noun, meaning "to divide" and "a share." Apparently a shortened form of "dividend," *divvy* is usually accompanied by *up* when used as a verb.

dizzy. This word derives from an Old English word meaning "foolish," "stupid," but for some odd reason is now considered informal or slangy in such expressions as *dizzy blonde*. Despite its sound origin, avoid using *dizzy* as a synonym for *scatterbrained*, *silly*, and *featherheaded*.

do. This useful word is informal or slangy when used to mean "serve as a prison term" (*doing* time); to "cheat" or to "swindle" (*do* someone out of his paycheck); and a "party" or "entertainment" (a big *do*). It appears in such slangy or trite expressions as *do away with* (dispose of, eliminate); *do in* (exhaust or kill); *do over* (refurbish, decorate); and *make do* (manage).

dodge. In the meaning of "shifty trick" or "evasive plan," *dodge* is considered no worse than informal usage, but it is tiresomely overused. Occasionally say *ruse, wile, artifice, stratagem, guile, maneuver, subterfuge, finesse, trick*, or *feint*.

dog. It is unknown why the name of a male canine animal should have been adopted for so many uses that are slangy, informal, or trite. Listed in one or another of these categories are *dog* meaning "a fellow" (you lucky *dog*); a dull or unattractive person (My partner was a real *dog*); an inferior product (That car is a *dog*); *dogs* (the feet); *go to the dogs* (degenerate); *put on the dog* (make a display); *dog collar* (clerical collar); *dog days* (hot, sultry period in late summer or early autumn); *dog-eat-dog* (ruthless, competitive); *dogface* (infantryman in the U.S. Army); *doggish* (stylish); *be in the dog house* (be in disfavor); *dog in the manger* (one who prevents another from enjoying what he himself has no use for); *dog's age* (a long time); *dog's life* (unhappy existence); *die like a dog* (meet a miserable end); *let sleeping dogs lie* (refrain from action or speech); *dog cheap* (inexpensive); *dog Latin* (mongrel or spurious Latin); *dog poor* (very poor); *dog tired* (exhausted).

doll. This word is slang when used to refer to a woman or girl (usually an attractive one), or to a helpful and generous person ("Be a *doll* and lend me some money"). *Doll up* is a slang term meaning to dress in a stylish or elegant way. The phrase *living doll* is especially trite and artificial.

done. This is the past participle of *do*. Be careful not to confuse *did* and *done;* say "He *did* that," not "He *done* that" and "This was *done* yesterday," not "This was *did* yesterday."

To have done with something is a grammatically correct but overused expression. *Done for* is an informal expression meaning "tired" or "defeated," meanings also expressed by the equally informal *done in. To be done with* someone or something is more accurately expressed by "to be finished with."

don't. This is a contraction of "do not." Avoid such illiteracies as *he don't, they don't got,* and *it don't seem.* Remember: *do* is a verb in the present tense and is not in the third person singular.

doodad. A rather meaningless term for a trinket, bauble, or generally unclassifiable object. Diction should be as exact and forceful as possible.

dope. This is a slang term for (1) narcotics; (2) information or data; (3) a stupid person; (4) a carbonated drink, especially Coca-Cola. It is also slang in expressions such as *dope out* (figure out, calculate); *dope fiend* (one addicted to narcotics); *dope sheet* (bulletin); and *dopey* (sluggish, befuddled).

doublecross. This informal term meaning "betrayal" or "swindle" should be avoided only because it has been so overused as to lose its effectiveness.

double negative. The phrase *double negative* is not itself a speech error of any sort, but it does name a construction generally considered illiterate or narrowly dialectal. Such a construction employs two negatives to express a single negation. Illiterate or unusually careless speech abounds with such expressions as *can't hardly, haven't scarcely, can't scarcely.* Such double negatives have been allowable in past centuries, but they are now out of style and unacceptable. You are not likely to say "I didn't get no money" or "I haven't seen nobody," but you should be careful to avoid using *not* with such negative words as *no, but, nor, only, hardly, barely, scarcely,* and *except.* ("I did *not* have *but* five hours sleep." "You *can't* help *but* love that child.")

doubt if, doubt whether, doubt that. Both *doubt* and *doubtful* are often followed by clauses introduced by *if, whether,* and *that.* A choice among the three depends upon the kind of sentence involved. *That* is used when a negative or interrogative idea is involved: "There is little *doubt that* you are mistaken." "Can you any longer be *doubtful that* you are mistaken?"

Whether is used in statements conveying genuine doubt and uncertainty: "It is *doubtful whether* he will live." "They *doubt whether* he was ever there." *If* is usually to be avoided after both *doubt* and *doubtful,* although some accomplished speakers feel that *if* and *whether* are interchangeable. Since the use of *if* is debatable in *doubt* constructions and the use of *whether* is limited, why not always use *that?*

dough. A slangy cliché for "money."

dozen. This collective noun is both singular and plural in the sense of "set of twelve" (*a dozen is; a dozen are*). In the sense of "a large number," the recognized plural is *dozens* (*Dozens* of people *were* present). In neither singular nor plural form is *dozen(s)* followed by *of* except with reference to a quantity that is part of a larger quantity. Say "a dozen apples" *not* "a dozen of apples"; say "several dozens of his friends"; "two dozen of those pears."

drag. The principal parts of this verb are *drag, dragged,*

dragged. Drug is nonstandard as a substitute for *dragged.* Never use *drug* as a part of the verb *drag.*

In the sense of "boring" or "annoying," *drag* is slangy, as it is in the sense of drawing on a cigarette, cigar, or pipe. As a noun, *drag* is slang when used to mean (1) something tiresome and tedious, (2) women's clothing worn by a male, (3) a puff of smoke, (4) influence, (5) a girl escorted to a party.

dreadful. Like *awful* (which see), *dreadful* and *dreadfully* are overused intensives often employed inexactly. Unless something really fills you with dread, avoid using either word. Like *awful, dreadful* is an adjective; its use before another adjective is nonstandard (*dreadful sorry, awful close*). If you must use such an expression, say "dreadfully sorry," "awfully close."

drop. Such expressions as *get the drop on* and *at the drop of a hat* were once picturesque but are now tired clichés. For comment on *drop dead,* see *dead.*

drowned. Some careless or illiterate speakers add a "d" sound to this word. It should be pronounced "drownd," not "drown*ded.*"

drunk. The principal parts of *drink* are *drink, drank, drunk.* Say "Joe *drank* the water," *not* "Joe *drunk* the water." *Drunken* is an adjective (a *drunken* driver); the use of drunk as an adjective (*drunk* driving, *drunk* driver) is highly informal, if not illiterate.

dry up. This phrase is slang (and rude slang, too) when used as a command to "stop talking."

duck. This word is a slang term for "an odd person" (*a queer duck*). *Duck soup* is overworked slang for "something simple or easy to do." *Ducky* is a slang term meaning "excellent," "good."

duds. An overworked and informal expression for "clothes" or "personal belongings."

due to. The phrase *due to,* when used in a prepositional sense meaning "owing to" and "caused by," is in common and reputable use. ("His accident was *due to* a fall on the icy pavement.") Many careful speakers avoid *due to* in introducing an adverbial construction, but actually *due to* is grammatically as sound and correct as the phrases it replaces: *owing to, because of, on account of,* and *through.*

However, *due to* and, especially, *due to the fact that* are wordy ways of saying *since* and *because*.

duffer. This is an informal, overworked term for an "incompetent" or "stupid" person ("I'm a *duffer* at golf") and is slang when used to mean something worthless or useless or "a peddler of cheap wares."

dumb. This term, when used to mean "stupid" or "dull," probably derives from the German word *dumm* rather than from Old English *dumb* (speechless). Whatever its origin, it is overworked or slangy in expressions such as *dumbbell, dumb bunny,* and *dumb blonde.* Occasionally use *dolt* or adjectives such as *slow, stupid, dull, obtuse,* and *dense.*

dump. This inelegant word is slang when used to mean "knock down" or "knock out" and "a low and disreputable place." *Dumps* may be considered informal or slangy when it means "a gloomy state of mind" (*down in the dumps*).

during the time that. A wordy way to express the meaning of "while."

dyed in the wool. A cliché. (The phrase refers to dyeing raw wool rather than finished garments and is now accepted as meaning "of high quality" or "thoroughgoing" and "altogether.")

each. This pronoun is singular and, even when not followed by *one*, implies *one*. Plural words used in modifying phrases do not change the number: "*Each has* his own reasons." "*Each* of the girls *has* her own reasons." When *each* appears after a plural subject to which it refers, the verb should be plural ("Bill and Jack *each have* their own reasons.")

each and every. This is a redundant (wordy) phrase; when used, it requires a singular verb: "*Each and every* one of you *has* his own reasons." Preferably, use *each* or *every*, not both.

each other, one another. In standard speech, *each other* is used when two persons are involved; *one another* is preferred when three or more persons are concerned. ("The man and his wife spoke to *each other* excitedly." "The six motorcyclists were arguing with *one another*.") Common usage (not recommended, however) permits such a statement as "The five culprits regarded *each other* with dis-

trust." Be safe: use *one another* when three or more persons
are involved.

eager. See *anxious*.

early on. A wordy and trite expression from which *on* can be
omitted. Say "early" or "soon" or "quickly" or "immediately."

easy. This word appears in numerous informal or trite or
slangy expressions. As often as you can, avoid saying *easy
does it, take it easy, easy money, go easy on, easier said than
done, easy street, slow and easy,* and *easy come, easy go.*

eatery. A slang term for "lunchroom" or "diner."

eats. A slang term for "food."

economic, economical. The former applies to material
wealth and to business or household enterprise. The latter
means "prudent in management," "not wasteful," "thrifty."
Thus one refers to "*economic* resources" and "*economical*
management," to "*economic* problems" and to "*economical*
living."

effect. See *affect*.

egg. Avoid using such slangy, informal, or trite expressions
as *a good egg* (well-liked person); *lay an egg* (fail, be defeated); *put all one's eggs in one basket* (risk all on a single enterprise); *teach one's grandmother to suck eggs* (try to teach
someone older or more experienced than oneself); *egghead*
(an intellectual).

egoism, egotism. Both words (and the adjectival forms,
egoistic and *egotistic*) refer to preoccupation with one's own
self, or ego. *Egoism,* less commonly used than *egotism,*
emphasizes self-importance in relation to other things: "Joe
has quite enough *egoism* to understand his role in society."
Egotism is an often-used word for excessive or boastful reference to, or emphasis upon, oneself: "His *egotism* made it
impossible for him to hold many friends." An *egoist* is one
"devoted to his own interests"; an *egotist* is a conceited,
boastful person.

either . . . or, neither . . . nor. The former means "one of
two"; *neither* means "not one of two." *Or* goes with *either,
nor* with *neither*. The use of either of these expressions to
coordinate more than two words, phrases, or clauses is held
permissible by some authorities but not by others: "*Either*

telephone *or* write." "*Neither* Jack *nor* Jill knows." *Either* may be pronounced EE·thuhr or AI·thuhr; *neither* may be sounded as NEE·thuhr or NAI·thuhr. (The long *e* sound, as in *equal*, is more widespread in the pronunciation of both words.)

elder, eldest, older, oldest. The first two words of this group apply only to persons, whereas *older* and *oldest* may apply to persons or things. Also, *elder* and *eldest* (much less common than the other two terms) apply principally to members of a given family or business establishment and indicate age or seniority ("elder brother," "eldest partner"). However, say "He is *older* (not *elder*) than his brother."

electoral. There is no short or long *i* sound in this word. Say ee·LEK·tuhr·uhl.

element. As a substance or as part of an entity, *element* is a vague word often used in a jargonish (meaningless, wordy) fashion. Avoid using it in a loose way; possibly *ingredient, component, part,* or *constituent* would come nearer to expressing your precise meaning.

elicit, illicit. The former, pronounced i·LIS·it, means "to draw out," "to bring forth" ("to elicit a response from the audience"). *Illicit*, pronounced il·LIS·it or i·LIS·it, means "illegal," "unlawful," "not allowed." Pronunciations of these words are similar, but meanings are not.

elite. This overused word meaning "choice" or "best of its kind" may be pronounced i·LEET or ay·LEET. The former pronunciation is more general in the U.S.A., the latter closer to that of this borrowed French word in its native language.

elm. Only in rare regional pronunciations does this word sound like *ell-um*. It should be sounded as one lengthened syllable, *elm*.

elude. See *allude.*

'em. A contraction of *them*, common in informal speech but not recommended for careful discourse.

emend. See *amend.*

emigrant, immigrant. These words (together with *emigrate* and *immigrate, emigration* and *immigration*) are related to the basic verb "migrate," which is used with reference to place of departure and to destination. *Emigrant* and *emi-*

grate refer specifically to a place of departure and emphasize movement from that place. *Immigrant* and *immigrate* refer mainly to destination and are followed by *to*, as *emigrant* and *emigrate* are by *from*: "Johnson *emigrated from* Sweden in 1965." "Johnson *immigrated to* England in 1965." A person moving from one country to another is an *emigrant*. One who has already moved to another area is an *immigrant*.

eminent, imminent. *Eminent* (pronounced EM·uh·nuhnt) means "distinguished," "high in rank," "noteworthy" (an *eminent* statesman). *Imminent* (pronounced IM·uh·nuhnt) means "about to occur," "impending," (an *imminent* rain squall).

enamored about, of, with. *Enamored* is a powerful word meaning "to inspire with love," to "captivate." Use it sparingly, and when you do, say "enamored *of*" (enamored *of* his new job) or "enamored *with*" (enamored *with* the new girl in the neighborhood). "Enamored *about*" is not acceptable idiom.

enclose, inclose. Although spelled and pronounced differently, these two words meaning to "surround, hem in, close on all sides" are interchangeable. Use either or both. *Enclose* and *enclosure*, however, are used much more often than *inclose* and *inclosure*.

enclosed. This word has the meanings stated in the preceding entry. Therefore, such expressions as *enclosed herewith* and *enclosed herein* are redundant. *Enclosed please find* is also a piece of business jargon that is not only wordy but silly.

end. This word is informal when used to mean "duty," "obligation," or "part" (your *end* of the bargain). It appears too often in such trite expressions as *go off the deep end* (behave recklessly or impulsively); *make both ends meet* (manage to live within one's means); *no end* (a great deal); *hold one's end up* (care for one's own responsibility); *at loose ends* (unsettled); *at one's wit's end* (at the end of one's resources); *put an end to* (finish, terminate); *ends of the earth* (remote regions, everywhere). *End result* is a wordy phrase: *result* conveys the idea of *end*. Since a *result* is an *end*, avoid this trite, redundant expression.

endemic, epidemic. The former word means "peculiar to a given country or people," and, in medicine, is applied to a disease characteristic of (or confined to) a particular locality. ("Malaria is *endemic* in certain warm, humid countries.") *Epidemic* means "breaking out suddenly in such a way as to affect many individuals at the same time": the term is used especially of contagious diseases. ("In that year an *epidemic* of cholera broke out.")

enervating, invigorating. Possibly because *enervate* looks and sounds something like "energy," many speakers confuse the meanings of *enervating* and *invigorating*. Almost antonyms, *enervating* means "weakening, devitalizing, sapping the strength of" (a humid, *enervating* climate); *invigorating* means "animating, giving energy or vigor" (a brisk, *invigorating* climate).

enough. This word, which can be used as a noun, adjective, and adverb, can also be overused as a sort of conversation filler. One grows tired of hearing such trite phrases as *oddly enough, strangely enough, peculiarly enough*, etc. If modifiers are needed, at least omit the *enough's*. See *ample* and *curiously enough*.

ensure, insure. The first of these words is a variant spelling of the latter. They are interchangeable when used to mean "to make certain or sure to come, to secure." When one is referring to a guarantee against loss, risk, or harm, he should use only *insure* (insurance.) The most common meaning of a related word, *assure*, is "to tell a person confidently that something exists or will occur."

enthuse. Meaning "to show enthusiasm," *enthuse* is nonstandard as a verb. Instead of saying "She *enthused* over the dance" say "She *was enthusiastic* over (or about) the dance."

entrance. As a noun meaning "entering" or "a passage that affords entry," *entrance* is pronounced EN·trans. As a verb meaning "to put into a trance" or "delight," the word is pronounced en·TRAHNS.

envelop, envelope. The first of these words, a verb meaning "to encase, enclose, or surround," is pronounced en·VEL·uhp. The noun *envelope*, meaning "something that envelops, an enclosing wrapping," is pronounced EN·vuh·lohp, ON·vuh·lohp, or AHN·vuh·lohp.

environment, environs. These related words, each meaning "surroundings, surrounding area," are pronounced en·VAI·ruhn·muhnt and either en·VAI·ruhnz or EN·vuh·ruhnz.

epic. This short word with powerful meanings and associated meanings should not loosely be used to refer to events, spectacles, or other matters unless they are notable for grandeur, scope, majesty, and heroism. It is doubtful that many sports events, films, TV shows, or books should really be called *epic*.

equal. Like *unique, perpendicular,* and other words with "absolute" meaning, *equal* should not be preceded by *more* or *most* because it is not capable of comparison. *More nearly equal* and *more equitable* are more acceptable and precise expressions than *more equal*.

equally as. The adverb *equally* is redundant (wordy) when combined with *as*. Omit *equally* in a statement such as "Hard work is (equally) *as* valuable as ability." Delete *as* from a remark such as "*Equally* (as) significant is one's desire to improve his lot."

escape. Possibly because so many English words begin with *ex, escape* is often mispronounced. It may be sounded as es·KAYP, e·SKAYP, is·KAYP, or i·SKAYP, but *not* as beginning with "ek" or "eks." In the sense of breaking out of confinement, *escape* should be followed by *from:* one *escapes from* prison; he does not *escape* prison. *Escape* has many meanings, some of which can be conveyed by *elude, evade, avoid,* and *shun.* Vary your vocabulary!

essential. This word is often used in the sense of "important" or "greatly desirable." Actually, it means something that is "necessary for the existence of something else." "Milk with meals" is not *essential* for growing children; it is *important* or *desirable*. Do not overuse or imprecisely use *essential*.

ethics. When meaning the moral sciences as a whole, *ethics* is a plural noun. It may be used with a singular verb when it refers to "fitness" or "propriety": "The ethics of his decision *is*—or *are*—debatable." The adjective form is always *ethical*, not *ethic* (which is the actual singular form of the noun).

ever, every. *Ever* means "constantly," "always," "at any time," "repeatedly." *Every* means "each and all without exception." Few speakers confuse these words except in the phrases "ever so often" and "every so often." *Ever so often* means "frequently," whereas *every so often* means "occasionally," "now and then." Trite phrases involving *ever* and *every* include *ever and ever, ever and anon, for ever and a day, every which way,* and *every now and then.*

everybody, everyone. These words are interchangeable in their meaning of "every person," although *everyone* is considered by some speakers as more "refined" and "euphonious" than *everybody*. Both pronouns, as subjects, require singular verbs; accompanying pronouns and adjectives should also be singular ("Everyone *has* (*not* have) an obligation to cast *his* (*not* their) vote."

Spelled as one word, *everyone* means "everybody." *Every one* (two words) refers to each person of a group and is followed by "of." ("*Every one* of them is loafing on the job.")

everyplace. This word is informal when used to mean "everywhere." Spelled as one word or two, *everyplace* is less standard than *everywhere*.

evident. See *apparent.*

evidently. This word, meaning "obviously" or "apparently," is frequently mispronounced. It has only four syllables, pronounced EV·uh·duhnt·lee or EV·i·duhnt·lee. The ending of the word is *not* pronounced TAL·li or TUH·lee.

exactly identical. A wordy phrase. *Identical* means "exactly the same," so that *exactly* is not needed.

except. See *accept.*

exceptionable, exceptional. These often confused words are not interchangeable. The former means "objectionable," the latter means "extraordinary," "uncommon," "unusual."

excerpt, extract. These words have several different meanings as both noun and verb, but each may refer to a passage or scene selected from a book, play, article, etc. Basically, to *excerpt* is "to pick out," "to pluck," whereas to *extract* is "to remove, usually with force."

excuse me, pardon me. The former is a weaker term than the latter, which implies guilt and a request for forgiveness. *Excuse me* is the correct term to use when asking someone to be allowed to pass or to overlook a minor matter. *Excuse me* should be used many times more often than *pardon me,* a term of mistaken gentility and affectation in most instances. See *apology*.

exemplary. This word, meaning "commendable," "worthy of imitation," may be pronounced eg·ZEM·pluh·ree or ig·ZEM·pluh·ree. Primary stress (strong accent) on the third syllable is not recommended by standard dictionaries.

expect. This word is often used informally to mean "suppose" or "presume." Say "I *presume* (or suppose) you are hungry" rather than "I *expect* you are hungry."

expectorate. This is another word for "spit," a euphemism thought to be less offensive than the term it replaces. Good speakers and writers avoid a roundabout way of expressing an "uncouth" idea on the grounds that if something can be mentioned or discussed at all — admittedly some topics and ideas are in questionable taste — it should be treated directly, forthrightly. *Expectorate* is not really more delicate than *spit*; it means to "clear out the chest by coughing up and spitting out" matter.

expertise. This term, meaning "specialized knowledge" or "great skill," has been accepted by modern dictionaries, but it is rapidly becoming a cliché through overuse.

explain about. Omit *about*, because *explain* conveys the complete thought of "making clear," of "defining." *Explain away* (to minimize, nullify) is a standard idiom, greatly overused. Possible substitutes for *explain* include *construe, elucidate, interpret,* and *expound*.

explicit, implicit. The former means "distinct," "specific," "clearly defined." ("The foreman gave us *explicit* instructions.") *Implicit* means "understood though not expressed." ("A commitment to duty was *implicit* in his every act and thought.") *Implicit* may also mean "complete," "unreserved" ("*implicit* faith in our system of government").

extant, extent. *Extant* (pronounced EKS·tuhnt or ek·STANT) means "still in existence, not destroyed or lost." *Extent* (pronounced ek·STENT or ik·STENT) means "scope," "comprehensiveness," "range." ("The *extent* of the land can be determined by *extant* property lines.")

extra. This common word meaning "something in addition, something beyond" is not firmly established in the mean-

ings of "very" or "unusually." Only in highly informal conversation should you say "*extra* good," "*extra* strong," "*extra*
fine," etc.

extract. See *excerpt*.

extrapolate. Anyone daring to use this big word meaning "to
estimate or infer by extending known information" probably
knows its pronunciation. For those previously unacquainted
with this term, the pronunciation is ek·STRAP·uh·late.

eye. This word appears in numerous informal, hackneyed, or
slangy meanings and expressions: *in the public eye; eye of
the wind; to catch someone's eye; to give someone the eye; to
keep an eye out (or on); to lay eyes on; to make eyes at; to see
eye to eye; in a pig's eye; with an eye to; eyeball to eyeball;
give one's eyeteeth; cut one's eyeteeth* (gain experience).

face. This word appears in several trite, informal expressions: *face up to, in the face of, face to face, to one's face, face
down, put a good face on.* Sometimes such expressions seem
necessary, but try not to overuse them.

fact. There is no such thing as a *false fact.* Therefore, *true
fact* and *true facts* are wordy expressions. *Loose facts* can be
better expressed by *suppositions* or *allegations.*

factor. This noun has several precise meanings, but it is
loosely and vaguely used to mean "element," "condition," or
"situation"—themselves also terms of jargon. "One *factor*
that made me take the job was the salary offered" can better
be expressed "I took the job partly because of the attractive
salary." Possible substitutes for *factor* include *ingredient,
component,* and *element,* although none is really precise.

factory. This word should be pronounced in three syllables:
FAK·tuh·ri. Do not say FAK·tri.

fact that. This is a wordy expression from which either *fact*
or *that* can usually be omitted. See *due to.*

fake. This word is informal or slangy when used to mean
"improvise," "act extemporaneously." *Fake out* is both
slangy and trite in the sense of "deceive," "outwit."

famed, famous, notorious. The first two of these words
have about the same meaning: "celebrated, acclaimed, renowned." Each, however, is overused in an exaggerated

sense of "well-known." *Notorious* has a meaning of "infamous, known widely and unfavorably." George Washington was *famed* and *famous*, Benedict Arnold was *notorious*.

fan. An informal term for "admirer." Instead of this shortened form of *fanatic*, occasionally say *devotee, habitué, follower, votary*, or *enthusiast*.

fanny. A slang term coyly used instead of the honest word *buttocks*.

farther, further. Distinction between these words has been breaking down for many years, but careful speakers use *farther* and *farthest* to refer to "a measurable distance" or "space" ("the ball traveled ten yards *farther*.") *Further* indicates "greater in quantity, time, and degree" and also means "moreover." ("We should discuss this problem *further*.") For *all the farther*, see *all*.

fast. This word appears in several informal or slangy expressions: *fast buck* (easily made money); *pull a fast one* (play an unfair trick); *play fast and loose* (act irresponsibly and deceitfully); *fast talk* (glib persuasion); *fast worker* (a quick, shrewd person).

fat. This useful word appears in the following informal and slangy expressions for which less trite synonyms can usually be found: *fat chance* (slight chance); *fat lot* (little or not at all); *chew the fat* (engage in informal conversation); *the fat is in the fire* (the action is started and cannot be stopped); *the fat of the land* (the best of anything); *fat cat* (wealthy or important person); *fathead* (stupid person); *fats* and *fatso* (overweight person). Among synonyms for *fat* in its basic meaning are *chubby, corpulent, fleshy, obese, portly, pudgy, plump, rotund*, and *stout*.

faux pas. This French phrase, meaning "false step" in English, is used to refer to a breach of etiquette, a social blunder. It should be pronounced FOE·paw or foe·PAW. The plural is spelled like the singular but is pronounced FOE·pawz or foe·PAWZ.

fault. This word is nonstandard (or informal) when used as a transitive verb: "Do not *fault* him." It is widely employed in this sense, however, and presumably will become standard. Until it does, why not employ *blame, censure, condemn, criticize, denounce, reprehend*, or *scold*?

feature. In the sense of "imagine" and "conceive of," *feature* is informal: "I cannot *feature* his getting married."

February. Through usage, *February* may correctly be pronounced FEB·roo·er·i or FEB·yoo·er·i, although the former is still considered preferable.

feed, fed. *Feed* is informal when used to mean "a meal" and is slang in the phrase *off one's feed* (without appetite, not feeling good). To *put on the feedbag* is a slang expression for "eating." *Feedback* has become a cliché meaning any information about the result of an action or process. To be *fed up* is considered an informal or slangy expression meaning "disgusted" or "out of patience."

feel. See *bad* and *believe*. *Feel like* is an informal phrase meaning "to be in the mood for." *Feel up to* (capable of, ready for) and *feel out* (investigate, try to find out) are clichés. *Feel up* (touch, caress) is slang. *Feel of* (to touch, finger) is a wordy phrase; omit *of*.

femme. This French word meaning "a woman" or "a girl" has become a cliché in English. So has the phrase *femme fatale* (an irresistibly attractive, seductive female).

fewer, less. Both of these words imply a comparison with something larger in number or amount. *Fewer* is preferred when "number" is involved (*fewer* houses on this street, *fewer* fish in the stream). *Less* is used in several ways: it is applied to material in bulk (*less* sugar in the coffee); with abstractions (*less* honor in business dealings); with matters involving degree and value (one is *less* than two). Although many speakers use these words interchangeably, *fewer* should be used to refer only to numbers or to units capable of being counted. ("The *less* money we have, the *fewer* supplies we can bring.")

field. In the meaning of "an area of human activity or interest," this word is greatly overused (*field* of endeavor, *field* of insurance, etc.). Also overused are phrases such as *play the field, hold the field, in the field, take the field,* and *out in left field.*

figuratively, literally. The former means *not* literal, that is, metaphorical (represented by a likeness or figure of speech). *Literally* means "really," "actually." *Literally* means "true to the *exact* meaning of the words it accompanies"; *figura-*

tively means "in a manner of speaking." ("The heavy work *literally* drained his remaining energy." "This author writes *figuratively* about the terrors of loneliness.")

figure. This is an overworked word for which the following might be substituted: *calculate, comprehend, compute, contrive, determine, reason, suppose,* and *think. Figure out* is both trite and informal, as are *cut a figure, figure on,* and *it figures.*

filet. This word from French is usually pronounced in the French manner FIL·ay or fi·LAY. The phrase *filet mignon* (meen·YON) means a choice cut of beef from the loin.

fill. This word appears in numerous informal, trite, or slangy expressions such as *fill me in, fill the bill, have one's fill, fill 'er up.*

fin. This is a slang term for an arm or hand and for a five-dollar bill.

finagle. An informal, overused term meaning "to trick, cheat, or deceive through slyness and cunning."

finalize. In the sense of "complete," "conclude," and "make final," *finalize* has been used so often that it is now accepted by most dictionaries as a standard word. Some careful speakers avoid it because of its associations with bureaucracy and "big business."

finally. In rapid speech, this word is often pronounced as though it were spelled "finely." Say FAI·nuhl·ee, with some emphasis on each of three syllables.

fine. This is one of the half-dozen most overused words in the language and is employed in a variety of loose meanings. Actually, its use as an adverb is considered informal or narrowly dialectal (*feeling fine*) and it can be replaced in some one of its many meanings as an adjective by *dainty, exquisite, minute, splendid, beautiful, finished, perfected, superior, select, consummate, aesthetic, choice,* and *elegant. Fine* is informal, slangy, or trite in such expressions as *doing fine, cut it fine, in fine* (in conclusion, finally), and *fine and dandy.*

fink. A slang term for an undesirable person, a strikebreaker, or one who informs against another. As a verb, *fink* is slang for "inform" ("He *finked* on me") and to deny or withhold help ("She *finked* out on the group").

first. There is little need or excuse for such phrases as *first of* *all* or for *firstly* (secondly, thirdly, etc.). "Of all" is unneeded, and the *ly* ending adds another syllable but no additional meaning. *First-rate* can be used informally as an adjective (a *first-rate* worker), but is substandard as an adverb ("He does his job *first-rate*"). *Of the first water* (high quality) is an overworked phrase.

fit. This hackneyed word can get some needed rest if you will occasionally substitute *suitable, appropriate, proper*, or *fitting*. Also, avoid such informal or trite expressions as *fits the bill, by fits and starts, throw a fit, fit to be tied, fit to kill, fit for duty*, and *let the punishment fit the crime*.

fix, fixings. *Fix* has a basic meaning of "place" and "fasten securely," but it is overused in a variety of meanings only loosely related to "establishing," "securing," or "repairing." Try to substitute a more exact word because it doesn't make sense to use the same expression in such locutions as *fix a toy, fix a drink, get a fix, fix your position at sea, fix your face, fix your hair, fix a bet on a game, fix an engagement, fix a sentence, fix a fight,* and *be in a fix. Fixings* is an informal word for "trimmings," "accessories" ("turkey and all the *fixings*, or *fixin's*").

fizzle. An informal or slangy word for "to fail," "to die out," or "a failure."

flabbergast. An informal word meaning "to confound," "to astound". See *amaze.*

flammable, inflammable. These words mean the same thing and are interchangeable. They are not contrasted as are, for example, *capable* and *incapable, mature* and *immature.* Although both words are correct, *flammable* is more often used by scientists and in technical pursuits, whereas *inflammable* is more common outside manufacturing contexts. Possibly someday everyone will settle on *flammable.*

flapdoodle. A slang term for "nonsense," "foolish talk."

flappable. Slang for "easily excited or upset," this is a term derived from *flap,* also slang when used to mean "an emerging situation" or "a state of excitement."

flaunt, flout. These words are often used interchangeably, but they have distinct meanings. *Flaunt* means "to show off," "to make a boastful display." *Flout* means "to scoff at," "to scorn." Say "This prisoner has continued to *flout* (*not* flaunt) the law." "The cook *flaunted* (*not* flouted) his skill in flipping flapjacks."

flick. Slang for a motion picture.

flimflam. An overused, informal word for "humbug," "nonsense," or "a swindle." As a verb, it means "to cheat, defraud."

flip. A slang word when used to mean "delight" or "be overwhelmed by": "That band *flipped* the young dancers." "The couples *flipped their lids* when the orchestra began to play." *Flip* is informal when used to mean "impertinent" or "rude": "The youngsters had a *flip* attitude toward their teachers."

flop. This word is considered informal and slangy when used to mean "a failure," "to fail," and "to go to bed."

flout. See *flaunt.*

flown. This is the past participle of *fly.* ("The birds have *flown.*") *Flowed* is the past participle of *flow.* ("The river *flowed* past the pier.")

flub, flubdub. The former is an informal or slang term for "blunder," "bungle," "perform poorly." *Flubdub* is slang for "nonsense," "bunkum," or "pretentious airs."

focus. This word of several meanings is often employed to mean "center of attention" and "to concentrate on." *Focus down on* is a wordy, trite phrase from which *down* should be dropped. See *center around.*

folks. This is an informal, even archaic, term for *people, folk, relatives,* or *race. Just folks* and *plain folks* are trite phrases implying simplicity and unpretentiousness.

foot. *Foot* and its plural, *feet,* are typically used in expressions such as *a five-foot board* and *a board five feet long. Foot* appears in such trite phrases as *put one's best foot forward, put one's foot in one's mouth, always under foot, footloose and fancy free, get off on the wrong foot, have one foot in the grave, put one's foot down, put one's foot into it. Feet* is tiresomely used in *set someone on his feet* and *feet first.*

for free. This is wordy slang, often used by careless speakers who forget that *free* means "for nothing."

foreseeable future. *Foreseeable* involves "seeing beforehand, exercising foresight." *Foreseeable future* (probably meaning "the future as far as we can now anticipate or predict it") is not only trite but lacking in good sense.

foreword, forward. The former is a preface or introduction; *forward* means "located in advance," "in front." Say FORE·WURD and FAWR·wuhrd.

for to. This is an illiterate or narrowly dialectal expression in such a statement as "He wanted *for to* tell me about something."

former, latter. *Former* applies to the first of two in a series. When you refer to the first of three or more, say either *first* or *first-named*. In the sense in which it contrasts with *former, latter* refers to the second of two things mentioned. When you mention the last of three or more, say *last-named*, not *latter*.

formula. The plural of this word is either *formulas* (FAWR·myoo·lahz) or *formulae* (FAWR·myoo·lee). Use whichever you prefer.

frank. An informal, widely used abbreviation of *frankfurter*, even better known as a *hot dog*. Say *frankfurter* only in formal speaking situations.

frank. See *candid*.

Frankenstein. This is the name of the person who created the monster, *not* the monster itself.

frankly. An overused, often insincerely used adverb. If you think some modifier is needed, occasionally say *unreservedly, candidly, plainly, openly*.

freak. This word is now accepted as meaning an odd happening or an abnormal person or event. *Freak out* is a slang term for "experiencing the influences introduced by drugs" and for "becoming, or acting like, a hippie."

freebie. Slang for "something given or received free of charge."

free gratis. *Gratis* means "freely," "for nothing," "without charge." Say *free* or *gratis*, but don't use both in the same phrase.

fresh. This word is informal or slangy in the sense of "bold," "impudent" (a *fresh* youth). *Fresh out* is slang in the meaning of "just run out" (*fresh out* of drinking water).

from whence. Although this phrase has been widely used

in previous centuries (even in the King James version of the Bible), it is wordy. Omit *from* or *whence* or just say *where*.

fuddy-duddy. An informal or slangy expression meaning "old-fashioned," "fussy," or "fault-finding."

-ful. In recipes, the plural of *cup full* is *cupfuls*, presumably because the same container is used more than once. If you fill two cups with coffee, however, you have *two cups full*. Because the "same container" rule usually applies, the plurals are *mouthfuls, armfuls, teaspoonfuls, handfuls,* etc. Note, however, that you serve four guests "four *glasses full* of water."

funeral, funereal. These words have related meanings, but *funeral* (FYOO·nuhr·uhl) usually means "burial rites," whereas *funereal* (fyoo·NEER·i·uhl) has an additional and more regularly intended meaning of "sad," "doleful," and "gloomy" ("a *funereal* expression on her face").

funny. This is an overworked word for which *odd, strange, queer, remarkable,* or *peculiar* often may profitably be substituted. Ask yourself, "Do I mean *funny-peculiar* or *funny-haha?*" In standard speech, "That's funny" can mean only "That's laughable" — or *amusing, diverting, risible,* or *droll.*

further. See *farther.*

future. See *foreseeable future.*

fuzz. A slang term for "policemen."

g. This seventh letter of the alphabet is the one most often omitted in pronunciation. In informal speech, it is permissible to drop *g* from words like *talking, walking, speaking, sitting, "gassing,"* and *drinking,* but it should form at least a slight sound in all speech other than the most relaxed, intimate, and informal.

gab. This is an informal word for "talk," "chatter," "prattle," etc. It appears in such hackneyed expressions as *the gift of gab, gabfest* (a slang term), and *gabby.*

gadget. An informal, vague term for any device or contrivance the exact name of which is unknown or forgotten. It is a "thingamajig," a "thingamabob," a "whatchumacallit."

gaff, gaffe. The former is an "iron hook," the latter a "social blunder," a "faux pas" (which see). *Gaff* appears in a slangy, hackneyed expression (*stand the gaff*, that is, endure strain or weather hardship) and is a slang term for "cheat," or "defraud." *Gaff* and *gaffe* are pronounced GAF.

gag. This is an informal, overworked term used to mean "joke" or "trick."

gal. "Girl" is almost as short as *gal* and sounds better to most ears, including those of girls.

gala. This word meaning, usually, a "celebration," "festive occasion," or "showy" may be pronounced GAY·luh or GAL· uh. Take your pick. If you live in England, you may prefer GAH·luh.

gam. A slang term for "leg."

gantlet, gauntlet, gamut. One may run a *gantlet* (a former kind of military punishment). One may also run a *gamut* (a series of musical notes or the whole range of anything). But one may not run a *gauntlet* because it is a kind of glove. "To take up the *gauntlet*" (accept a challenge) and "throw down the *gauntlet*" (challenge to combat) are now hackneyed expressions.

garage. The preferred pronunciation is guh·RAHZH, but guh· RAHJ is also acceptable. The British are more likely to say GAR·ahzh or GAR·ij.

gas. This word is slang when used to mean (1) "long-winded talking" or "to talk excessively"; (2) something exciting or satisfying ("The party was a real *gas*"); (3) to evoke a strong reaction ("The remark *gassed* them"); (4) *gas-bag* (talkative person); (5) *gassy* (talkative). *Gas up* and *step on the gas* are trite, informal expressions.

gee. This is an exclamation of surprise (derived from "Jesus") and is a verb when used informally to mean "fit" or "go with" ("This plan doesn't *gee* with yours"). *Gee* (also spelled *G*) is slang for one thousand dollars.

geek. Slang for "a carnival performer," "a freak."

general, generally. Each of these words is often slurred in speaking. *General* is pronounced JEN·uhr·uhl; *generally* should be pronounced JEN·uhr·uhl·ee. *General* and *generally* are loosely overused in many expressions: *generally speaking, in general, in a general way,* etc. Possible substitutes: *prevailing, customary, ordinary, regular, popular, catholic, common, universal* and their corresponding adverbial forms (*universally*, etc.). *Generally always* is a wordy, trite expression.

gent, gents. *Gent* and *gents* are informal terms for a *man, men,* or *gentleman (gentlemen)*. *Gents* is also slang for "men's room."

genteel, gentile, gentle. *Genteel* means "well-bred, cultivated, polished" (*genteel* customs). A *gentile* is a non-Jew. *Gentle* means "mild" (a *gentle* massage).

get. This little word of many meanings has a primary one: "obtain," "come into possession of." It has numerous informal, idiomatic, or slangy meanings and appears in several hackneyed expressions. Among informal meanings of *get* and *got* (the past tense of *get*) are *comprehend* ("I don't *get* you"); *get the advantage of* ("overeating will *get* him"); *to be forced or obliged* ("I have *got* to leave soon"); *to strike or hit* ("The bullet *got* him in the arm"). Among slangy or trite uses may be mentioned *to puzzle* ("That remark *got* me"); *to observe* ("Did you *get* that look?"); and *get about, get ahead of, get across, get along, get around, get around to, get away with, get back at, get by, get down to business, get nowhere, get something off one's chest, get out of, get together, get through to someone, get up and go.* Do you *get* the idea that *get* is overused?

get-up. An informal or slangy phrase for "overall arrangement," "appearance" ("Leslie appeared in an odd *get-up*.")

gimcrack. This word for "a useless, gaudy object" is pronounced JIM·krak.

gimme. It requires only a moment longer to say *give me.*

gimmick. A slang term for "a novel or tricky feature or detail added to increase the appeal of something." *Gimmicky* is a slang word meaning "full of gimmicks."

girl friend, girl Friday. See *boy friend.*

gismo. A gismo is a *gadget* (which see) and of the same degree of informality.

give. This inoffensive little word appears in many informal or hackneyed expressions, among them *to give tongue to, to give to understand, give-and-take, give a good account of, give birth, give forth, give off, give out, give rise to,* and *dead giveaway.*

glad. This is an overworked word for which you can occasionally substitute *cheerful, lighthearted, joyful, joyous,* and *happy.* Also, avoid overusing such slangy or trite or informal expressions as *glad eye, glad hand,* and *glad rags.*

go. It's inconceivable that we could do without the word *go,* but perhaps we can lessen its use in such trite or informal expressions as *to go without saying, to let it go, no go, on the go, to go through with, to go over big* — or *like a lead balloon, to go out with, to go one better than, to go in with, to go hard with, to go halves, to go against the grain, to go after, to go begging, to go back on.* *To go for,* meaning "like" or "admire," is a widely used slang expression.

goat. This term for "the butt of a joke or trick" is slang. *To get one's goat* is a tiresomely used slang expression.

gob, gobs. *Gob* is slang for "sailor." *Gobs* is slang for "a large amount or number" (*gobs* of money).

goings on. An informal, trite term for "action" or "behavior."

gone. This word appears in such slangy and trite uses as *goner* (someone ruined or doomed); *real gone* (exciting, great); *gone on* (infatuated with); *all gone; done gone and done it; far gone* (deeply involved); *gone with the wind, gone to glory, gone to the dogs, gone where the woodbine twineth, gone to seed.*

good, well. *Good* is an adjective: "to see a *good* play"; "to have a *good* time." *Well* is both an adjective and an adverb, but with different meanings; as an adjective, "in good health," and as an adverb, "ably." ("Since my illness, I have felt *well.*" "The cast performed *well* in the first act.")

Good appears in such trite, informal expressions as *make good, good for nothing, come to no good, all to the good, good and sick, good and tired, as good as new, for good and all, good egg, good Joe, good-oh, goodies,* and *goody-goody.*

gook. A slang term for any dirty or slimy substance; offensive slang for "an Oriental" or other foreigner.

goon. Slang for a "stupid person."

gooney bird. Slang for "an albatross."

goop. Slang for a rude, ill-mannered person.

goose. This word is slang when used to mean (1) giving someone a playful poke in the backside and (2) accelerating a gasoline motor in spurts. *To cook one's goose* is a hackneyed, informal expression meaning "to spoil or ruin one's chances." *Goose egg* is slang for "a score of nothing."

gorgeous. An overused word, usually an exaggeration. Try *dazzling, colorful, brilliant, resplendent, beautiful, attractive, delightful.*

got, gotten. See *get. Got* is the standard form of the past tense and past participle of *get. Gotten* is also a correct form of the past participle. Both *have got* and *have gotten* are suitable in spoken English, but each term is wordy in that the idea could be expressed by "have," "possess," or "own."

gotta. Take a split second longer and say "got to" or "have got to." Better still, say "should" or "must."

gourmand, gourmet. A *gourmand* is one who delights in eating well and heartily. A *gourmet* is a fastidious lover of good food and drink. While on the subject of eating, note that a *glutton* is one with a huge appetite and an *epicure* is one with refined table tastes. *Gourmand* and *glutton* are related in meaning, as are *gourmet* and *epicure.*

government. This word has three full syllables. Say GUHV·uhrn·muhnt, *not* GUHV·uhr·muhnt. Similarly, *governor* has the standard pronunciation of GUHV·uhr·nuhr, *not* GUHV·nuhr.

graduate, graduate from. Both *graduated* and *was graduated* are acceptable terms, provided *from* is also used. Say "He *graduated from* college last year" or "He *was graduated from* college last year." Do *not* say "He *graduated* college last year."

grand. See *great.*

grass. This is a slang term for "marihuana," which is also slangily known as *pot, weed, Mary Jane, gage, tea,* and, in cigarettes, as *reefers* or *joints. Grassroots* (basis, origin, or fundamental quality) is another overused expression. *Go to grass* and *let the grass grow under one's feet* are also clichés.

gratin. See *au. Gratin* is pronounced GRAT·in or GRAHT·in.

gratis. See *free gratis.*

gravy. This is a slang term for "money easily gained." *Gravy train* is slang for any "occupation that requires little effort."

grease. This is a slang term when used as a verb to mean "bribe." *Grease monkey* is slang for "a garage attendant."

The preferred pronunciation for *grease* is GRES (Greece),
but as a verb it is often sounded as GREEZ.

great. Both *great* and *grand* are overused exaggerations for
characteristics which are *impressive, large, huge, distinguished, renowned, eminent, noted,* and *celebrated.* Also,
great often sounds "gushy."

Greenwich. This word is pronounced GREN·ich, GRIN·ij, or
GREN·ij. The first pronunciation is favored in the United
States.

grin. See *Cheshire cat.* Possible substitutes for *grin* include
smile, simper, and *smirk.*

grievous. Many speakers add a sound to this word that
doesn't belong. Say GREEV·uhs.

grocery, groceries. Each of these words has three syllables,
not two. Say GROH·suhr·ee and GROH·suhr·rees.

groom. This is a word for "manservant," but it is widely used
as a shortened form of *bridegroom.* Actually, one should say
"bridegroom" rather than "groom" when this meaning is
called for, because in Old English *bryd* meant "bride" and
guma meant "man." However, it would be silly to recommend that *groom* be used only when one refers to a person
who cares for horses, especially since a man's *bride* might
well be considered his "filly."

guess. See *allow.*

gum. When combined with *up,* this is a slang expression
meaning "to ruin," "to spoil." *Gum up the works* is one of
the most overused clichés in the language. *Gumshoe* is
slang for "detective." *Gumdrop* is silly slang when used to
mean one's beloved.

gun. This word appears in several informal, trite expressions
that border on slang: *give her the gun, stick to one's guns,
jump the gun, big gun* (eminent person), *gun for* (try to destroy or overcome), *gun moll* (female companion of a gun-
carrying person), *spike one's guns.*

gung ho. A slang term presumably meaning "enthusiastic,"
"loyal," or "dedicated."

gunk. An informal or slangy expression meaning "a slimy,
greasy, or filthy substance." It is related to *guck,* another
slang term for any substance, such as "sludge."

gumption. An informal word meaning "shrewdness," "boldness," or "enterprise," any one of which would sound better than *gumption* in a question such as "Do you have the *gumption* to tackle the work?"

guts. This is a slang term meaning "courage," "bravery." The word is in such widespread use that it would be absurd to suggest that you never use it in this sense. *Intestinal fortitude* is stuffy and pretentious, but you might occasionally use *fortitude, resolution, tenacity, mettle, spirit, boldness, audacity, grit, pluck, backbone, heroism, gallantry,* or *valor.*

habeas corpus. Translated literally from Latin, this phrase means "you shall have the body." In English usage, *habeas corpus* is a writ (written order) designed to secure the release of someone from unlawful restraint. The term is pronounced HA·bee·us KOR·poss.

had. This past tense and past participle of *have* is used with varied meanings. It expresses cause in *I had my car washed,* and in a statement such as *I had my arm twisted,* it suggests "suffering an experience from an outside source." *Had better* is used in giving advice or issuing a mild comment or threat ("You *had better* apologize to her"). *Had rather* and *would rather* indicate a preference ("I *would rather* stay than go"). *Had of* and *had have* are wordy because *had* expresses the complete thought. *Had ought to* and *hadn't ought to* are wordy and nonstandard. *Better had* ("You *better had* do what you're told") is illiterate. *Hadda* is an unrecommended way of saying "had a" or "had to" ("I *hadda* go"). *Had it,* meaning "disgusted" or "resigned" ("After that trip, I'd *had it*"), is slangy.

hair. This word appears in such trite or slangy expressions as *let one's hair down, the hair of the dog that bit me, get in one's hair, split hairs, wearing a hair shirt, hairy* (meaning something hazardous or difficult, as in *a hairy trip*), *tear one's hair, make one's hair stand on end, to a hair,* and *not turn a hair.*

half. See *a half.*

hand. Careless speakers tend to omit the sound of *d* in this word and in *handle, handful, handbag, handball, handbook, handcuff, handlebars, handwriting,* etc. The *d* should be sounded. *Hand* appears in numerous hackneyed expressions: *with a heavy hand, bite the hand that feeds one, at the hand(s) of, by one's own hand, try one's hand at, eat out of someone's hand, from hand to hand, force one's hand, hand in glove, hand over fist, have one's hands full, on the other hand, show one's hand, throw in one's hand, take in hand, tip one's hand, put one's hand to, with a high hand, with clean hands, get out of hand, hand and foot, hands down, hands off, lay hands on,* and *the handwriting on the wall.*

hanged, hung. People are *hanged*; objects (such as curtains and pictures) are *hung. Hang around* (to loiter) is an informal expression, as are *hang one on* (to strike a person or to become drunk) and *give a hang* (care). *Hang fire* is hackneyed. *Hung over* (be ill from dissipation) is slang.

hardly, scarcely, barely. See *double negative.* These three adverbs are interchangeable when they refer to sufficiency in quantity, ability, or capacity. Avoid saying *couldn't hardly, hardly never, wouldn't scarcely, not barely,* etc.

has-been. A wornout, slangy term for someone no longer popular or influential.

hassle. This word for "argument," "fight," and "to argue, to contend" has ascended from the level of slang but remains a hackneyed, informal term.

have got to. Say *should, must,* or *ought to.* See *get* and *got.*

hay. The phrase *hit the hay* (go to bed) is slang. *That ain't hay* (a trifling amount of money) is also slang. *To make hay* (succeed, get ahead) may be considered either informal or slangy. *Haymaker* is slang for "a powerful blow with the fist." *Hayseed* is a derisive slang term for an unsophisticated man from the country. *To go haywire* (break down, become crazy) is a slang expression.

head. Watch out for these overused, often informal, occasionally slangy expressions: *head and shoulders above, on one's head, head something off, come to a head, go to one's head, head over heels, keep one's head above water, over one's head, talk one's head off, put our heads together, turn one's head, out of one's head, take it into one's head, hang one's head in shame, keep one's head, heads up, give someone his head, lose one's head,* and *make head or tail of. Headhunting* is slang when used to mean "getting rid of political enemies" and "the procurement of executive personnel." A *headhunter* is a slang term for "a recruiter of personnel." *Headshrinker* is slang for a psychiatrist.

healthful, healthy. These words are often used interchangeably, but *healthful* means "conducive to health" and *healthy* means "possessing health." ("This is a *healthful* climate." "Eleanor is a *healthy* woman.")

heap, heaps. A *heap* is an old or run-down car, in slang talk. (Actually, *rattletrap* is a more colorful term.) *Heaps* is an informal word meaning "a great deal, lots of."

heart. Like other bodily organs, *heart* appears in many overworked informal expressions, several of them approaching slang: *set one's heart on, to one's heart's content, with all one's heart, near to one's heart, wear one's heart on one's sleeve, break one's heart, after one's own heart, do one's heart good, from the bottom of my heart, have a heart, have one's heart in the right place, heart and soul, heart-to-heart, lose one's heart, eat one's heart out, cross one's heart, have a change of heart, have one's heart in one's mouth, in one's heart of hearts, set one's heart at rest, take heart, America's heartland, hearts and flowers* (maudlin sentimentality), and *heart-whole and fancy free.* Incidentally, *heart failure* is a loose, vague term. Doesn't everyone die of *heart failure*? Try to be specific about the coronary ailment or disease that is (or was) involved.

heel. This is a slang term for "a cad, a scoundrel," and, as a verb, for "furnishing someone with something." *Well-heeled* is a slang expression for "provided with plenty of money."

height. Pronounce this word HITE, not HITH. (*Length* has a *th* at the end; *height* has not.)

hell. This ubiquitous noun is ludicrously stretched in meaning to include everything from *hot as hell* to *cold as hell.* *A hell of a time* may mean "enjoyable" or "harrowing." *He played like hell* may mean "well" or "badly." Wholly aside from moral scruples, be careful and sparing in the use of such a slippery term. Among trite or slangy expressions may be mentioned *hell for* (concerned about, insistent upon), *be hell on* (be rough to), *catch hell* (receive punishment), *give someone hell* (harm, scold), *hell and high water* (troubles or difficulties of whatever size), *hell to pay* (trouble to be faced), *play hell with* (cause damage), *raise hell* (cause uproar or difficulty), *to hell and gone* (far away), *what the hell* (used to express resignation, indifference, or boredom), *a heller* (reckless, wild person), *hell-fired* (extremely, great), *hell-for-leather* (at high speed), *hell's bells* (interjection indicating surprise or annoyance), and *hellbent* (determined, stubborn). While on the subject of *hell*, try to think of all the expressions you know involving *heaven*. Many are current, each one hackneyed.

help but. See *cannot (can't) help but*.

he-man. An overused term for a strong, muscular, or virile man.

hen. A slang term for "woman." *Henpeck* is informal for "nag, harass." *Henparty* is slang for "a gathering of women."

hep. This is an older form of *hip*, both of which mean "aware of," "wise to." One is as slangy as the other.

hi. This variation of *hello* is constantly used, as are *hey* and *hiya*. Each is informal, each is threadbare from overuse, but each will continue as salutations that no one can banish.

hiccup, hiccough. Both spellings are standard; both words are pronounced HICK-up. HIC·KOFF is an unrecommended regional pronunciation.

high. This word is slang when used to mean "intoxicated by narcotics or alcohol." It appears in the following expressions that are hackneyed, informal, or slangy: *high and mighty, high and dry, high and low, flying high, highbrow, higher-up* (person in authority), *high hat* (to snub), *high muck-a-muck* (important person), *high sign* (gesture, glance), and *high tail* (leave hurriedly).

him, himself. The former is the objective case of the third person personal pronoun *he*. *Himself* is a pronoun that suggests emphasis ("He, himself, will go") and that turns action back on the grammatical subject ("He bathed himself carefully"). Use *him*, not *himself*, in a statement such as "Sandy remarked that his aunt would spend the week with Mrs. Sandy and *him*."

hindrance. Do not confuse this word with *hinder;* say HIN·druhns, not HIN·der·uhns.

hip, hippie. See *hep*. Both *hip* and *hippie* are slangy, but constant use may move them into the category of informal or even unrestricted usage. Each refers to an awareness or possession of supposedly advanced attitudes and tastes or to those who advocate them.

hisself. An illiteracy; say "himself."

historic, historical. The senses of these words overlap, but *historic* should be used to refer to something that is renowned, influential, or history-making (the *historic* meeting of Livingstone and Stanley). *Historical* means "concerned with" or "contained in" history (a specialist in *historical* studies). Pronounce them hi·STOR·ik and hi·STOR·i·kal. *Historically* has five syllables: hi·STOR·i·kal·ly. *History* should be pronounced HIS·tuh·ri, not *HIS*·try. See *a, an.*

hoi polloi. This is a Greek term meaning "the masses," "the many." If you use it, do not say "*the* hoi polloi," because *hoi* is Greek for *the.*

hold. This innocent word appears in several trite, informal, or slangy uses and expressions, among them *hold out, hold-up, hold back, hold one's own, hold one's peace, hold forth, hold down, hold off, hold one's tongue, hold water, hold for, hold with, hold fast, hold over,* and *hold a candle to.* The expression *get a hold of* is wordy, trite, and borders on illiteracy.

holy. These trite and slangy expressions seem silly and meaningless: *holy cow, holy smoke, holy terror, holy cats, holy dollar, holy Joe, holy mackerel,* and *holy Moses.*

homey. A sentimental and informal substitute for *homelike, familiar, comfortable.*

hook. Watch out for such hackneyed or slangy expressions as *by hook or crook; hook, line, and sinker* (entirely, completely); *off the hook* (freed from something); *on one's own hook* (independently); *get* (or *give*) *the hook* (receive or cause a dismissal); and *on the hook* (involved). *Hooked* is slang for "addicted to narcotics or alcohol" and "being married." A *hooker* is slang for (1) a prostitute and (2) an alcoholic drink.

hootenanny. A respectable term for a gathering of folk singers but an informal term for an "unidentifiable gadget."

horn. These terms are clichés or slang and occasionally both: *blow one's own horn, pull* (or *draw*) *in one's horn(s), on the horns of a dilemma* (see *dilemma*), *horn in* (intrude), *lock* *horns* (disagree, fight), *horn of plenty* (cornucopia), *horn-swoggle* (cheat), and *horny* (lustful).

hors d'oeuvre. This is a French term for an appetizer or canapé served before a meal. In literal French it means "outside of work," that is, "apart from the ordinary meal." It is pronounced or·DURV. The plural, *hors d'œuvres*, is sounded or·DURVZ.

horrible. An overused term. If you must use an intensive of great strength, occasionally say *shocking, appalling, fearful, frightful, horrendous, detestable, repugnant, obnoxious,* or *loathsome.*

horse. Do you really need to use this word as often as you probably do? Each of the following expressions is hackneyed or slangy: *straight from the horse's mouth, hold your horses, horse of another color, get on one's high horse, back the wrong horse, beat a dead horse,* and *look a gift horse in the mouth. Horse* is slang for "a man," for "horsepower," and for "heroin." *Horse around* is slang for "fool around." *Horse collar* is baseball slang for "preventing a team from scoring." *Horse feathers* is slang for "rubbish" or "nonsense." *Horsehide* is slang for "a baseball." *Horse's ass* is slang for "a fool." *Horse sense* is an informal term for "common sense."

hot. This short word is employed in several senses that constitute slang: good or impressive (a *hot* player); ridiculous or incredible (that's a *hot* one); recently stolen (*hot* goods); sexually aroused; wanted for criminal activity (a *hot* fugitive); following closely (*hot* on the trail of); sensational or scandalous (a *hot* news item); a speedy vehicle (a *hot* new jet plane). *Hot* also appears in such dubious expressions as *hot air* (empty talk), *hotcha* (meaning approval or delight), *hot foot* (practical joke), *hot lick* (jazz), *hot money* (funds suddenly transferred), *hot potato* (difficult or risky situation), *hot rod* (a car altered for increased speed), *hot rodder* (fast, reckless driver), *hot seat* (electric chair), *hotshot* (successful person), *hot stuff* (person of interest or merit), *hotsy-totsy* (perfect), and *hot water* (trouble).

how. Among the most common and tiresome expressions in the language are *and how!* and *how come?* Closely following these two in overuse and staleness is *how about that?*

human, humane. *Human* refers to the form, nature, or qualities characteristic of man. Formerly, *human being* was recommended over *human*, but both expressions are fully acceptable now. *Humane* refers to such good qualities in man as mercy, compassion, and kindness (a *humane* citizen of this town). *Human* is pronounced HYOO·muhn, *humane* is sounded hyoo·MAYN.

humble. Although the initial *h* sound is often omitted, standard pronunciation is HUHM·b'l. If you don't like this pronunciation, try *modest, lowly, meek, subdued, resigned, submissive, acquiescent, compliant,* or *unassuming*.

hump. Among tiresome phrases to avoid are *over the hump* and *get a hump on*.

hung. See *hanged*.

I, me. The former is nominative case, the latter objective. Be careful in using either in a compound phrase after a verb or preposition. Say "This problem concerned only him and *me*" (*not* him and I). "The way he acted in front of you and *me* made me angry" (*not* you and I). "Leaving early were both he and I" (*not* he and me).

ice. This word is slang when used to mean (1) a diamond or diamonds; (2) to remove any question of victory (clinch—*ice* —the game); (3) protection money paid by the operator of an illicit business; and (4) fees paid by brokers to theater managers for tickets. Also, try not to use such clichés as *break the ice, cut no ice, on ice* (in readiness), and *on thin ice* (in a risky situation).

I'd. This contraction of "I would," "I should," "I had," etc. is permissible in rapid, informal talk but generally should be avoided.

idea. This word is not only overused in such an expression as *What's the big idea?* but in many other expressions. Occasionally try substituting *conception, thought, notion, concept, impression, opinion, belief, view, conviction, theory,* or *hypothesis*. Any word you choose may be as vague as *idea*, but at least you will avoid overworking a threadbare term.

identical. Every letter in this word is sounded in standard pronunciation: ai·DEN·ti·kal. Avoid the wordy phrase *same identical* ("He made the *same identical* mistake day after day") because *same* and *identical* are synonymous.

identity. Sound every letter: ai·DEN·ti·ty.

ideology. This is a word used loosely and vaguely to apply to almost any conceivable body of ideas. If you use it, say AI· dee·OL·uh·gee or ID·ee·OL·uh·gee, but be careful not to extend its meaning to absurd lengths. Often, *ideology* could effectively be replaced by *idea, notion, thought,* or *concept.*

idiot. An *idiot board* is a television term for an apparatus that serves as a prompter during a program. You can decide for yourself whether the slang term for a television set, *idiot box,* is deserved. An *idiot* is completely helpless, totally incapable of learning. An *imbecile* may be able to communicate a little but cannot provide for himself. A *moron* may take a place in society but requires supervision.

I don't think. This expression is loose and inexact, because whoever uses it obviously is thinking. It is more logical to say "*I think that you don't* love me" than "*I don't think* that you love me." Regardless of the attitude of your loved one or any other circumstance, *I don't think* is an expression here to stay, illogical or not.

if and when. This is a hackneyed and wordy phrase from which "and when" can be dropped without loss of meaning. Other related wordy phrases that need excision are *when, as, and if* (only *if* is needed) and *unless and until* (*unless* expresses the thought).

if, whether. In formal use, *if* introduces one condition only; *whether* introduces alternate conditions, usually with *or not* expressed or implied. ("*If* we try hard, we can do the work." "We were wondering *whether* we could do the work.") In less precise use, both *if* and *whether* are used to introduce clauses of varied kinds, but *if* is not used when it causes doubt about meaning; for example, the sentence "The physician asked to be telephoned *if* the patient was in a coma" could mean *at what time* or *whether* the patient was in a coma. Also, prefer *whether* in a sentence such as "*If* I was going to pay the bill was the question raised by the letter."

illicit. See *elicit.*

illusion. See *allusion.*

immigrant. See *emigrant.*

imminent. See *eminent.*

immoral. See *amoral.*

impeach. This word means "to bring to trial with the intent of removing from office," "to attack," "to degrade." It does *not* mean "to remove from office." (Only one president, Andrew Johnson, has ever been *impeached;* but he was found not guilty in subsequent proceedings.)

implement. As a verb meaning "to carry out," "to provide a definite plan for action," *implement* is tiresomely overused. Related words that might be used include *execute, fulfill, accomplish, achieve, perform, enforce, materialize, administer*, and *carry out.*

implicit. See *explicit.*

imply, infer. *To imply* is "to suggest a meaning only hinted at, not explicitly stated." *To infer* is "to draw a conclusion from statements, evidence, or circumstances." ("Your remark *implies* that Bill was untruthful." "The officer *inferred* from the fingerprints that the killer was left-handed.")

impractical, impracticable, unpractical. Distinctions in the meanings of these words have largely broken down, but *impractical* actually means "theoretical" or "speculative." *Impracticable* means "not capable of being used," "unmanageable." ("The architect's recommendations are *impractical* and his blueprints are *impracticable.*") *Unpractical* is interchangeable with *impractical* but is considered not quite so formal and refined.

in. This little preposition indicating position, condition, and location is indispensable, but perhaps one does not have to use it so often in such trite expressions as *have it in for* (hold a grudge), *ins and outs* (twists and turns, changing conditions), *all in* (fatigued), *in for* (guaranteed, about to receive), *in that* (since), *have an in* (access, favor), *in group* (incumbent, favored), *in with* (on friendly terms), *in apple-pie order, in black and white, in the last analysis, in the same boat, in spite of the fact that*, and a rash of "new" terms such as *laugh in, teach in, talk in, sit in, be in*, etc.

in, into. As distinguished from *in* (see above), *into* indicates movement or direction *to* an interior location. Say "Molly was *in* the kitchen" and "Molly walked *into* the kitchen." If you pause between *in* and *to* — say *in to* rather than *into* — *in* becomes an adverb ("You may now go *in to* see the new baby.")

in addition to. A standard phrase, this is a wordy way of saying *moreover, besides, further, also,* and *too.* Even *in addition* without *to* is one word longer than necessary.

in back of. See *back of.*

in behind. A wordy phrase from which *in* should be omitted.

incidentally. *Incidently* is an illiteracy. Say IN·si·DENT·ly, but think of and spell the word as *incidentally.*

inclose. See *enclose.*

in connection with. A wordy phrase which means "about" or "concerning."

incredible, incredulous. The former means "unbelievable," the latter "skeptical," "unbelieving." ("The story Bill told us was *incredible*." "The speaker's remarks left his audience *incredulous*.")

index. The plural of index is both *indexes* (IN·deks·iz) and *indices* (IN·duh·SEEZ). The former is generally used; the latter is considered more formal and "refined."

individual. This word is overused to refer to "one person only" and frequently has a contemptuous or facetious meaning. Phrases such as *individual person, each individual member,* and *individual self* are wordy. As nouns, *individual* and *person* are synonymous.

induce. See *deduce.*

infectious. See *contagious.*

infer. See *imply.*

inferior than, to. Say *inferior to* ("This motor is *inferior to*— not *inferior than*—that one.")

inflammable. See *flammable.*

infra dig. This Latin phrase, an abbreviation of *infra dignitatem,* means "beneath one's dignity," "undignified," and is pronounced IN·frah·DIG.

ingenious, ingenuous. *Ingenious* means "inventive," "resourceful," "talented," "imaginative." *Ingenuous* means "naïve," "frank," "unsophisticated," "artless." ("Alex's suggested solution is *ingenious*." "She is an *ingenuous* little child.")

innards. An informal and uncouth term for the "viscera," "internal bodily organs."

in order, in order that. These phrases are usually deadwood and should be avoided. "He was sent into the field *in order* to encourage the salesmen" means the same thing without "in order." The sentence would be even wordier if it read "He was sent into the field *in order that* he might encourage the salesmen."

in regard to, in regards to. The phrase should be *in regard to*. *Regard* should not be used carelessly in its plural form. *In regard to* is wordy but it does have a specific meaning of "consideration for."

inside of, outside of, off of. In each of these phrases, *of* is superfluous. Say "*inside* the room," *not* "*inside of* the room," etc. Note, however, the use of *inside* and *outside* as nouns: "He bought new upholstery for the *inside of* his car." "The *outside of* the barn needs painting."

in spite of the fact that. This is an excessively wordy way to say "although."

intents and purposes. This is a standard legal phrase ("to all intents and purposes"), but unless you are a lawyer, why not use *practically*?

inter-, intra-. *Inter-* means "between," "among" (*intermarriage, international, intercollegiate*). *Intra-* is a prefix meaning "within" (*intracranial, intravenous, intrauterine*). When two universities play a game against each other, they engage in *intercollegiate* athletics; when two colleges of one university play each other, they engage in *intracollegiate* athletics (or *intramural* athletics—"within the walls").

in the midst of. A wordy phrase for *amid, in, within,* or *inside*.

intrigue, interest. *Intrigue* suggests an element of mystery or suspense and is often used where the speaker probably means only *interest* (curiosity, absorption, fascination). The distinction is clear when you realize that synonyms for the noun *intrigue* are *plot, scheme, design, maneuver, ruse, stratagem,* and *trick*.

in under. A wordy phrase ("the cat was *in under* the chair") from which *in* should be dropped.

invent. See *discover*.

invigorating. See *enervating*.

invite. As a noun, *invite* may be considered an impropriety or slang. Say "invitation," "summons," or "bidding."

irregardless. See *disregardless*.

irrelevant. Don't transpose letters in saying this word meaning "not applicable," "without relation." It should be pronounced ir·REL·uh·vuhnt.

irrevocable. This word meaning "irreversible," "not to be called back or repealed," is pronounced i·REV·uh·kuh·b'l, *not* i·re·VOK·uh·b'l.

is when, is where. The use of *is when* and *is where* in explaining and defining something is a common error in speech and writing. Rather than misuse an adverbial clause ("Anemia *is when* the blood is deficient"), you should employ a noun or a noun with modifiers ("Anemia is a disease in which deficiencies appear in the blood.") To say, for instance, "Stealing *is where* you take . . ." instead of "Stealing is the act of taking . . ." is to be awkward and childish.

it. This short word is often used in a vague or indefinite way to stand for, or refer to, a variety of things and ideas. The term also appears in expressions that are trite or slangy, such as *to get with it, be with it, have it* (be attractive), *had it* (reach the end of endurance or patience). *It* is a singular pronoun in the third person; *it don't* and *it weren't* are illiteracies.

it's. This contraction means "it is" ("It's raining) and "it has" ("It's been raining"). Awkward and stilted though the expression may sound, you should say "It's I" rather than "It's me," because a predicate complement is in the nominative case. If you don't like to say "It's I" (or "It is I" or "This is I"), then say "This is" followed by your name. Similarly, as a careful speaker, watch out for such expressions as *it's us, it's them, it's her, it's him.* If you think the correct forms of *we, they, she,* and *he* in these constructions sound strained, then use names: "It's Jane," "It's Jim," etc.

-ize. This suffix has aided in the creation of hundreds of standard words such as *pasteurize, dramatize, sterilize,* and *hospitalize.* Unfortunately, many weird improprieties have also resulted, such as *powerize, concertize,* and *headlineize.* Most verbs and adjectives in the language *can* be treated with *-ize,* but don't "finalize" or "permanentize" your attachment to such coinages until they are widely accepted.

jack. This word is slang for "money" and for a stranger ("Hey, Jack"). It appears in hackneyed expressions such as *every man jack* (everyone without exception), *jack of all trades* (one who can perform a variety of tasks), *hit the jackpot* (experience success, good fortune), *jack up* (increase, raise), *dumb jackass* (fool, ass), and *to jackass* (act the part of a fool or wrestle or hoist something into place).

jag. Slang for a "spree," a "bout" (a shopping *jag*, a crying *jag*), and for being intoxicated (have a *jag* on).

jalopy. Once considered slang, *jalopy* is now an informal term of unknown origin for an old or dilapidated automobile or other conveyance.

jam. An informal or slangy term for "a predicament" ("in a jam"). A *jam-up* is slang for "congestion" or "obstruction" ("orders were in a *jam-up*"). *Jamboree*, an informal name for a "carousal" or "merrymaking," appears in shortened form in *jam session* (an impromptu gathering of jazz musicians).

jaw. This is a slang term for "argument," "backtalk" ("Don't give me any *jaw*") and for talking and gossiping ("They *jawed* all night"). *Jawbreaker* is slang for a word difficult to pronounce.

jazz. A slang term for "exaggeration," "wild talk" ("Don't give me that *jazz* about your good luck"). *Jazz it up* is a slang expression meaning "put some life into it" and to "act with vigor." *Jazzy* is a slang term meaning "lively," "active."

jealous, zealous. A *jealous* person feels resentment or suspicion because of rivalry or competition of some sort ("Sue was *jealous* of her beautiful sister"). A *zealous* person is active, diligent, devoted ("He was the most admired, *zealous* worker in the plant"). *Jealous* is pronounced JEL·uhs; *zealous* is sounded as ZEL·uhs.

jewelry. This word is pronounced JOO·uhl·ree or JYOO·uhl· ree. Avoid transposing letters as in the common mispronunciation JEWL·uh·ree.

jiffy. The phrase *in a jiffy* is informal and trite. For *jiffy* occasionally substitute *moment, trice, flash, minute,* or *second.*

Jim Crow. Also spelled with lower-case letters, this term is slang for the systematic practice of suppressing blacks and for favoring or promoting their segregation.

jim-jams. Slang for a state of nervousness or great excitement. A less slangy substitute for *jim-jams* is *jitters.*

jive. This is a slang term for (1) jazz or swing music, (2) the jargon of jazz enthusiasts or of narcotic addicts and (3) any meaningless or unintelligible talk.

job. This word, although overworked, is standard usage for "position" or "station." It is slang when used to mean a theft or similar crime and "a person" ("She was a sweet *job*"). *Lie down on the job* and *on the job* are trite expressions. As a verb, *job* is slang when used to mean "cheat" or "defraud" ("He *jobbed* me on that deal").

John Hancock. This term, after the name of a signer of the Declaration of Independence, is a trite expression meaning a person's signature ("Put your *John Hancock* on the dotted line"). In fact, to put any signature *on the dotted line* is a cliché.

Johnny. Both *Johnny-come-lately* (a recent arrival) and *Johnny-on-the spot* (on hand when needed) are hackneyed expressions. *John* and *johnny* are slang for "a toilet."

join together. *Join* means "to unite," "to connect," so that *together* is here wordily unnecessary. Since marriages are sometimes shaky, perhaps they require the statement, "What therefore God hath *joined together*, let no man put asunder," but in other instances avoid redundancy.

joint. Slang for "a marihuana cigarette" and for "a place of low repute, a cheap place." *The times are out of joint* may be a true statement but is definitely a trite one.

juice. Slang when used to mean "vitality" or "electricity."

jump. This word appears in several informal and either trite or slangy expressions: *the place was jumping, to jump a claim, to jump at* (accept hastily), *to jump on* — or *all over* (to scold, abuse), *jump the gun* (start prematurely), *jump ship* (desert, leave), *jump the track* (get off course), *on the jump* (working speedily, very busy), *get the jump on* (attain an advantage), *jumping-off place* (outer limit or place to make a start), *jumpy* (nervous), *jump down one's throat* (answer sharply, angrily), and *jump bail* (forfeit one's bail by absconding).

junkie. A slang term for "narcotics addict."

just. As an adverb, *just* means "precisely" (*just* perfect); "narrowly" (*just* missed the bus); and "recently" (*just* got here). Phrases such as *just exactly* and *just recently* really say the same thing twice. *Just about* (I'm *just about* to leave) seems

self-contradictory, since the words mean "precisely approximately." However, this book is not *just about* going to deny
that the idiom is common and deep-rooted, although you
might occasionally say "very nearly" or "almost."

keep. Try not to use as often as you probably do such time-
worn expressions as *keep tabs on, keep in with, keep to oneself, keep track of, keep up on, keep up with, keep up to, for
keeps, keep up with the Joneses*, and *keep at it*. There's nothing incorrect with any of these locutions, but each is worn
and weary.

kept. This word has a *t* which should be sounded. The pronunciation *kep* is nonstandard. Such phrases as *kept press,
kept woman, kept man*, and *kept writer* are trite.

khaki. Formerly, only KAH·kee was standard pronunciation,
but usage has caused KAK·ee also to become acceptable.

kibitzer. This term from Yiddish, via German, for an "on-
looker" or "meddler" was once considered slang, then an
informality, and now bears no restrictive label.

kibosh. Meaning "nonsense," *kibosh* is considered either
slangy or informal. A trite phrase, *put the kibosh on*, means
"to render ineffective, to check, to squelch."

kick-back. This term is slang for "a percentage payment"
and, as a verb, for making such a refund and for returning
stolen goods.

kike. A slang term, both derogatory and offensive, for a Jew.

kind. This word has many meanings, among them "belonging to a class" (a *kind* of preacher); "a subdivision of a category" (that *kind* of orange); and "rather" or "somewhat"
(*kind* of sorry). *Kind* is singular, so that one should not say
"*these* (or *those*) *kind* of shoes" but "*this kind* of shoes" or
"*these kinds* of shoes." (The same principle applies to *sort*
as to *kind*.) Both *kind of a* and *sort of a* are wordy phrases
from which *a* should be omitted.

kindergarten. This word is often mispronounced, perhaps
because it is often misspelled. It has only one *d* in spelling
and in sound. Say KIN·duhr·gart·en.

knock. The following meanings and uses of *knock* are slang:
(1) to criticize, (2) to kill, (3) to burglarize. *Knock around* (or
knock about) is slang for "to wander aimlessly." *Knock
down* is slang for "earning" ("He *knocked down* a good sala-

ry"). *Knock off* is slang for "ceasing work." *Knock up* is slang for "making pregnant." Phrases that are trite or slangy include *knock-down, drag-out* (violent); *knockers* (breasts); *knockout drops* (drug put into a drink); *knock one-self out; knock out of the box; knock me over with a feather;* and *knock for a loop.*

knot. This word has several meanings, one of which is "unit of speed." The words *an hour* should never follow *knots.* A ship can travel at *six knots* or at *six nautical miles an hour* but *not* at *six knots an hour.*

know. This term appears in several hackneyed, informal, or slangy expressions, among them *know the ropes, in the know, know-it-all, know-how, know from Adam,* and *know enough to come in out of the rain.* As a verb, *know* should never be followed by *as* ("I don't *know as* I am able"). Instead of *as,* use *that, whether,* or *if*—in that order of preference.

knowledge. One has *knowledge about* something and *knowledge of* something but not *knowledge on* something. If you are overusing the word *knowledge,* try *learning, information, enlightenment, lore, erudition, scholarship, discernment, comprehension,* or *judgment.*

kook. This is a slang term for a peculiar or foolish person. A *kooky* person is, slangily, someone who is eccentric or zany.

kudos. In Greek, *kudos* means "glory" or "fame." The final "s" is not the sign of a plural; no such thing exists as *a kudo. Kudos* is singular ("Kudos *was* due the first astronaut").

laissez-faire. Pronounced LEZ·ay fare, this term from French is used, possibly overused, to mean "non-interference in the affairs of others." In French, the phrase means "allow to act" or "let (them) do."

landlord. This word contains two *d*'s, both of which should be sounded. Say LAND·lawrd.

latter, later. See *former.* The word *latter* refers to the second of two things, not to the last of any series. *Later* means "subsequently" and is not directly related in meaning to *latter.* The phrase *later on* is wordy; *on* should rarely, if ever, be included.

laundry. Say LAWN·dree or LAHN·dree, but *never* LAWN·duh·ree and LAHN·duh·ree.

lay, lie. The former means "to place" and is a transitive verb requiring an object. *Lie*, in the context here, means "to recline," is intransitive, and takes no object. ("I shall *lay* the rug on the floor." "Please *lie* down here.") The principal parts of *lay* are *lay, laid — laid, laying;* the principal parts of *lie* are *lie, lay — lain, lying.* Among hackneyed expressions employing *lay* and *lie* may be cited *lay down the law, lay of the land, lay oneself open, lay by the heels, lay down one's life, lay heads together, lay one's cards on the table, lay a course, lay about one, lay for, lay it on with a trowel (or shovel), lay it on thick, lie low, lie down on the job, take lying down, lie in wait,* and *uneasy lies the head that wears a crown.*

lay off. This expression is now standard in its meanings of "suspension," "dismissal," and "to suspend," "to dismiss." It is slang when used to mean "quit," "give up." ("I *laid off* the mashed potatoes.")

lead, led. These words are sometimes confused because the past tense of *lead* is *led*, which is pronounced like the metal *lead*. When an object is covered or treated with lead (the metal) it is *leaded*, but such a condition bears no relationship to the verb that means "to show the way," "to conduct or escort."

learn, teach. In standard usage, *learn* (meaning "to gain knowledge") is never acceptable in the sense of *teach* ("to instruct," "to impart knowledge"). One can *learn* something, but he cannot *learn* someone else anything.

leave, let. These words are interchangeable only when accompanied by *alone* ("Leave — or let — Eleanor alone.") In correct usage, *let* normally means "allow," "permit," "cause" ("*Let* me do that for you.") *Leave* usually means "go away from" or "cause to remain" ("If you *leave* me undisturbed, I can finish the work quickly.")

led. See *lead.*

leg. This word is now fully acceptable in its meaning of the limb or appendage of anyone, male or female. *Leg* is trite or slangy, however, in numerous expressions: *stretch one's legs, shake a leg, pull one's leg, give a leg up, not have a leg to stand on, on one's last legs, leg it* (walk, run), *leg art, legwork* (research), and *crooked as a dog's hindlegs.*

legible, readable. In the sense of "capable of being read," these words are interchangeable. *Readable* has an additional meaning: "interesting," "fascinating," or "pleasurable." Corresponding nouns are *legibility* and *readability*.

lend, loan. The latter has long been established as a verb, especially in business circles (*"loan* the firm some money"), but *lend* is considered preferable ("I refused to *lend* — not *loan* — him my car for the evening.") *Loan* (not *lend*) should be used as a noun.

less. See *fewer*. As a comparative of *little, less* refers to quantity, *lesser* to importance (less *money,* a lesser *official*).

let's. As a contraction of *let us, let's* is informal but standard. *Let's us* ("Let's us leave early") is a wordy expression; omit *us* or *'s*.

lettuce. A slang term for "paper money."

level. This word appears in such overworked expressions as *on the level, level with me, seek one's own level,* and *dead level*.

lever. This word may be pronounced LEE·vuhr or LEV·uhr. Use the pronunciation most widespread in your area.

liable. See *apt*.

libel, slander. *Libel* involves *written* or *pictorial* expression injurious to reputation or character. *Slander* applies to *oral* expression that is false, defamatory, or malicious. If you wish to avoid both terms, try *defame, malign, vilify, revile,* or *traduce,* and corresponding nouns (*defamation,* etc.)

library. Say LAI·brer·ee, *not* LAI·berry.

lid. Slang for "a hat." To *flip one's lid* is a slangy way of "losing one's composure."

lie. See *lay*.

lief. In the sense of "readily," "willingly," *lief* sounds like "grandfather talk," but it is the proper form in *had as lief go as stay*. More modern (and more wordy) approximate synonyms are "just as soon" and "would rather." ("I would as *lief* leave now as later" *or* "I would *just as soon* leave now as later.") *Lief* and *leave* (*let*) are *not* synonymous.

lifelong, livelong. The former means "continuing for a lifetime" ("Johnson dwelled in *lifelong* poverty"). *Livelong* (pronounced LIV·lawng) means "long in passing," "whole." ("She spent the *livelong* day in the meadow.")

light, lit. The past tense of *light* is *lighted* or *lit*. Thus, one may say "Bill *lighted* a cigar" or "Bill *lit* a cigar." *Litten* ("She *litten* the fire) is nonstandard. *Light* may also mean "to descend" or "to land." Both *lighted* and *lit* may be used to refer to all things that come down, whether planes, snow, or rocks. Both words in varying parts of speech appear in expressions that are trite or slangy: *see the light of day, in the light of, make light of, light into* (attack), *light out* (leave), *light-fingered, shed light on the subject, light as a feather, trip the light fantastic* (dance), *lit up like a Christmas tree, being lit* (intoxicated).

lightening, lightning. The former (pronounced LAIT·un·ning) means "making lighter in weight," "lessening." *Lightning* (pronounced LAIT·ning) is an "electrical discharge."

like, as. In recent years, *like* (for *as, as if*) has been used so increasingly that it is now accepted as popular or informal in constructions formerly considered nonstandard. When *like* precedes a noun that is not followed by a verb, its use is standard: "He talked *like* an expert." As a subordinating conjunction, the use of *like* is not recommended, however, ("He drank beer *like* it was going out of style.") In standard usage, say *as* or *as if* in clauses of comparison ("You should do *as* I tell you" *not* "You should do *like* I tell you.") No longer do you need to avoid *like* "like" you once did, but it is preferable to use it only in a prepositional sense. In other situations, use *as if, though,* and *as though* not only for "correctness" but for effective variety. You will then speak *as* — not *like* — a good speaker should.

like for, like to. These phrases are nonstandard in expressions such as "I'd *like for* you to have it" and "She *like to* have drowned." From the first example, omit *for*; for *like to have* in the second, substitute *nearly* or *almost*.

likely. See *apt*.

likes of. This is a nonstandard expression when used to mean "of a kind," "of a sort." Avoid a statement such as "She wore a hat the *likes of* which I'd never seen before."

line. Try to cut down on your use of such hackneyed or slangy expressions as *hold the line, all along the line, get a line on, in line for, along this line, out of line, what's your line?, hard lines, draw the line, in line of duty, lay it on the line,* *read between the lines, toe the line, bring into line,* and *line of fire.*

lip. This word is slang in the sense of "impudent talk" ("Don't give me any more *lip*.") It is slangy or hackneyed in expressions such as *button one's lip, bite one's lip* (or *tongue*), *hang on the lips of, smack one's lips, keep a stiff upper lip,* and *lip music* (talk, chatter.).

listen at, listen to. *Listen to* is preferred idiom ("She *listened to* — not listened at — the concert.")

lit. See *light.*

literally. See *figuratively.*

literature. This word may be pronounced LIT·uhr·uh·choor, LIT·uhr·uh·chuhr, or LIT·uhr·uh·tyuhr. The word is loosely applied to any kind of printed material such as pamphlets, circulars, and handbills, but in accurate use should refer only to writings of universal and permanent interest. When you request a company to *send literature,* you are asking for a commodity it does not stock — unless the company is a bookstore or publishing firm.

littler, littlest. These are juvenile terms. Say *less* and *least* when importance or quantity is concerned, *smaller* and *smallest* when referring to size.

live at, in, on, to, for, by, off. *Live* combines with each of these prepositions to form standard idiomatic phrases with distinct meanings. One may live *at* a certain address, *in* a certain town, and *on* a certain street. Another person may live *to* eat, *for* a certain cause, and *by* a certain faith. Finally, one may live *off* the land or *off* the proceeds of insurance. However one lives, he should avoid using such hackneyed expressions as *live down, live high off the hog, live high, live up to, live on the fat of the land, live in hopes, live and let live,* and *live it up.* The adjective *live* (LAIV) is constantly overused for *alive* ("I feel *live*").

livelong. See *lifelong.*

loan. See *lend.*

loath, loathe. *Loath,* pronounced LOHTH and sometimes spelled *loth,* means "reluctant," "unwilling." *Loathe,* pronounced LOHTH with the *th* sound hard, or distinct, means "to abhor," "to detest." ("A kind person, Jack was *loath* to say that he *loathed* the foreman.")

locate. This word is informal when used to mean "settle" or "take up residence." ("John's parents *settled in* — *not* located in — Columbus, Ohio.")

loner. An informal and overworked term for one who avoids others.

lollapalooza. Slang for "an unusual person, place, or event."

looksee. Slang for "a quick glance," "a rapid survey."

loose, lose. The former means "free" as an adjective and "to free" as a verb. *Lose* means "to suffer a loss." ("Please *loose* me before I *lose* my temper.") *Loose* (pronounced LOOS, to rhyme with "goose") is trite in *at loose ends, to cut loose, loose-tongued, a loose liver,* and *have a screw loose.* From the expression *lose out,* delete *out.*

lost. *Get lost* is rude slang; *the lost generation, lost cause, lost in thought, lost nation,* and *lost tribes of Israel* are weary expressions.

lot, lot of, lots of. *Lot of* and *lots of* are informal, wordy substitutes for "many." *The lot* (meaning "all") is also informal. *Draw lots* and *cast one's lot in with* are clichés.

louse, lousy. *Louse* is a slang term for a contemptible person. *Louse up* is slang for "botch" and "spoil." *Lousy* is slang for "well-supplied" (*lousy* with money) and "unpleasant," "inferior," "worthless" (a *lousy* cold, a *lousy* meal, a *lousy* show). *Lousy* also means "infested with lice"; if you wish to impress friends, say "pediculous."

lovely. An overworked term usually involving exaggeration and having little precise meaning. Occasionally say *delightful, enjoyable, pleasant, attractive, graceful, appealing, comely,* or *fair.*

lump. To *take one's lumps* is an unattractive, informal expression meaning to "suffer one's setbacks or punishment." To tell someone to *lump it* is an inelegant way to tell him to tolerate what must be endured. *Lump in the throat* is a cliché.

luxuriant, luxurious. The former means "growing vigorously or abundantly" ("The foliage was *luxuriant.*") *Luxurious* means "fond of or given to luxury." Approximate synonyms of *luxurious* are *epicurean, sensuous,* and *voluptuous.*

luxury. Pronounce this word as LUHK·shoo·ree or LUG·shoo·ree.

mad. See *angry. Mad* is informal when combined with *about* or *over* to indicate enthusiasm (*mad* about football). It is slang when used to mean "unusual" or "pointless" (*mad* conversation) and "gay" or "frantic" (a *mad* dash for the train). *Like mad* is slang for "wildly" (driving *like mad*). To *have a mad on* is slang for "to sulk," "to be angry." *Mad as a hatter* is a hackneyed expression.

madam. Spelled as *madam* and pronounced MAD·uhm, the term is a title of respect and a form of address to a woman. Spelled as *madame* and pronounced mah·DAHM, the word is a French title of courtesy and is roughly equivalent to *Mrs.* The plural of both *madam* and *madame* is *mesdames* (MAY·dahm). It is safe enough to call any woman *madam*, but you should be careful not to refer to one as *a* madam, unless you are in a brothel. *Ma'am* is an informal abbreviation of *Madam* and *Madame. Missus* and *missis* are illiteracies. *Mrs.* (pronounced MIS·iz) has a plural of *Mmes.* and is a title prefixed to the names of married women only.

mainline. A slang term for injecting narcotics directly into a major vein.

maitre d'hôtel. This is a French term, often shortened to *maitre d'*, for a head butler or steward. The full phrase is pronounced MET·tre·dough·TEL.

majority, plurality. One meaning of *majority* is "more than half." *Plurality* means "the highest number within a given number," "the excess of votes received by the leader over the next candidate when three or more are competing." If Joe got eighty votes, Jack sixty, and Bill forty, Joe would have a *plurality* of twenty but not a *majority* because he received fewer than half the votes cast. *Majority* is often used as a loose substitute for *many*.

make. This word is slang when used to mean (1) gain or acquire (*make* the big time) and (2) to seduce. It appears in scores of trite or slangy expressions, among them *make a play for, make away with, make do, make like, make off with, make time, make up to, make or break, make with, make bold, make a face, make eyes, make hay, make tracks, on the make, make things hum, make a habit of, make a clean breast of, make bricks without straw,* and *make no bones about.*

marbles. A slang term when used to mean "senses," or "brains," as in the phrase "to lose one's marbles."

marihuana (or marijuana). Pronounce it MAHR·uh·WAH·na. See *grass*.

marital, martial. The former pertains to "marriage," the latter to "war." Only cynics would maintain that the words are interchangeable. Note both spelling and pronunciation: MAR·uh·tuhl and MAHR·shuhl.

marvelous. Because of a felt need to add strength to word choices, many speakers use *marvelous* when they probably have in mind something much less "miraculous" or "astonishing." Other words in this "big stick" category are *amazing, awful, breathtaking, colossal, gigantic, spectacular, stupendous, terrible, titanic,* and *wonderful.* Use each of these words sparingly and thoughtfully; each packs power.

masterly, masterful. These terms imply having the skill or art of a master. *Masterly* is usually restricted to a meaning of "skillful," however, whereas *masterful* suggests authority, dominance, and force. ("Napoleon, a *masterful* man, deployed his troops in a *masterly* way.")

material, matériel. The more common of these words, *material* (muh·TIR·i·uhl) means "matter," "substance," "constituent element." *Matériel* (muh·TEER·i·el) is usually limited to equipment or supplies and is distinguished from *personnel* (people).

mathematics. Although plural in form, *mathematics* is used with a singular verb. ("Mathematics *is*—not *are*—a study of form, number, and arrangement.")

matinée. A *matinée* (pronounced MAT·uh·NAY or MAT·i·NAY) is a daytime, especially an afternoon, performance. Never say *matinée performance*; it's a wordy expression.

may. See *can*.

me. See *I*.

meal ticket. Slang for a person or thing looked to as a source of financial support.

mean. See *average*.

means. As a noun signifying resources (property, money, etc.) *means* requires a plural verb. ("His means *are* apparently unlimited.") When denoting "a way to an end," *means* may take a singular or plural verb: *a means, any means,* *every means*, and *one means* are followed by singular verbs; *all means* and *such means* take a plural verb. Phrases like *by all means, by no means, not by any means,* and *by means of* are hackneyed and wordy.

measles. This is a "mass" noun without a singular form (there is no such thing as *a measle,* although one can refer to *a measle epidemic). Measles* cannot be used with a numeral; you can say "two cases of measles," but whoever heard of "two measles"? Other nouns of this general kind are *morals, munitions, news, riches,* etc. Because they are not real plurals, such nouns require special attention, but most of them take singular verbs. However, when some mass nouns are modified by plurals (*these* savings, *their* morals), following verbs should be plural.

media. This is a plural noun (the singular is *medium*). One should not refer to television, for example, as "*a* powerful media," nor should he use *medias,* an incorrect plural.

median. See *average.*

meet up with. This is a wordy, nonstandard expression. "I *met up with* some girls on the beach" is better expressed by "I *met* some girls on the beach" or "I *encountered* some. . . ."

memo, memorandum, memos, memoranda. A *memo* (a short note or written record) is a standard abbreviation of *memorandum* (MEM·uh·RAN·duhm). *Memos* and *memoranda* (MEM·uh·RAN·dah) are standard plural forms.

might. This word is the past tense of *may* (see *can, may*). Avoid such nonstandard expressions as *might of* and *might could* (for *might have* or *might.*) In the senses of "possibility" and "permission," *may* is more intense than *might. He may die* is stronger than *He might die,* and *May I stay?* is more forceful than *Might I stay?* As a noun, *might* appears in such trite expressions as *with might and main* and *with all his might. Mighty* is informal in the sense of "very" (*mighty* scared).

mike. An informal abbreviation for *microphone.*

mind. You should *mind* how you use this word in numerous hackneyed expressions: *put in mind, in the mind's eye, keep in mind, presence of mind, make up your mind, mind your p's and q's, on one's mind, bear in mind, give someone a* *piece of one's mind, have a good mind to, half a mind to, know one's own mind, out of your mind, a meeting of minds,* and *never mind.*

miniature. This word for "reduced in scale," "small," loses a syllable in the speech of many persons. MIN·ee·uh·chuhr is the preferred pronunciation, although MIN·i·chuhr is now also acceptable.

mischievous. This word is difficult to spell and to pronounce. Say MIS·chuh·vuhs or MIS·chi·vuhs. Unless you are trying to be humorous, don't say mis·CHEE·vuhs or mis·CHEE· vee·uhs.

modern. Say MOD·uhrn, not MOD·run.

monopoly. Say *monopoly on,* not *monopoly of* (although *of* is common usage in Great Britain). If you tend to overuse *monopoly,* perhaps one of these words will prove an adequate substitute: *cartel, combination, corner, pool, syndicate,* or *trust.*

mooch. A slang term meaning "to obtain free by begging or cajolery." A *moocher* slangily *mooches.*

moola. This word, also spelled *moolah,* is a slang term for "money." Just for fun, see how many slang terms you can think of for money. Here are starters: *bread* (which see), *long green, spondulicks* (spondulix).

moonshine. Slang for "illegally distilled whiskey," *moonshine* is an informal term for "foolish talk or acts."

moot point. This is a trite phrase. At least occasionally, say *dispute, (argue, debate, talk over,* etc.).

mop up. A trite, informal term meaning "to complete a task or operation."

moral, morale. These words are distinct in pronunciation and meaning as well as in spelling. *Moral* (MOR·uhl or MAWR·uhl) is concerned with the goodness or badness of human action and character. *Morale* (muh·RAL or muh· RAHL) refers to the state of spirits of a person or group. No exact one-word synonyms exist for *morale,* but for *moral* you can use *ethical, upright, righteous, virtuous, noble,* and *scrupulous.*

more. This word appears in several wornout expressions that should be used sparingly or not at all: *the more the merrier, more than meets the eye, more honored in the breach than in* *the observance, more in sorrow than in anger, more than I bargained for, more and more,* and *more or less.*

more of a. This is a wordy phrase from which *of a* can be dropped without loss.

most. See *almost.*

mouth. As noted elsewhere, every organ of the body is used in expressions now considered trite. *Mouth* is no exception: *down in the mouth, say a mouthful, talk poor mouth, mouthwatering, by word of mouth, big mouth, loud mouth, shutmouth,* etc.

muchly. This is an unnecessary adverb, really an illiteracy, which conveys nothing not covered by *much.*

mug. This is a slang term for "face" and for photographing someone. A *mug shot* is slang for an identifying picture.

must. In the sense of "something not to be missed" or "a requirement," *must* is tiresomely overused: "Paris is a *must* on any European trip." "A college degree is a *must* for this position." *Musta* is a clipped, unrecommended pronunciation of *must have.* Another nonstandard substitute for *must have* is *must of.*

mutual. See *common.* Especially to be avoided is the wordy phrase "mutual cooperation." *Cooperation* implies "working together."

myself. This word is a reflexive pronoun, normally used in a sentence with *I* as the subject ("I hurt *myself*"). The use of *myself* for *me* as the object of verbs or prepositions is nonstandard; say "The supervisor spoke to Jane and *me,*" not "to Jane and *myself.*" Also, do not use *myself* as the subject of a verb; say "The policeman and *I* saw the accident," not "The policeman and *myself* saw the accident." See *him.*

nail. Avoid the overuse of such trite expressions as *hit the nail on the head, hard as nails, right on the nail, nail to the cross, nail down,* and *nail one's flag to the mast.*

naïve. Pronounced nah·EEV, this word and its related noun, naïveté (nah·EEV·TAY), are overused. Suitable substitutions for *naïve* include *artless, guileless, ingenuous* (see *ingenious, ingenuous*), *innocent, natural, simple, unaffected,* and *unsophisticated.*

name. *By the name of* is a wordy way of saying "called" or "named." Wornout expressions involving *name* include *to one's name, in the name of, thy name is legion, name to conjure with, name names,* and *name-dropping.*

natch. Slang for "naturally," "of course," "certainly."

nature. In many uses, *nature* is either meaningless or superfluous. Instead of "the risky *nature* of the task," say "the risk of the task." Also to be avoided are trite phrases like *in the very nature of things, Mother Nature, in a state of nature, in the nature of, by nature,* and *against nature.*

naught. Also spelled "nought," *naught* is a rarely used word meaning "nothing," "zero." It is an approximate antonym of a word with which it is sometimes confused, *aught,* which means "all." ("For *aught* we know, his efforts came to *naught.*")

nauseous, nauseated. *Nauseous* (NAW·zee·us) means "causing sickness"; *nauseated* means "feeling sickness," "being queasy." A gas, for instance, is *nauseous* and causes a person to become *nauseated.* (*Nauseous* is related in meaning to *noisome,* which means "foul," "filthy," or "dangerous," as in "a *noisome* odor").

near. Don't overuse such trite expressions as *a near miss, the near future, near at hand,* and *near-record.*

neat. This is an overused slang term when used to mean "appealing," "stylish," or "the greatest." A current slang phrase is *a neat tell-off.*

neck. Here we are with the body again! The following are slangy or hackneyed, sometimes both: *save one's neck, break one's neck, neck and neck, neck or nothing, neck of the woods, stick one's neck out, get it in the neck, neck and crop, win by a neck,* and *neck and heels. Necking* is slang for "kissing and fondling," *necktie party* for "lynching by hanging."

needle. This is an informal word in the sense of "to tease or provoke" and is slang when used to mean "increasing the alcoholic content" of a drink. *Needle* appears in such trite expressions as *needle in a haystack* and *give someone the needle.*

needless to say. This is a cliché with two objectionable qualities: (1) it is overused as much as any expression in the language and (2) it is redundant and silly. (After all, the speaker who uses this phrase promptly proceeds to state what is *needless to say.*)

neither . . . nor. See *either . . . or.* Do you ever use such trite expressions as *neither fish, flesh, nor good red herring,* and *neither rhyme nor reason?* If so, desist.

nerve. This word is judged either slangy or informal in the sense of "audacity," "impertinence," or "rudeness" ("What a nerve!") *Get on one's nerves, an attack of nerves,* and *nerve-racking* are wornout expressions.

never. This word means "not ever," "on no occasion." Despite this absolute meaning, it is often used to mean "well, hardly ever." Remember that *never* is a negative, so that *won't never* and *hardly never* are double negatives (which see). *Never no more* is an illiteracy. To call someone a *never-was* (unimportant or worthless from the beginning) is fully as slangy and twice as insulting as to call that someone a *has-been* (which see).

new. Among the most overused clichés in English are *new wine in old bottles, a new broom sweeps clean,* and *a new lease on life.*

news. Like *measles* (which see), *news* is used with a singular verb, although it is plural in form. Say "What *is* the news today?" *not* "What *are* the news today?"

nice. This is a blanket word used and overused to describe persons, things, or events that more exactly may be *agreeable, pleasing, delightful, kind, choice, delicate, minute, accurate, respectable, dainty,* and *refined.* When *nice* can mean so many things, it is no wonder that it is rarely used *nicely* (that is, *suitably*).

nigger. This is a vulgar slang term referring to a black or to any dark-skinned person. *Nigra* and *darky* are equally objectionable. Like *Jewess, Negress* (female) is often used derogatorily and is usually considered offensive. *Negro* is a proper term, but many Negroes prefer to be called *blacks,* or, in this country, *Afro-Americans.*

nit. The egg of a parasitic insect, a *nit* is small and unimportant. *Nitpicking* (concern with minor details) is a colorful but now trite slang expression.

no. A narrowly regional or illiterate term for a worthless, good-for-nothing person is *no-account.* A term with the same meaning, *no-good,* may be considered either slang or an illiteracy. *No how* is an illiteracy; say "in no way" or "not at all." *No-show* is slang for a traveler who reserves a seat but neither claims nor cancels his reservation. *No-wheres* is an illiteracy. *No more* is illiterate when used to mean *anymore* ("I'm not going there *no more*"). *No place* is a sound expression but, like *no more*, is often used in a double negative ("I'm *not* going *no place* today"). *No such a* is wordy; omit *a*. *No use for* ("She has *no use for* me") is either illiterate or highly informal. Among hackneyed expressions involving *no* are: *no respecter of persons, no expense has been spared, no man in his right mind, no thinking man.*

not. This contraction of *nought* (*naught*, which see) means "in no way, to no degree" and is used to express denial, refusal, etc. It appears in such to-be-avoided double negative expressions as *not never, not nothing, not none* (of us), and *not no more*. It also appears in such trite expressions as *not worth the paper it's written on* and *not wisely but too well.*

notorious. See *famed.*

not too. Isn't it true that in almost every instance you can think of where *not too* is used, the *too* can be dropped? What does *I'm not feeling too good* mean other than *I'm not feeling good*? When *not* and *too* come together, the construction is similar. "*Not too* many people came" means what? Probably *not many*, unless you wish to say that *not more* people arrived than could be accommodated.

nowhere, nowheres. The former is standard, the latter is an illiteracy. However, *nowhere* should not be used in a construction already containing a negative (*not* traveling *nowhere*); also, *nowhere* is often followed by an unnecessary *that* ("*Nowhere that* I have wandered . . ."). *Nowhere near* is common in informal speech; *nowheres near* is an illiteracy. Better than either is to say *not nearly.*

nth degree. Popular usage, not mathematics, has caused this expression to mean "to the utmost extent." Inexact as it is, the phrase also has the handicap of triteness.

nuclear. Even television announcers occasionally have trouble saying NYOO·klee·ar.

number. See *amount.*

of, off. Until a few centuries ago, *of* and *off* represented different pronunciations of the same word. Today, *of* has a basic meaning of "derived or coming from," whereas *off* means "at or to a distance from a nearer place," "no longer attached or supported." In constructions indicating possession, *of* may be followed by an uninflected noun (friend of my brother) or by a noun or pronoun in the possessive case (friend of my brother's, friend of *his*). One objection to the use of *of* is that it performs too many functions to be really useful. Another is that it is often used unnecessarily: one should omit *of* in expressions like *stay off of* and *alongside of*. *Of* is also used illiterately as a substitute for *have* (*must of, should of*). Similarly, *off* should not be followed by *from* or *of*: "He walked *off* (not *off from* or *off of*) the stage." *Off* is illiterate when used to indicate a source; say "I got a meal *from* (not *off*) her."

Avoid such clichés or slang terms as *off and on, on and off, offbeat* (unconventional), *off the record*, and *ofay* (a white person).

often. In singing and in some verse, the *t* in *often* is occasionally pronounced, but in ordinary speech, one should say AWF·uhn, OF·uhn, or OF·'n.

O.K. This term of debatable origin is acceptable in general speech. When used as a noun or as a verb, no one objects to it (*get his O.K., O.K. the arrangement*). Some experts advise against the use of *O.K.* as an adjective ("things are not O.K. with us") and as an adverb ("the car was running O.K."). As noun, verb, adjective, and adverb, *O.K.* is overused.

old. This overused word (for which *aged, ancient, elderly*, and *venerable* are available synonyms) appears in many loose, trite, or slangy expressions: *old hat, old bean, old oaken bucket, good old times, old boy, old chap, old country, old fellow, old goat, old Harry, Old Nick,* and *Old Scratch* (Satan), *old lady, old man, old school tie, old-timer, old wives' tale, old fogy, old guard, old world, in days of old, old Adam,* and *old head on young shoulders*.

older, oldest. See *elder*.

on account of. This is a wordy phrase, especially when, as often happens, it is combined with *cause* or *due to* ("The cause of his absence was *on account of* his illness"). Remove the deadwood: "The cause of his absence was illness."

on an average of. From this phrase you can usually drop *on*. ("We sell *on an average of* one dozen every day" does not need *on*.)

on balance. See *balance*.

one and the same. Try dropping *one and* from this phrase. Does its removal make any real difference in meaning?

one of the. This is a redundant phrase. "One of the ideas I have . . ." can be better expressed "One idea I have. . . ."

one of those who. Should the verb following this expression be singular or plural, since *one* is singular and *those* is plural? Because *who* refers to *those*, use a plural verb. But if you were to say "Jack is the only one of those boys who was tardy," you would be correct in using a singular verb because only one boy was tardy.

on the part of. This is a wordy way to say *by, for,* or *among*. Either *by* or *among*, for example, can replace *on the part of* in "There was no objection on the part of many of those present."

oneself. This word may be spelled and pronounced as *oneself* or *one's* self (wuhn·SELF, wunz·SELF). *Oneself* is generally preferred because it is shorter and easier to spell and pronounce.

only. A frequent error in speech, a mistake made by nearly everyone, is misplacing a modifier such as *only*. When you say "Hank *only* wanted to borrow five dollars," you have said that *the only thing Hank wanted* was to "borrow five dollars." What you probably had in mind was "Hank wanted to borrow *only* five dollars." Words like *only, scarcely, hardly, not, even, today, tomorrow,* etc. are associated with the word or phrase immediately preceding or following. Place such modifiers in your sentences so that they convey precisely the meaning you intend. And remember: *not only* requires as much care in placement as does *only*. "He *not only* saw Jack at the game but Jill, too" should read "He saw *not only* Jack at the game but Jill, too."

onto. This word and *on* are used interchangeably, but *onto* more strongly suggests "movement toward." "The dog jumped *on* the table" may mean that he was already on the table, jumping. "The dog jumped *onto* the table" means that he leaped to the table from somewhere else. In constructions where *on* is an adverb and *to* a preposition, pronounce them as separate words: "We then moved *on to* the next room."

oral, verbal. *Oral* means "spoken rather than written" and "of or pertaining to the mouth." *Verbal* means "associated with words." *Verbal* can and does refer to what is written; *oral* does not. Be careful in using "oral" and "verbal" with words like *agreement, promise, understanding,* etc. If the agreement (promise, understanding, etc.) is not in writing, *oral* makes that sense clear. That is, *verbal* is less precise than *oral* in conveying the idea of *by mouth.* When you can choose between a word that means two things (*verbal*) and one that can mean only one (*oral*), try to be precise. Why not use *oral* and *written* for clear contrast?

orgy. Even if you never attend a revel or indulge in secret rites, you should know how to pronounce the term for such activity. Say AWR·ji.

ought. This word, followed by *to*, indicates obligation, duty, desirability, and likelihood. ("You *ought* to pay me what you owe." "You *ought* to have gone with me." "The rain *ought* to stop soon.") Sometimes, the infinitive following *ought* may be omitted, provided it is understood. ("Should we start now? We *ought* to.") *Ought* used without *to* is nonstandard in such expressions as *we ought go, we ought buy,* etc. Auxiliary verbs (*could, did, had, should,* etc.) are nonstandard in combination with *ought.* Do not say "They *had ought* to stop" and "We *should ought* to go now." *Oughta* is an informal pronunciation and spelling of *ought to.*

out loud. See *aloud.*

out of, outside of. See *inside of.* Not all "double prepositions" are incorrect: one can walk *out of* a store, stroll *up to* a house, and go *over to* a friend's room. However, "looking *out of* a window," "waiting *outside of* an office," and "falling *off of* a stairway" are wordy, nonstandard phrases.

outstanding. This is an overworked word. Vary your word choice with *prominent, salient, excellent,* or *distinguished.*

over with. From this phrase *with* can be omitted. "The pain will soon be *over*" means precisely what is conveyed by "The pain will soon be *over with.*" Also, you can use "ended" or "finished."

oyster. This word, slang for "a close-mouthed person," also appears in the tiresome expression *the world is his oyster.*

pad. A slang term for one's room or apartment.

paint. This is a narrowly dialectal word when used to mean "a spotted horse or pony." To *paint the town red* is a cliché for "going on a carousal." *Paint job* is slang for a "fresh coat of paint."

pair, pairs. As a noun, *pair* can be followed by a singular or plural verb, but the singular is always used when *pair* emphasizes "unity" or "oneness" ("This pair of shoes *is* black"). A plural verb may be used when the members of a pair are treated as individuals ("The pair are running rapidly now"). After any numeral other than "one," say "pairs," not "pair." ("Sue bought three *pairs* of stockings.")

pair of twins. Do not say "a pair of twins" unless you are referring to four people.

pal. This word, formerly considered slang, is now informally and tiresomely overused to mean "friend," "close companion."

pamphlet. Say PAM·flit or PAM·flet.

pan. This is a slang term for "face" and an informal word for "criticize," "find fault with." *Deadpan* is slang for an "emotionless face or manner." *Pan out* is slang for "be successful," "turn out satisfactorily." *Panhandle* is an informal term for "begging."

pants. This is a term meaning "a pair of trousers." An abbreviation of *pantaloons, pants* refers to one garment but is treated as a plural in "*these* pants *are* dirty." To use the word with a singular verb, say "This pair of pants *is*. . . ." Some "experts" feel that *trousers* is a more genteel term than *pants*, but *pants* is a word calculated to stay in and, possibly, up.

panty. This is a term for women's or children's underpants. The plural is spelled *panties*. A *pantywaist* is slang for a "weak, effeminate male."

pap. A slang term for "money" or for "favors" received as political patronage. *Pap* is also an archaic word for "teat," "nipple."

pardon me. See *excuse me*.

park. In informal speech, park is used to mean "place" or "leave" not only one's automobile but many other possessions: *park your hat, park your carcass*, etc. *Parking* has also become a slangy euphemism for "necking" and "love-making."

particular. This word has four syllables, each of which should be pronounced: pahr·TIK·yoo·luhr.

partner, pardner. There is no such word as *pardner* in standard usage. Pronounce the word correctly: PAHRT·nuhr. If you overuse *partner*, occasionally substitute *ally, accomplice, confederate, colleague,* or *associate.*

party, person. *Party* implies a group, and, except in legal and telephonic diction, should not be used to refer to one person. For *person,* see *individual.*

pass. This word appears in several hackneyed phrases that are idiomatically sound but informal or slangy: *make a pass at* (make a sexually inviting gesture, action, or remark); *pass out* (lose consciousness, faint); *pass away* and *pass on* (euphemisms for *die*); *pass the buck* (refuse responsibility); *pass off as* (dispose of, or treat, deceptively); *come to pass* (happen, occur); *a pretty pass* (ironic situation); *pass up* (reject, refuse to take advantage of); and *pass over* (ignore, disregard).

passé. This term from French meaning "out-of-date," "no longer current," has become a cliché because of its brevity and exactness. To avoid monotony, occasionally say *aged, outmoded, faded, antiquated, past its prime, archaic, superannuated.*

pat. In the senses of "a stroke or tap" and "exactly" or "steadfastly," *pat* is overused in expressions like *stand pat, sit pat, have down pat, stay pat,* and *pat on the back.*

patent. As a noun meaning "grant" or "license," *patent* is pronounced PAT·uhnt. As an adjective meaning "plain," "evident," "obvious," *patent* is preferably pronounced PAY·tuhnt, although PAT·uhnt is "acceptable."

pavement, sidewalk. What in England is called a *pavement* is termed a *sidewalk* (a walk at the side of a street or road) in the United States. In America, a *pavement* (the paved part of a paved road) in England becomes a *roadway.*

payola. A slang term for "bribery."

peeve. Here is an overused word meaning "to annoy" or "a vexation," "a grievance." Instead of saying "that peeves me" or "my pet peeve," why not substitute some form of *aggra-vate, annoy, bother, irritate, irk, provoke,* or *vex*? For *peevish* ("fretful," "discontented"), try *querulous, contrary, fractious, irritable, waspish, irascible,* or *testy.*

pep. This is an acceptable, although informal, term for "high spirits," "vim," "energy." Also informal, and also overused, is the adjective *peppy.* It won't make you seem stuffy occasionally to use adjectives such as *active, forceful, dynamic, vigorous,* or *strenuous* and nouns such as *dynamism, power, force, strength,* and even *puissance. Pep talk* and *pep meeting* are overused phrases.

per. Linguists once argued that since *per* is a Latin word it should be followed only by another Latin word: *per annum, per diem,* etc. Our language, however, has never paid attention to such a prescription, and hybrids abound in English. However, *per* is overused to mean "in accordance with." As often as possible, avoid saying "As *per* your instructions" and, where the meaning is clear, say "*a* day" and *a* year" rather than "*per* day" and "*per* year."

percentage. This term is a slangy cliché for "gain" or "advantage" ("What's the *percentage* in hard work without some fun?").

perfect. In addition to being overused to mean "complete," "excellent," "flawless," "exact," "thorough," "delightful," etc., *perfect* is often accompanied by *more* and *most* ("What could be *more perfect* than this?" "It was the *most perfect* weather we had all summer.") As an absolute, *perfect* is logically incapable of comparison. See *absolute.* Instead of using *perfect* as a loose, coverall term, why not choose a word that more nearly conveys what you have in mind? (Possibly some of the terms used above in defining *perfect* will be useful.)

perhaps. Many speakers transpose the letters in some words beginning with *per* and *pre. Perhaps* often sounds like PRE· haps. It should be pronounced puhr·HAPS or puhr·APS.

period of time. The word *period* conveys the idea of time; therefore *of time* is redundant. Also wordy is the phrase *lapse of time,* since *lapse,* like *period,* connotes time. When a specific amount of time is mentioned ("a lapse of ten hours"), no wordiness is involved.

perk, perky. These are standard words involving "liveliness," "sprightliness," "good spirits," etc. *Perk* (and *perky*) come from a French word meaning "to perch," (roost) however, and bear no relationship in meaning to *percolate*, which derives from Latin words meaning "to filter" or "strain." It is slangy to refer to *perking* (or *percing*) coffee. Similarly, it is slangy to say that someone is *percolating* (being lively or active).

perm. An abbreviation of "permanent," *perm* is overused as a slangy substitute for "a long-lasting hair setting."

persecute, prosecute. To *persecute* someone is to "harass, annoy, bother, or oppress" him. To *prosecute* is "to institute legal proceedings" or "to follow up something undertaken." *Persecute* is pronounced PUHR·si·kyoot; *prosecute* as PROS· i·kyoot.

person. See *party*.

personal friend of mine. How many friends do you have who are not *personal*? *Personal* can be omitted from this phrase and, in removing deadwood, why not change *of mine* to *my*? Only in a society where everyone becomes a number or an item for computer input is it pitifully necessary to say "He is someone whom I know *personally*." Avoid such wordy expressions as *personally, I believe . . .* and *in my personal opinion*.

personal, personnel. See *material*. *Personnel* means "a group of persons." *Personal* involves a particular person, an individual. *Personal* is pronounced PUHR·suhr·uhl; *personnel* is pronounced puhr·suh·NEL.

perspective, prospective. The former term (puhr·SPEK· tive) involves techniques for representing dimensions and surfaces as well as "point of view." *Prospective* (proh·SPEK· tive) means "looked forward to." ("His *perspective* on this problem is logical." "The *prospective* rate of return on this investment is low.")

perspire, sweat. Perhaps because *perspire* has its origin in Latin, whereas *sweat* comes from Anglo-Saxon, some persons feel that *perspire* is more elegant and genteel than *sweat*. Both are standard words. Keep in mind, though, that *sweat* appears in a number of trite, informal, or slangy expressions: *no sweat* (easily done); *sweat blood* and *sweat* *out* (endure or await anxiously); *sweat out of* (extort, force from); *sweatbox* (torture cell): and *by the sweat of his brow.* *Perspire* is too fastidious a word to admit the intrusion of slang and too unpopular to fit into hackneyed expressions. *Persweat* is a coy, nonstandard neologism.

persuade. See *convince.*

phase. Do not overuse this word as a synonym for *appearance* or *aspect.* It can be used precisely to mean "a distinct stage of development" but it is often employed in a vague way, as are other such "jargonish" terms as *factor, instance, nature, case,* and *thing.* To *phase out* something is to "eliminate by one stage, or step, at a time."

phenomenon, phenomena. The former is singular (*"This phenomenon* is hard to understand"); *phenomena* is plural (*"These phenomena* impressed several observers"). *Phenomenons* is an alternate, less preferred, plural. *Phenomenon* is pronounced fi·NOM·i·non; *phenomena* is pronounced fi· NOM·i·nah.

phony. A slang term for something fake or spurious. The plural is *phonies.* The term is also spelled *phoney,* with a plural of *phoneys.*

pickle, pickled. To be *in a pickle* is a slangy way of describing being in an embarrassing or troublesome situation. *Pickled* is a slang term for "drunk."

picture. Pronounce this word PIK·chuhr or PIK·tyuhr. Do *not* pronounce it like *pitcher* (PICH·er). You can go to see a film, movie, cinema, or motion picture, but you can see a *moving pitcher* only on a baseball diamond. *Pretty as a picture* and *picture of health* are clichés.

piece. Avoid such trite expressions as *go to pieces, piece of one's mind, of a piece, speak one's piece,* and *pièce de résistance* (principal event, outstanding quality). *See cake.*

pile. A slang term for "a large sum of money." *Piles* is informal when used to mean "a heap," "a mass," "an accumulation," as are *lots* and *heaps* in the same sense.

pill. This word is slang when used to refer to a baseball, to an unattractive person, and to an oral contraceptive (usually spelled with a capital *P* and preceded by *the*).

pin. Watch out for such trite expressions as *pin money, pin-*

point, pin something on someone, and *pin down. Pin-up* is an informal term for a picture of an attractive girl.

pinch. Avoid overusing such trite expressions as *pinch pennies, make a pinch,* and *in a pinch.*

pip. A slang term meaning "someone, or something, wonderful."

pipe. This word is slang for "an easy task." *Pipe down* is slang for "stop talking"; *pipe up* is slang for "speaking." *Pipes* is slang for the voice, the throat, or the human respiratory system. *Pipe dream* is a cliché. To *pay the piper* is a wornout expression.

pistol. This term is slang for an unusual or dynamic person. *Hot as a pistol* is a hackneyed phrase.

pitch. This word is slang in *make a pitch* (a talk designed to persuade, such as that made by a hawker, lover, or other salesman). Informal and trite are expressions such as *pitch in* (assist, work hard), *pitch into* (attack, assault) and *pitch on* (choose, select). *Sales pitch* is business jargon; *pitchout* is shoptalk (in baseball) as are *pitch-and-run shot* and *pitch-and-putt* (in golf).

pizzazz. A slang term for "flair," "zest."

plan on. Preferable to *plan on going* (or any other gerund like "going") is *plan to go* (or any other infinitive like *go.*)

plank down, plank out. These idioms are informal (or slangy) when used to mean "pay up" or "pay promptly." *Walk the plank* is a cliché suggesting "being forced to do something against one's will."

plastered. A slang term for "drunk."

play. Avoid as many of these trite expressions as often as you can: *play the game, play fast and loose, make a play for, play both ends against the middle, play by ear, play for time, play into the hands of, play off one against another, play one's cards, play up to, play with fire,* and *played out.*

plenty. An informal term when used to mean "quite" or "very" (*plenty* angry, *plenty* tired). When *plenty* refers to "supply" or "quantity," it should be followed by *of:* say "plenty *of* time," not "plenty time."

ploy. This is a useful word meaning "stratagem," "maneuver," but it has been so overused that it has lost its pristine effectiveness.

plug. This word is slang when it means "gunshot" or "bullet" (a *plug* in the leg) or "to shoot" (to *plug* with a bullet). It is also slang for "anything worn out" or "useless" (a *plug* horse). *To plug* is slang for "giving favorable mention of something." *Plug-ugly* is slang for "a gangster." *Plug hat* is slang for "a high silk hat." *Plug in* is slang for "begin to listen." *Plug along* and *plug ahead* are informal clichés meaning "to work steadily."

plumb. This is an informal, overworked word used to mean "completely," "entirely."

plurality. See *majority.*

plus. This word is incorrectly and tritely used in the meaning of "something added or extra." ("That's a *plus.*") *Plus* does not have the conjunctive force of *and*; say "Mike *and* his friends" *not* "Mike *plus* his friends." Since *plus* is a preposition rather than a conjunction, a following verb is singular or plural depending on the number of the subject: "Three plus three [a unit] *equals* six." "Their purposes (plural) plus our general plan *are* excellent."

poem, poetry. These often-mispronounced words should be spoken as POH·em (or POH·im) and POH·i·tree. The word pronounced POME refers to a fleshy fruit, such as an apple or pear.

point. This word is redundant in many sentences. From a statement such as "The speaker stressed *the point* that the fires were accidental," delete *the point.* The term also appears in such hackneyed expressions as *get the point, get to the point, in point of, make a point, make a point of, upon* (or *on*) *the point of, stretch a point, point-blank range, point of departure, point of order, point of view,* and *point of honor.*

politics. This word usually takes a singular verb ("Politics *is* an art, a science, a business, and a profession.") When *politics* indicates opinions and principles, it may be used with a plural verb ("His politics *are* his own affair"). When in doubt, use a singular verb.

pooh-pooh. *Pooh* is an informal but standard interjection used to express disdain. When doubled into the expressive formation *pooh-pooh*, the term becomes a trite and slangy verb meaning "to reject," "to scorn," "to consider unworthy."

poorly. An informal term for "in poor health," "not well."

pop. As an abbreviation of "popular," *pop* is overused in terms such as *a pop singer, pop concert, pop art, pop music,* etc. *Pop off* is slang for "leaving abruptly" and "speaking angrily." *Pop out* is baseball shoptalk. *Pop the question* is a weary expression.

pork barrel. This is a slang term meaning "a government appropriation, policy, or bill that aids a specific area and its inhabitants."

positively. See *absolutely.*

posted. An overused substitute for "informed." If you like neither *informed* nor *posted,* how about *acquainted, apprised, advised,* or *notified?*

pot. This word is slang when it refers to "a large sum of money," to "a fat stomach" (really a *potbelly*), "to shoot," and "marihuana." Trite terms to avoid include *go to pot* (become ruined, deteriorate), *get potted* (become intoxicated), and *take potluck* (eat food that is available without special preparation).

practical, practicable. See *impractical.* Both *practical* and *practicable* follow the reverse distinctions made in this cross reference.

practically. This word (pronounced PRAK·tik·lee) is not an exact synonym for "virtually" or "essentially" and should never be used to mean "nearly" or "almost." Say "This species is *virtually* extinct," not "*practically* extinct." Say "He has *nearly* stopped breathing," not "*practically* stopped."

precede, proceed. The former means "to come before," "to go in advance of." *Proceed* means "to go forward," "to carry on." ("Senator Blup *preceded* his staff into the room and *proceeded* to justify his vote on the measure.")

prefer, preferable. Pronounce these words with the accent on different syllables: pri·FUHR and PREF·uhr·uh·b'l. *Prefer* is followed by *to* (prefer to), never by *than* (prefer than) when the object of *prefer* is not an infinitive. "She prefers sewing *to* cooking." "They prefer to play football rather than watch it," or, revised, "They prefer playing football *to* watching it.")

pretty. This word is overused to mean many things: *attrac-*

tive, graceful, pleasing, delicate, comely, fair, and *lovely.* It is also overused to mean "moderately," "somewhat," or "to a degree" (*pretty* tired, *pretty* lucky). Slangy or trite phrases to avoid include *sitting pretty, pretty up, a pretty penny,* and *pretty much.*

preventive, preventative. These words mean "serving to hinder," "to keep from occurring." They are interchangeable, although the former is primarily an adjective, the latter a noun.

priority. See *top.*

pro. As an abbreviation of "professional," *pro* is overused in referring to anyone skilled in an occupation or activity, including some that have no relationship whatever to any acknowledged profession. Your skilled friend may be startled, but not upset, if you refer to him (or her) as a *virtuoso,* an *expert,* an *artist,* an *artiste,* or even a *wizard.*

probably. This word is often slurred. Say PROB·uh·blee. But if you say *probably* too often, occasionally try *presumably* or *likely* or *possibly* or *plausibly* or *in all likelihood.* (Remember, however, that *one* word is normally preferable to more than one.)

prophecy, prophesy. The former term is a noun only, pronounced PROF·i·see. *Prophesy* is a verb (to predict, to reveal) and is pronounced PROF·i·sai.

propose, purpose. In the meaning of "intend," these words are interchangeable: "I *propose* (or *purpose*) to go to headquarters myself." *Propose,* much the more commonly used word, also means "to suggest" and "to nominate." ("I *propose* that we send Jim.") *Propose* is pronounced pruh·POHZ; as a noun *purpose* is pronounced PUHR·puhs, but as a verb it may be pronounced PUHR·puhs or puhr·POSE.

proposition. This word for "plan" or "scheme" is widely overused, especially in the sense of a matter requiring careful handling. *To proposition* is an informal term meaning "to propose," "to suggest" — often with illegal or immoral intent. Approximate synonyms for the noun *proposition* are *suggestion, overture, design, recommendation,* and *proposal.*

prosecute. See *persecute.*

proved, proven. The preferred form of the past participle of "prove" is *proved* ("David has *proved* his point"). *Proven* is

standard (and preferred) as an adjective used before a noun
(a *proven* belief). Also, *not proven* is more commonly used
than *not proved*, although both phrases are standard.

provided, providing. In the sense of "if" or "on the condition," both *provided* and *providing* are standard terms. *Provided,* however, is preferred to *providing* (in this sense) by
a majority of language students. ("You may leave *provided*
—preferably not *providing*—you have finished eating.")

psychological moment. This is a trite and vague expression.

pull. This word is slang in the sense of "drawing out a knife
or gun" and is slangy or informal in the meaning of "special
influence or appeal" ("Jim has *pull* with the coach"). The
term appears in several hackneyed expressions such as *pull
oneself together, pull one's own weight, pull through, pull
together, pull out, pull back, pull down,* (receive as salary,
etc.), *pull apart, pull off* (perform successfully), and *pull
someone's leg.*

punk. A slang term when used to mean (1) of poor quality,
(2) an inexperienced youth, (3) a young hoodlum, (4) a homosexual. It is informal or narrowly dialectal in the sense
of "not well," "ill" ("I feel *punk* today").

pupil, student, scholar. These words have related meanings, but *pupil* is usually applied to someone in elementary
school, *student* to one in high school or college, and *scholar*
to a mature person who is devoted to learning.

pure. Among the more wornout clichés in English are *pure
and simple, poor but pure, pure as the driven snow, pure
drivel,* and *pure nonsense.*

purpose. See *propose.*

put. One of the most overworked words in English is *put.*
Note its appearance in these hackneyed expressions: *put
across, put through, put upon* (be imposed on), *put aside, put
away, put by, put forth, put in, put off, put down, put up with,
put-up job, put a spoke in someone's wheel, put one's shoulder to the wheel, put back the clock, put one's foot down, put
on the dog, put all one's eggs in one basket, put up to,* and
stay put. This list of tired expressions could be doubled. *Put
your mind* to avoiding *put* as often as you can.

put on. A current slang term in widespread use, *put-on* is a noun meaning an affected manner or act; *put on*, a verb meaning to make fun of, ridicule, or tease someone.

quantity. In casual conversation, speakers often fail to sound both *t*'s in this word. The standard pronunciation is KWON·tuh·tee (or KWON·ti·tee).

quasi. This Latin term meaning "resembling but not being," "to some degree," and "almost" is pronounced KWAY·sai or KWAH·zee.

quay. This word for "dock" or "reinforced bank where ships are berthed or unloaded" has only one pronunciation: KEE.

queen. Slang for an effeminate male homosexual.

queer. This slang term for "counterfeit," "fake," and "homosexual" is overused in the sense of "odd," "unconventional." Other possible substitutes for "queer" include *strange, quaint, peculiar, eccentric, singular, outlandish,* and *unusual.*

quick, quickly. The former is a noun, an adjective, and an adverb. *Quickly* is an adverb only. Although such expressions as "come quick" and "move quick" are often heard, experts agree that a pure adverb, *quickly,* is preferable. It is better to use *quick* only as a noun (*cut to the quick* and *the quick and the dead* are trite expressions illustrating this use) and as an adjective (*a quick mind.*)

quid pro quo. This Latin term ("something for something") in English means "an equal exchange." Pronounce the phrase KWID·pro·KWOH but use it sparingly because it has become a cliché.

quiet, quite. Careless speakers sometimes fail to distinguish between the sounds of these words. *Quiet* is pronounced KWAI·uht; *quite* sounds like KWITE. In the senses of "really," "truly," and "to the greatest extent," *quite* is always proper. In the meanings of "somewhat" or "rather" (*quite* warm today), *quite* is also standard usage. *Quite a* used to indicate an "extraordinary quality or personality" (*quite* a man, *quite* a performance) is permissible but informal. *Quite a spell* is informal for "an extended period (time)."

quiz. The use of *quiz* as both verb and noun is informal (*quiz* the suspect, a *quiz* by a panel of experts), but a greater objection to it is that it is overused to the point of triteness.

quote. As an abbreviation for the noun "quotation," *quote* is considered an informal neologism. In careful speech, say "quotation" and "quotations" rather than a "quote" and "quotes."

rabbit, rarebit. The correct term for a certain kind of cheese dish is *Welsh rabbit*, but *rarebit* has been so widely substituted that both *Welsh rabbit* and *Welsh rarebit* are now acceptable—in one's diction, although perhaps not always in one's stomach. *Rabbit* appears in several overworked expressions: *rabbit punch* (boxing shoptalk); *rabbit ears* (sensitivity to jibes or insults, television antenna); *rabbit's foot* (good-luck charm).

rabies. This term for a certain kind of acute infection may be pronounced RAY·beez or, much less common, RAY·bi·eez.

racket, racquet. *Racket* has a basic meaning of "din," "uproar," and "clamor." It is a slang term when applied to any business or job and trite when used to describe any dishonest or illegal practice. *Racquet*, once the only word used to name a light bat employed in such games as tennis and badminton, is still so spelled in the game of *squash racquets*. Today, *racket* has superseded *racquet* to the extent that some modern dictionaries do not list *racquet* as a main entry. *Racket* and *racquet* are both pronounced RAK·it or RAK·et.

rag. This is a slang term for "newspaper" and an informal one for "tease" or "scold." *The rag game* is a slang phrase for "the garment industry." *Rag* appears in such trite, informal phrases as *chew the rag* (talk), *from rags to riches* (from poverty to wealth), *ragtime* (jazz), *rag and bone man* (junk collector), *on the ragged edge* (in a dangerous, precarious position), *ragtag and bobtail* (rabble, riffraff), and *glad rags* (party clothes).

ragout. This term from French cookery names a highly seasoned stew. It is pronounced ra·GOO (with the *a* sounded like the *a* in *rag*).

raise, rear, rise, raze. Once it was maintained that people *raised* pigs and corn and *reared* children. Careful speakers preserve this distinction, but the general public does not; therefore, you can *raise* or *rear* as many children as you can afford, with no purist in language to prevent you. The noun *raise* (a raise in pay) is also standard, although *rise* (a rise in pay) was once considered the only proper term in this construction. One's arm *rises;* one *raises* his arm. *Raise* and *raze* are antonyms in the sense that the former means "to elevate," "to lift," whereas *raze* means "to tear down." ("The workmen *raised* the scaffolding and then *razed* it.") Try to avoid such clichés as *raise one's sights, raise Cain, raise hell, raise money, raise a siege, rise to the occasion, rise above the commonplace, rise in the world, rise to one's responsibilities, rise from the dead, rise on one's hind legs, feel the yeast rising, rear guard,* and *bring up the rear.* A horse *rears* (REERS) up on its hindlegs, not *rares* (rhymes with DARES) up.

rake-off. A slang term for "a share of the profits," particularly in an enterprise involving a bribe. *Rake-off* is an informal expression when used to mean "a discount."

rap. This word is slang for (1) talking in a rambling fashion and (2) a reprimand, censure. *Take the rap* is slang meaning "to accept punishment, especially when one is not guilty of any crime." *Beat the rap* is a slang phrase meaning "to escape punishment." *A bum rap* is "a frameup" or a "faulty conviction for a crime." *Don't care a rap* and *rap on the knuckles* (or *shins*) are hackneyed expressions.

rarely ever. This widely used phrase is wordy, unidiomatic, and illogical. Instead of saying "Sue *rarely ever* talks," say "Sue *hardly ever* talks" or "Sue talks *rarely, if ever*" or "Sue talks *rarely or never.*"

rat. This is a slang term for (1) a scoundrel, (2) an informer, (3) one who deserts companions in time of trouble, (4) to desert, and (5) to inform ("squeal"). *Rats* is a slangy exclamation. *Smell a rat* (suspect or surmise deceit or trickery) is a trite, slangy expression. *Ratfink* is slang for "a despicable person." *Rat race* is slang for "a ceaseless round of activity," "a hectic routine." *Ratty* is slang for "shabby," "disreputable," dowdy."

rate. In the meaning of "deserve" and "possess influence or status," *rate* is nonstandard. Use "deserve" or some other word in a statement such as "Bill doesn't *rate* such excellent service." Avoid *rate* in saying "Judy doesn't *rate* with her boss as she should."

raw. Watch out for such trite, informal phrases as *in the raw* (in a crude state, or naked) and *raw deal* (unjust treatment).

read. Do you ever use such trite expressions as *read between the lines, read someone like a book, read oneself to sleep, read the riot act,* and *read someone's thoughts?*

readable. See *legible.*

real, really. See *actual* and also *actually. Real* can be a noun but functions mainly as an adjective. *Really* is an adverb only. Use *really* to modify verbs, adjectives, or other adverbs (*really* ill, *really* fast, *really* moving). Do not say *real cool, real soon,* or *real* rapid. You may insist that *real* means "very" (*real* pretty), but such use is nonstandard. *Really* can be used as an intensive: "*Really,* you should have spoken to her."

really and truly. This phrase is both trite and wordy. Say *really* or *truly* but not both in the same phrase.

rear. See *raise.*

reason. This word appears in numerous trite expressions such as *it stands to reason, theirs not to reason why, within reason, by reason of, bring someone to reason,* and *any reasonable person.* Note that one word, *because,* can replace five words: *for the simple reason that.* If you overuse *reason* by itself, try *understanding, intuition, judgment,* or *discernment.* In the sense of "cause" or "basis for action," you can substitute *purpose, motive, end, object,* or *objective.*

reason is because. See *because.*

reason why. The word *why* is an adverb, conjunction, noun, and interjection and should not be used as a pronoun. Instead of saying "The reason *why* he left is unknown," say "The reason *that* he left is unknown." When *why* is used as a "conjunctive adverb" (that is, part conjunction and part adverb) it properly appears in a remark such as "I never realized *why* he was upset."

receipt, recipe. Only a few years ago, *receipt* had a basic meaning of "receiving" and was never used, except by uneducated persons, in the sense of *recipe* (a formula for preparing something, a set of directions for mixing measured ingredients). Today, *recipe* is still preferable to *receipt* in the sense of "formula," but widespread usage is gradually removing all restrictive labels from *receipt.*

recess. As a verb (and as a noun meaning "a remote, secluded place," "an alcove," and "a period of intermission or suspension of activity") *recess* once had only one standard pronunciation: ri·SES. Usage has caused REE·ses to become more popular than ri·SES, but both are standard pronunciations.

reckon. See *calculate.*

recognize. Don't slur the distinct sounds of this word. Say REK·uhg·NAIZ.

red. How often do you hear—and do you use—any trite expressions involving *red?* How about *paint the town red, red as blood, see red, red-blooded man, roll out the red carpet, red-carpet treatment, not a red cent, redeye* (whiskey, ham gravy), *red-faced, caught red-handed, a red herring* (misleading clue), *red-light district, red-hot, in the red* (in debt or operating at a loss), *red dog* (football shoptalk), *hot as a red fox, a red-letter day,* and *red tape* (complicated forms and procedures)? *Run up a red flag* when tempted to use any of the foregoing clichés.

refer. See *allude.*

refer back. The word *refer* conveys the idea of "back." (It comes from two Latin words meaning "back" or "again" and "carry.") Omit *back* and avoid wordiness ("The speaker *referred* to—not *referred back* to—his earlier comments").

regard, regards. See *in regard to.* Both *regard* and *regards* suggest *esteem* and *respect, admiration,* and *approbation.* With these synonyms to choose from, you can avoid the trite request, "Give my regards to. . . ."

regular. The only *regular,* standard pronunciation of this word is REG·yoo·luhr. Don't omit the second syllable.

remainder. See *balance.*

remembrance. Because this word resembles *remember,* many speakers incorrectly add a syllable in pronouncing it. Say ri·MEM·bruhns, *not* re·MEM·ber·uhns.

rendezvous. Say RAHN·duh·voo or REN·duh·voo. French people say RAHN·day·VOO.

repeat again. See *again.*

répondez s'il vous plaît. You are more likely to say "R.S.V.P." than this French expression meaning "please reply." If you do use the full form, say ray·pohn·DAY·see ·voo·PLEH.

representative. This word has five syllables. Sound them all: REP·ri·ZEN·tuh·tiv.

research. The preferred pronunciation of this word as both noun and verb is ri·SUHRCH. Also standard and often heard is REE·suhrch. The word means "scholarly or scientific inquiry" and is used frequently when all that is involved is *study, examination, investigation, spot check, breakdown,* or *canvass.*

respectfully, respectively, respectably. The first of these terms means "with respect" ("He addressed the supervisor *respectfully*"). *Respectively* means "each in the order named" ("Harry, Ned, and Steve were known as the Ace, the Banker, and the Nightcrawler respectively"). *Respectably* means "in a manner worthy of esteem" ("That family lived *respectably* in this community for thirty years").

restaurant, restaurateur. The former term, which derives from a French word meaning "to restore," is a somewhat more genteel word than *eating house, eatery, beanery,* and *hash house* (all slang) and *café, luncheonette, coffee shop, tavern, grill,* and *lunch counter.* It should be pronounced RES·tuh·ruhnt or RES·tuh·rahnt. A *restaurateur* (pronounced RES·tuhr·uh·tur) is the manager (or owner) of a restaurant.

return back. *Return* implies "going back" or "coming back" to a former place, position, or condition. Omit *back* from this expression ("It is not easy to *return* — not *return* back — to one's childhood home.")

revenge. See *avenge.*

reverend, reverent. The former means "deserving of reverence and respect" and is primarily an adjective as well as a title applied to clergymen. This title of *Reverend* should not be used with merely a surname (Reverend Baker); say, instead, "The Reverend Thomas Baker," "The Reverend Mr. (or Dr.) Baker," or "Reverend Thomas Baker." *Reverend* is not a noun in standard usage; do not say "the Reverend." *Reverent* means "feeling or indicating reverence" (a *reverent* feeling in church).

rich. This word appears in several hackneyed expressions for which less trite substitutes can be found: *rich as Croesus, rich beyond the dreams of avarice, rich in tradition, a rich harvest, a rich voice, a rich joke, rich in kindness, rich with color, rich in beauty, a rich feast, a rich odor, rich soil,* and *rich supply.* Possible synonyms for *rich* in one or more of its meanings include *affluent, opulent, moneyed, abundant, wealthy, plentiful,* and *ample.*

right. This is a word of many meanings, as is the plural form *rights.* We could not get along in speech without them, but we can avoid overusing such already hackneyed expressions as *be in one's right mind, put things right, the right thing at the right time, right of way, right wing, right about face, right away, out in right field, let the left hand know what the right hand is doing, right to work, in one's own right, in the right, by rights,* and *set to rights. Right along, right soon, right off,* and *right smart* are informal phrases indicating the use of *right* as an adverb.

ring. The past tense of *ring* (as a verb) is *rang,* not *rung.* Say "The telephone *rang* many times" *not* "The telephone *rung* many times." Say "has *rung,*" not "has *rang.*" *Ring* appears in such to-be-avoided trite expressions as *ring a bell, ring down the curtain, ring the changes,* and *ring true.*

riot. A slang term for a person or event considered "hilarious," "ludicrous," or "highly entertaining." Hackneyed expressions: *run riot, let one's imagination run riot, riotous living,* and *read the riot act.*

rise. See *raise.* Watch for such trite expressions as *get a rise out of, give rise to, rise to the emergency.* The past tense of *rise* is *rose,* the past participle is *risen.* ("The moon *rose* early." "The sun *has risen* later every day this week.")

rocker. This word appears constantly in the slang phrase *off one's rocker* (out of one's mind).

rough. This word is informal when used to mean "unpleasant," "difficult" (a *rough* experience). It appears in several trite expressions, among them *a rough diamond* (a worthy but uncultivated person), *in the rough* (in an unfinished state), *rough it* (get along without the usual comforts), *rough and ready* (crude but usable), *rough and tumble* (without regard for rules), *roughneck* (a rowdy person), *ride roughshod over someone* (treat inconsiderately), and *rough spoken* (coarse in speech).

round. See *about. Round* is an adverb, a verb, a preposition, an adjective, and a noun. In one or more of its parts of speech, and in the plural noun (*rounds*), *round* appears in several clichés: *a round of beef, a round of applause, the* *daily round, in the round, go the rounds, make the rounds, round off, round out, round the world, roundhouse* (slang for a blow delivered with a sidearm movement), *round robin, round the clock,* and *round and round the mulberry bush.*

rout, route. *Rout* has several meanings, but some of them indicate "a way," "a course," or "a road," which are the specific meanings of *route. Rout* is usually pronounced ROWT. This is the pronunciation often given *route,* but the preferred pronunciation of *route* is ROOT. As a verb, *route* is pronounced both ROOT and ROWT.

rubber. This word appears in such overworked expressions as *rubber check* (check drawn against insufficient funds), *rubberneck* (a gawking tourist), and *rubber stamp* (perfunctory approval).

rumble. Slang for "a gang fight."

rumpus. This word means "a noisy clamor." A *rumpus room* is a place for parties and games. *Rumpus* is not a verb; do *not* say "He *rumpused* around" or "He went *rumpusing* about the town."

run. This word appears in dozens of trite expressions, among them *run across, run afoul of, run after, run around with, run away, run away with, run down, run in, run in with, run off, run out on, run through, run up, a run for his money, on the run, in the long run, out of the running, run-of-the-mill, cut and run, my blood ran water, runner up,* and *run (butt) one's head against a stone wall.*

sack. A slang word when used to mean (1) a bed or mattress, (2) to discharge from employment, (3) to sleep (*sack out*). *Hit the sack* is a slang term for "go to bed." *Get the sack* is slang for "being dismissed." A *sad sack* is slang for a disconsolate or unattractive person.

sacrilegious. This word meaning "disrespectful," "irreverent," is often misspelled and therefore mispronounced. Do not confuse this term with "religious"; it should be associated with "sacrilege." Say SAK·ruh·LEE·juhs, or, also standard, SAK·ri·LIJ·uhs.

sadism. This term was once associated only with sexual gratification and the infliction of pain on others. It, and the adjective *sadistic,* now refer to "delight in cruelty." *Sadism* may be pronounced SAY·DIZ·um (preferred) or SAD·iz·um. *Sadistic* is pronounced SAY·DIS·tic.

saga. A *saga* (pronounced SAH·guh) refers to any long narrative in verse or prose dealing with legendary or historic events. Like *epic* (which see), *saga* is loosely used in place of such words as *story, tale, adventure, exploit,* and *event.*

said, same. As an adjective, *said* should not be used except in legal jargon (the *said* claimant). In general speech, this use of *said* is wordy because it is unneeded. If clarity demands some modifier, say *specified, aforementioned,* or *referred-to.* In a similar way, *same* is often used outside legal and commercial contexts in wordy, useless ways. Substitute *it* for *same* in a statement such as "I have your book and will return it (not *same*) tomorrow."

same as, same like. *Same as* is established idiom in a sentence such as "Your problem is the *same as* mine." It is nonstandard, however, to use *same as* as an equivalent of *just as:* "He was angry, *same as* you said he would be." Also nonstandard is *same like* ("I want more crullers *same like* I bought yesterday.") In such constructions, use *such as* for *same like.*

sank. The principal parts of *sink* are *sink, sank, sunk.* Say "The oar *sank – not* sunk – beneath the water." Say "The blast has *sunk – not* sank – the freighter."

sap. This is slang for "a fool," "a dupe." *Saphead* is a slang term with the same meaning. *Sappy* is a slangy adjective meaning "silly" or "mawkish."

savoir faire. If you must employ this overused French term for "tact" and "adroitness," pronounce it correctly: SAV· wah·FARE. Other words you might use: *diplomacy, subtlety, finesse.* But don't use *savvy,* a slang term for "understanding" and "common sense."

saw, seen. The past tense of the verb *see* is *saw;* the past participle is *seen.* Say "I *saw –* not *seen –* him yesterday." Say "I have *seen –* not *saw –* him every day this week." As a noun, *saw* appears in the cliché *an old saw* (wise saying). *Sawbones* is slang for "a surgeon." *Sawed-off* is a slang description of a short or runty person. *Sawbuck* is slang for a ten-dollar bill. *Sawdust trail* is slang for "the way to conversion for a sinner or a criminal."

say. Don't use these trite expressions if you can avoid them: *it goes without saying, on your say-so, they say, have your say,* and *that is to say* (a pretentious, wordy expression as well as a cliché). To avoid overusing *say,* try *affirm, assert, aver, declare,* or *state.*

scarcely. This word has a negative sense and should not be accompanied by another negative. See *double negative* and also *hardly.* Avoid such expressions as *couldn't scarcely, didn't scarcely, without scarcely,* etc.

scissors. This word is plural in form but may take a singular or plural verb. One may say "A pair of scissors *is* . . ." and "My scissors *are* or *is.* . . ."

scram. A slang term meaning "to leave abruptly."

scratch. This word is slang for "money." It also appears in such trite phrases as *up to scratch* (adequate, satisfactory) and *from scratch* (from the beginning). *Old Scratch* is a slang term for Satan (the devil).

screw. This term appears in such trite or slangy expressions as *have a screw loose* (be eccentric, behave oddly), *put the screws to* (apply pressure on someone), *screw out of* (extort, cheat out of), *screwball* (eccentric person or, in baseball, an erratic curve), *screwy* (odd, eccentric), *screw around* (waste time), *screw up* (ruin through bungling), and *screwed* (cheated).

scrumptious. Slang for "splendid," "delightful," "delectable." It is related in meaning to the word from which it was probably corrupted, "sumptuous."

sculp, sculpt. Once considered nonstandard, both words are accepted as shortened forms of "to sculpture." Both *sculp* and *sculpt* are derived from a Latin verb *sculpere* (to carve). But doesn't *sculpture,* a perfectly good verb, sound better than *sculp* and *sculpt?*

secondly, second of all. See *first.*

secretary. This word has four syllables. Sound each of them: SEK·ri·TER·ee.

see. This word has so many synonyms that there is little excuse for its overuse: *observe, notice, behold, discern, espy, regard, note, view, perceive,* etc. It appears and reappears in many expressions idiomatically standard but annoyingly prevalent in everyone's speech: *see about, see after, see off,*

*see out, see through, see what I mean?, do you see?, see to, I
don't see that, see beneath the surface* (skin), *see a man about
a dog, see beyond the nose on his face,* and *see both sides of
the question.* The phrase *see where* is nonstandard for *see
that.* Say "I *see that—not* see *where—*rain is predicted for
tonight."

see where. See *where.*

seldom ever. This is a wordy, illogical phrase, from which
ever should be dropped. See *rarely ever.*

sell. This word is slang when used to mean "to cheat," "to
trick." A *sell* is slang for "a hoax," "a swindle." *Sell* appears
in such trite or slangy expressions as *a hard sell, a soft sell,
to sell someone a bill of goods, sell off, sell out, sell short,* and
sell like hot cakes. To *be sold* on something or someone is to
be tritely pleased or convinced.

semimonthly. See *biannual. Semimonthly* means "twice a
month." Words containing *semi-* are easy to remember because *semi-* is a Latin element meaning "half."

senior citizens. This is a euphemism now well-entrenched in
the language. If you prefer exactness to tact, say *the aged,
the elderly, the old,* or even the slightly condescending *old-
sters* (which is modeled on *youngsters*).

sensitive. One is *sensitive to* light or beauty or pain, etc. and
is *sensitive about* an infirmity, such as deafness.

sensual, sensuous. Several terms refer to "satisfaction of
the senses," among them *sensual, sensuous, epicurean, luxurious,* and *voluptuous. Sensual* applies to the "physical"
senses only. *Sensuous* refers to what is experienced through
all the senses, especially those involved in appreciation of
art, music, literature, nature, and the like. One refers to
sensual pleasures, such as eating and drinking, and to *the
sensuous sounds and delights* of music, sculpture, etc.

set, sit. Predominantly a transitive verb, *set* means "to put,"
"to place." ("*Set* the box on the floor, please.") *Sit* is predominantly an intransitive verb with a basic meaning of "place
oneself." ("When I *sit* down, you come and *sit* beside me.")
Set used for *sit,* and *sit* for *set,* in the meanings indicated,
are nonstandard. Do not say "*Set* yourself down" nor "*Sit* it
here."

Both *set* and *sit* have special meanings. The following are standard usage: "The sun *sets* behind that mountain every afternoon." "The house *sits* in a valley." "*Sit* the baby in the chair and then *set* her on her feet." The following expressions involving *set* and *sit* are hackneyed: *set one's face* (or *one's mind*) *against, set one's heart on, set by the ears, set one's hand to the plow, set the world on fire, set one's teeth on edge, set about, set against, set down, set aside, set forth, set in, set off, set-up, set apart, set upon, all set, get set, set store by, sit in on, sit on, sit out, sit pretty, sit tight, sit-down strike, sit-in,* and *sitting duck.*

shake. These expressions are trite, slangy, or both: *shake down, shake off, shake one's head, shake the dust from one's feet, shake up, two shakes of a lamb's tail, no great shakes, shakeout, shaking in his boots, give someone the shakes, have the shakes, give* (or *get*) *a fair shake,* and *shake a leg.*

shall, will. Distinctions in the use of *shall* and *will* have broken down, but some careful speakers still observe these principles: (1) Use *shall* in the first person and *will* in the second or third persons to express future time: "I (we) *shall* leave soon." "You (he, they) *will* leave soon." (2) For expressing command or determination, use *will* in the first person and *shall* in the second and third: "I *will* speak, no matter who tries to stop me." "You *shall* speak" (meaning "You *must* speak"). (3) To express willingness, promise, or intention, use *will* (same verb, different meaning) with all personal pronouns. "I *will* help you now." "You *will* be a success."

In general, use *should* and *would* according to these recommendations for *shall* and *will.* Both *should* and *would* also have specialized meanings: *should* in the sense of "ought" and *would* in the sense of "habitual action." ("You *should* go now." "He *would* take a walk every day.") Also, see *ought.*

shanks's mare. A slang term for using one's own legs as a means of transportation.

shape. This term is informally used to mean "condition" or "form" (in great *shape,* have a good *shape*) and appears in such overused expressions as *shape up, be in bad shape,* and *take shape.*

sharp. This word has so many different meanings ("keen," "acute," "piercing," "biting," "clever," "alert," "incisive," "quick," "deceitful") that it is a difficult term to use exactly. Perhaps one of the words listed above will help you to avoid the overuse of *sharp* and make your speech *sharper*.

shell. Watch out for such informal, slangy, or trite expressions as *shell out* (pay), *be shelled* (defeated or tricked), *shell game, shell shock, shell fire*, and *shellback* (a veteran).

shillelagh. Even if you're Irish only on St. Patrick's Day, you should be able to say sha·LAY·lee.

shoot. Perhaps you never use *shoot* as a mild interjection (*Oh, shoot!*), but you probably do overuse the word in one or more of its forms: *shoot the works, shoot the chutes, shoot the breeze, shoot the bull, shoot down, shoot at, shoot up, shot through with, shot with luck, shooting* (or *gunning*) *for someone, be shot, half shot*, and *shoot one's bolt*.

should. See *shall*.

show. As a verb, *show* has several synonyms: *display, exhibit, parade, flaunt, expose, present*, etc. As a noun, its meaning can be expressed by words like *demonstration, exhibit, presentation*, and *display*. With such a list to choose from, we should be able to curtail the use of such trite or slangy expressions as *give away the show, steal the show, stop the show, a great show, show of hands, show business* (or *show biz*), *showdown, show me, a showoff, showpiece, show place, show up, show stopper, put on a show, show a clean pair of heels*, and *show the white feather*.

shrink. This, like *headshrinker*, is a slang term for a psychiatrist or psychologist. The analogy is somewhat obscure; the verb *shrink* means "to draw together," "to constrict," "to become reduced in amount or value."

shut. The following expressions are only too familiar: *shut up, shut one's eyes to, shutdown, shuteye* (sleep), *shut in* (an invalid), *shutout*, and *shutoff*. In the sense of "shed" or "free," *shut* is an illiteracy ("*shut* of his debts.")

sick. *Ill, indisposed, infirm, ailing*, and *unwell* are synonyms for *sick* in its primary meaning. However, *sick* has acquired several other meanings, among them "disgusted," "ghoulish," and "sadistic," so that *sick* appears in several trite expressions with loose, inexact meanings: *a sick show, sick society, sick humor*, etc. One of the most often used clichés in speech is *sick and tired*. Both "sick *at* one's stomach" and "sick *to* one's stomach" are heard. Each is idiomatically acceptable, but "sick *at*" is preferred.

side. Be wary of hackneyed expressions such as *take sides, side by side, this side of the grave, side with, side against, on the side, on the side of the angels,* and *wrong side of the tracks. To have no side* is an informal way of describing a lack of dignity or imposing bearing. *Sidekick* is slang for "a close friend and follower."

sidewalk. See *pavement.*

sight. This word is slang for something "shocking" or "unusual" ("Her clothes were a *sight*"). It appears in these trite and slangy expressions: *sight unseen; on sight; out of sight, out of mind; sight for sore eyes; at first sight; catch sight of; know by sight; upon sight; sight gag;* and *not by a long sight.*

simple reason. These words appear often in "for the *simple reason* that." Why use five words to express the thought of one: *because*?

simply. When used in such phrases as *simply wonderful, simply great, simply perfect, simply gorgeous,* etc., *simply* simply contributes nothing but triteness.

sit. See *set.*

situated. This word, meaning "located" or "placed," is often deadwood. Omit it in a statement such as "This town is *situated* in central Texas."

size up. Whether this term is informal or slangy is immaterial; it is trite in the sense of "forming an estimate," "arriving at an opinion about." *Size up the situation* is as prevalent a cliché as the language possesses.

ski. This word is pronounced SKEE.

skin. As you would expect, this term for "body covering" appears in many hackneyed expressions: *by the skin of one's teeth, get under one's skin, have a thick skin, no skin off one's back* (or *nose*), *skin and bones, skin-deep, skin game, skinny dip,* (swim in the nude), *thin-skinned* (sensitive), *save one's skin, skin someone alive,* and *skintight. Skin* is slang when used to mean "swindle," "cheat".

skip. This is an informal term when used to mean "leave hastily or secretly" (skipped town). *Skip it* is widely used as an informality meaning "to forget," "to ignore," or "to overlook" something.

skirt. This term is slang for "woman" or "girl." As a verb, *skirt* means "to go around the edge of," so that one should delete *around* from *skirt around* and *about* from *skirt about*.

skunk. A slang term for "a mean, contemptible person." As a verb, *to skunk* is "to defeat thoroughly." To say that someone is *drunk as a skunk* is to insult a sober mammal whose only flaw is his fetid odor.

slander. See *libel*.

slant. What's your *slant* on *slant*? Experts agree that in the meaning of "point of view" or "opinion" *slant* (as well as *angle*) is greatly overused.

slick. An overused term for "clever," "wily," or "sophisticated." A *slick chick* doesn't "click" with language experts.

slow, slowly. Each of these words is an adverb, so that one can say "Drive *slow*" or "Drive *slowly*." Careful speakers use *slowly* in such an expression. *Slow* is preferred in statements such as "This watch runs *slow*."

slug. A slang term when used to mean "drink" or "portion" (a *slug* of gin) or "a lazy person." *Slugfest* is slang for "a fight." *Slugger* is baseball shoptalk for "a hard hitter."

small. Consider these synonyms for *small: diminutive, little, miniature, miniscule, minute, petite, tiny, wee*. Any of these should enable you to avoid overusing *small*. Also, watch out for such overworked expressions as *feel small, small fry, small beer* (weak beer or a person of little importance), *small change, small-minded, small potatoes* (a person or thing of little value), *small-scale, small stuff, small talk*, and *small-time* (minor, insignificant).

smart. Be *smart* and avoid overusing *smart money, smart aleck, get your smarts back* (return to your senses), *the smart crowd* or *smart set, smarty-pants* (an impertinent person), *smart guy*, and *smart cookie*.

smell. As an intransitive verb, *smell* may be accompanied by an adjective ("The roses *smell good*," *not* "The roses *smell well*" or *smell bad, not badly*.) *Smell of* as in "She *smelled of* the flowers" is a wordy phrase. Unless you mean that she had acquired the odor of flowers, omit *of*.

smidgen. An overworked, informal word for "a bit," "a small portion."

smithereens. Slang for "fragments," "splintered pieces."

smooch. Slang for "a kiss" and also for "to kiss."

snafu. Slang for "a state of confusion" and, as a verb, for "causing confusion or chaos."

snap. An informal term for "an easy task" or "simple assignment." *Snappy* is an informal expression for "brisk" or "chic."

snitch. Slang for "stealing" and for "turning informer."

snoop. An informal term meaning "to pry," "to prowl." A *snoopy* person *snoops*.

snoot. This is a variation of *snout*, a slang expression for the human nose. A *snooty* person is "snobbish" and "haughty," presumably because he keeps his *snoot* in the air. *Snoot* is pronounced as it is spelled; *snout* is pronounced SNOWT. Better still, never pronounce either; *nose* sounds better.

snooze. An informal term meaning "to doze" and "a light nap."

snow. To *snow* someone is a slangy way of overwhelming him with flattery or favors. *Snow job* has much this same meaning.

so. See *as . . . as. So* is an adverb, a conjunction, an interjection, and a pronoun and appears in such combinations as *so as* and *so that*. Two objections to *so* are (1) its overuse in the phrase *so as* in constructions where "therefore," "thus," and "consequently" would serve as well, or better, and (2) its overuse as an intensive—a general substitute for "indeed," "extremely," etc. ("I'm *so* tired").

sock. Slangy and trite are such expressions as *sock it to me*, *socked in* (closed in by bad weather or other unfavorable circumstances), *socked away* (saved, stored), *sockdolager* (something unusual, noteworthy), *a sock* (a blow, punch), and *Old Sock* (term of familiarity). *Pull up your socks* is an inelegant, informal suggestion to pull yourself together. *Sockeroo* is slang for "a success." *Socko* is slang for "impressive," "successful" (a *socko* performance).

soft. This word is informal when used to mean "easy," "simple," "feeble," (a *soft* job, a *soft* assignment, *soft* in the head). Instead of saying that so-and-so is *softhearted*, couldn't we avoid an overworked term and say that he is *kind, tender, merciful, considerate, easily moved,* or *indulgent*? It should not be difficult to find other phrases for such hackneyed expressions as *have it soft, softheaded, soft pedal, soft sell,* *soft shoulder to cry on, soft soap* (cajolery), *soft spot in one's heart, soft-spoken, be soft on someone, soft breeze, soft music, soft landing, soft focus, soft shoe, soft touch* (person easily persuaded or influenced), and *softy* (a sentimental or effeminate person).

soiree. This is a party that takes place in the evening. Say swah·RAY.

some, somewhat. The former is an adjective of indefinite number (*some* money, *some* fruit). Applied adverbially in the sense of *somewhat* (rather, to some degree), *some* is nonstandard. Say "The patient is *somewhat*—not *some*—better today." *Some* is informal or slangy in the sense of "remarkable": "He is *some* swimmer."

somebody. This term is synonymous with "someone," a word usually considered more refined than *somebody*. Both words are standard; each takes a singular verb ("*Somebody* or *someone is* in the house"). The proper form of the possessive is *somebody else's*, not *somebody's else; someone else's* not *someone's else.*

someplace. This is an informal term for "somewhere." Say "I left my coat *somewhere*" (preferably *not* someplace.)

somersault. Pronounce this word as SUHM-uhr·sawlt.

something. These phrases are trite: *something in the wind, something on his mind, get something off one's chest,* and *something rotten in the State of Denmark.*

something like. This phrase may be considered informal or slangy in the sense of "approximately," "close to." ("It's *something like* twelve o'clock.") Why not say "about" or "approximately?"

someways. This word is nonstandard. Say "someway," "somehow," or "in some ways."

somewheres. This is an illiteracy. Say "somewhere."

sore. This word is informal and slangy when used to mean "angry." *Sorehead* is slang for "a person easily offended or annoyed." *Sore at heart, in sore need, in sore distress,* and *sore in mind* are clichés.

sort, sort of. See *kind. Sort of* is informal when used to mean "rather" or "quite" (*sort of* sorry). *After a sort* and *out of sorts* are hackneyed expressions.

S.O.S. These letters, when represented by a radio telegraphic signal, signify "a call for help." The expression is overused in daily speech.

sound. As an intransitive verb, *sound* is accompanied by an adjective, not an adverb. Say "The story sounds *strange* (not *strangely*)" and "The news sounds *good*." Some experts recommend that *out* be omitted from *sound out*, but the expression is valid and well-established. *Sound off* is slang for "speaking in a loud, complaining way."

specie, species. The former is the singular of the latter but is also a word with an entirely different meaning: "coin" or "coined money" ("The debt was paid in *specie*"). *Species*, used as both singular and plural, refers to a category of classification: "This is an odd *species* of public servant." Say SPEE·shi (singular) and SPEE·shiz or SPEE·sheez (plural).

specs. An informal abbreviation of "spectacles" (eyeglasses). Another slang term for *spectacles* is *cheaters*.

speed. This is a slang expression for a drug (amphetamine). *Speedball* is slang for an intravenous dose of heroin and cocaine. *Full speed ahead, the speed of light, with the speed of sound, at full speed, speed the parting guest*, and *speed up* are overused terms. Among possible substitutes for *speed: velocity, rapidity, quickness*, and *celerity*. The past tense and past participle of *speed* are *sped* or *speeded*. Synonyms for the verb *speed* include *hurry, hasten, accelerate, expedite*, and *quicken*.

spell, spell out. In the sense of "a short distance," *spell* is informal ("Walk with me a *spell*"). *Spell out* (state explicitly) is overused but is standard idiom; *spell out particulars* (or details) is wordy. The past tense and past participle of *spell* are *spelled* (preferred) or *spelt*.

spit. See *expectorate*.

sponge. This is a slang term for "a drunkard," for "obtaining free" (*to sponge*), and for someone who looks to others for his support (a *sponger*). *Throw in the sponge* (give up, surrender) is a cliché.

sport. A slang term for "a carefree or careless person," *sport* also appears in such hackneyed expressions as *make sport of, in sport, a good sport, sport of circumstances, sport a new car* (or any possession), *sport with someone's emotions* (particularly that of "love"), *sporting chance* (fair opportunity), *sporting house* (a brothel), *sporting lady* (a prostitute), and *sporty* (flashy).

spread. A slang term for "an abundant meal." *Spread oneself thin* and *spreadeagle the field* are hackneyed expressions.

square. This is slang for "a rigidly conventional person." ("Get with it; don't be a *square*.") Trite phrases to be wary of: *square peg in a round hole, on the square, squareshooter, square off* (assume a fighting position), *square up* (settle, pay), *square the circle* (attempt the impossible), *square with one's conscience, square meal,* and *square deal.*

stand. Among trite expressions involving *stand* may be cited *stand on one's own two feet, stand one's ground, stand a chance, it stands to reason,* and *stand in with.* Idiomatically sound but overused phrases include *stand in for, stand up with, stand on, stand over, stand up to, stand up for, stand out, stand down, stand by,* and *stand for* (endure or permit).

statue, stature, statute. A *statue* (STACH·oo) is "an image," *stature* (STACH·uhr) means "height" or "status," and a *statute* (STACH·oot) is "a law." ("This is a *statue* of Senator Smith who helped frame many *statutes* and who achieved great *stature* as an orator.")

status. If you must use this overworked term for "standing" or "position," pronounce it STAY·tus or STAT·us.

stay, stop. As a verb, *stay* has several synonyms: *remain, linger, tarry, sojourn, abide, wait,* etc. As a verb, *stop* is related to *arrest, check, halt,* and *terminate.* As these parallel words suggest, *stay* and *stop* do differ in meaning. For example, one *stays* rather than *stops* at a hotel. *Staying power* is a descriptive but overworked expression.

stems. A slang term for "legs."

stick. This is a slang term for "a marihuana cigarette" and for "an unbending, humorless person." Trite phrases to avoid: *be stuck on* (in love with or in difficulty), *stick to the ribs* (be filling, substantial), *stick up for* (support), *stick-in-the-mud* (an old fogy), *stick-to-it-iveness* (perseverance), *stick up* (a robbery or "to rob"), *in the sticks* (backwoods), *stick together, stick it out* (hold on, persevere), *stick around* (remain), *stick one's neck out, the sticking point* (stalemate, impasse), *a stick out* (outstanding person), *stick-up man* (a robber), *sticky-fingered* (thievish), *stick in one's craw*, and *stick to one's guns.*

stiff. A slang term for (1) a corpse, (2) a drunk, (3) a priggish person, and (4) a hobo. Watch out for such clichés as *frozen stiff, lucky stiff, a stiff right to the jaw, a good stiff drink, a stiff price to pay, keep* (or *hold*) *a stiff rein,* and *stiff-necked.* Usable synonyms for *stiff* include *inflexible, rigid, tense, taut, firm,* and *unyielding.*

still and all. A wordy way to say "nonetheless" or "however" or just plain "still."

stink. Principal parts of this verb are *stink, stank* or *stunk, stunk. Stink* is slang for "of poor quality" ("This book *stinks*") and for "making a fuss." *Stinking* and *stinko* are slang for "drunk." *Stinkpot* and *stinker* are slang for "a mean person." *Stinkaroo,* also spelled *stinkeroo,* is slang for "something bad." *To make a stink* and *raise a stink* are clichés.

stir. This is a slang term for prison. *Stir crazy* is slang for "being upset or restless from long confinement." *Not stir a finger to help, to stir oneself, to stir one's stumps* (or *legs*), *stir pity, stir one's heart,* and *not a leaf stirred* are hackneyed expressions.

stock. Among many overused expressions involving *stock* are *take stock in, lock, stock, and barrel, on the stocks* (under construction), *out of stock, rolling stock,* and *stock in trade.*

stomp. This word means "to tread heavily," "to press down." It is nonstandard when used to mean "stamp." Say "The mob *stomped* the victim to death," "Jane *stamped* her foot against the floor." *A stomp* is a kind of heavy-footed dance.

stool pigeon. A slang term for an informer or for a person acting as a decoy or spy. (The term, sometimes shortened to *stoolie,* derives from decoy pigeons' originally having been tied to stools.)

strangely enough. See *enough.*

strangled to death. Leave out *to death; strangled* means "to kill by stopping the breath."

stratum, strata. *Stratum* is the singular form of this noun and is nonstandard when used with a plural verb. Say "Each *stratum is . . .*" and "All *strata are. . . .*" Neither *stratums* nor *stratas* is acceptable as a plural. *Stratum* is

pronounced STRAY·tuhm or STRAT·um; *strata* is pronounced STRAY·tuh or STRAT·uh.

strength. This word has a definite *g* sound. Say STRENGTH
or STRENGKTH. Useful substitute words include *energy,
force, might, power, puissance,* and *potency.*

strike. The past tense of *strike* is *struck;* the past participle is
either *struck* or *stricken. Strook* is an obsolete form of the
past tense. Try to use sparingly such trite or slangy expressions as *strike it rich, the hour has struck, strike a pose, it
strikes me that, struck terror to our hearts, strike dumb,
strike up the band* (tune, etc.), *lightning struck, struck my
ears, strikes my eyes, how does this strike you?, strike one's
fancy, strike a balance, strike a compromise, struck him
down, strike camp, strike home, strike oil,* and *have two
strikes against one.*

string. Principal parts of the verb *string* are *string, strung,
strung.* No such word exists as *strang; stringed* is an adjective, not a verb form. *String* is informal (some language
students say it is slang) when used to mean (1) to fool or
deceive and (2) to hang someone. In its forms as noun and
verb, *string* appears in such hackneyed expressions as *no
strings attached, to string along, to pull strings, to play on
one's heartstrings, stringbean* (tall, thin person), *make the
first string, like a string of beads, string of lights, have two
strings to one's bow, on a string, string words together,
string along with,* and *string out* (extend, stretch).

stuff. This word is slang for "money" and is informal when
used to mean "belongings," "possessions," "facts," "refuse,"
"junk," "and "foolish ideas." It appears in such slangy or
hackneyed expressions as *have good stuff, kid stuff, cut out
the rough stuff, stuff and nonsense, plenty of stuff on the ball,
knows his stuff, stuffed shirt, a head stuffed with, stuff the
ballot box,* and *the stuff of life.*

stump. As a verb, *stump* is informal when used to mean
"dare" or "challenge" and "perplex" or "baffle." *Stumps* is
slang for "legs" ("stir your stumps"). *Up a stump* is a hackneyed expression meaning "being puzzled, in a quandary."
In the sense of "stub" (strike), *stump* is narrowly dialectal
(really nonstandard) as in "Don't *stump* your toe."

subsequent to. This is a standard idiomatic phrase but a wordy way to say "after" or "later."

succinct. This is a helpful word to prevent overuse of *terse, pithy, laconic,* and *brief.* Pronounce it suhk·SINGKT.

such and such. An overused expression meaning "undetermined" (at *such and such* a place).

sugar. A slang term for "money" and for "sweetheart." *Sugarcoat* is an informal term meaning "to make more attractive or palatable" ("The treasurer *sugarcoated* the offer"). *Sugar daddy* is slang for "a wealthy man who spends freely."

suicide. As a verb, *suicide* constitutes an impropriety. Say "He committed suicide," *not* "He suicided" or, even worse, "He suicided himself."

suit, suite. These words have a common origin but are used in different ways. One speaks of "a *suit* of clothes," "a *suit* at law," "a *suit* of cards," etc. *Suite* means "a company of followers," "a connected series of rooms," "a musical composition," etc. *Suit* is pronounced SYOOT; *suite* is pronounced SWEET. In standard usage, only *suite* can be applied to "matched furniture pieces," but in this usage *suite* is often pronounced (incorrectly) like *suit.* Why not avoid difficulty and say "*set* of furniture"?

superfluous. Pronounce this word syoo·PUHR·floo·uhs. (Be careful *not* to accent the third syllable.)

sure, surely. See *certain, certainly.*

sure and. A nonstandard phrase; say "sure *to.*" See *come and.*

surprise. See *amaze.* When you use *surprise,* remember that it contains two *r* sounds. Say suhr·PRAIZ.

suspicion. The use of *suspicion* as a verb meaning "to suspect" may be considered an impropriety or an illiteracy. By whatever name, such use is nonstandard. Say *suspect, suppose, assume, presume, surmise, infer, deduce, deem, mistrust, distrust,* or *doubt.*

svelte. If you use this elegant word for "willowy," "slim," "graceful," or "slender," say it as though it contained an *f:* SFELT.

sweat. See *perspire.*

swell. This word is slangy or informal when used to mean "smart," "stylish," "elegant," or "excellent" (a *swell* meal, a *swell* dress, a *swell* party). *A swell* is slang for "a dandy," "a fashionably dressed person." Among trite and slangy expressions to avoid are *swelled with pride, swelled head,* and *a swollen stream.*

swing. This word is slang for (1) to manage successfully, (2) to participate in juvenile fads, and (3) to be hanged. Do you need to say *swing this deal, in full swing, he's a swinger, on the swing shift,* and *a swinging party*? The principal parts of *swing* are *swing, swung, swung.* The form *swang* is no longer standard in English. Say "The workman *swung* (*not* swang) from the scaffold."

swipe. A slang term when used with the meaning of "to steal."

switcheroo. Slang for "a sudden or unexpected change or reversal in attitude, plan, etc." The same meaning is slangily conveyed by a statement such as "But here's the *switch.*"

swop. This is a nonstandard version of *swap,* meaning "to trade," "to barter" or "an exchange."

synthesis. See *analysis.*

tab, tabs. *Keep tab on* and *keep tabs on* are informal, trite expressions meaning "to keep an account of," "to check on," "to observe."

table d'hôte. This French phrase ("the host's table") means "a meal of prearranged courses served at a fixed time and price." Say TAB·el·DOTE.

tablespoonfuls, tablespoons full. See *-ful.*

taboo. Occasionally relieve this overworked word by saying *ban, prohibition, embargo, injunction, denial,* or *proscription.* Useful adjectives are *forbidden, disallowed, banned, unlicensed,* and *untouchable.*

tacky. An informal term meaning "shabby" or "dowdy."

tactics. This word, although plural in form, is used with a singular verb when it refers to the art, science, or general mode of procedure used in gaining success or advantage. When *tactics* refers to the maneuvers themselves, the verb is plural. *Tactic,* singular in form, is always used with a singular verb: "His *tactic* is to upset his opponents." "The *tactics* of military strategy *is* a complicated study." "The generals' *tactics* in that battle *were* masterly."

take. See *bring. Take and* ("I *took and* hit him on the nose") is an illiteracy. In the expression *take, for example, take* is unnecessary and should be omitted. *Take in* is informal when used to mean "attend" ("We *took in* a show"). *Take on* is informal in the sense of "showing emotion" ("Don't *take on* so over the loss"). *Take sick* is informal for "become ill" ("He *took sick* and nearly died"). *Take it easy* and *take care* are clichés. In fact, *take it easy* and *don't take any wooden nickels* are among the most tiresome of all hackneyed expressions.

tank. This word is slang for "jail" or "jail cell." *Tanked* and *tanked up* are slang for "drunk."

tape. To *have something taped* is a slangy way to express the meaning of "thoroughly planned" or "completely understood."

tasteful, tasty. *Tasteful* is standard in the sense of "having or displaying good taste." *Tasty* means only "having a pleasing flavor," "savory." One should usually refer to a *tasteful* affair or ceremony and to a *tasty* meal (which might also be served in a *tasteful* manner).

teach. See *learn.* Useful words related to *teach* are *discipline, drill, educate, instruct, school, train,* and *tutor.*

tee. *Teed off* is slang for "begin" ("They *teed off* the campaign at noon"), for "angry," "upset" ("Jim was *teed off* over the insult") and for "hitting" ("The boxer *teed off* on his opponent with a left to the jaw").

teeny. This is a rather coy, but standard, variation of *tiny.* The word *teenybopper* is slang for an adolescent girl addicted to fads and novelties.

teeth. For no particularly good reason, one has a *toothache,* not a *teethache,* even if more than one tooth is hurting. *Teeth,* the plural of *tooth,* outscores the singular form in the number of hackneyed expressions in which both appear: *long in the tooth* (old, elderly), *tooth and nail* (fiercely, as hard as possible), *a toothsome invitation, by the skin of one's teeth, a kick in the teeth, put teeth in*—or *into, show one's teeth, put* (or *set*) *one's teeth on edge, to the teeth* (entirely, fully), *to throw into someone's teeth* (reproach), and *cut one's teeth on* (action during one's youth).

tell. *To tell off* (rebuke, scold) is slang. *To tell on* (to tattle on or to exhaust) is highly informal. *All told* (including everything) is a cliché, as are *to tell tales out of school, with telling effect,* and *tell it not in.* . . .

tend. This verb used with *to* is informal for *attend to.* Say "It is your job to *attend to* the problem," *not* "tend to the problem."

tentative. This word meaning "experimental," "hesitant," or "uncertain" contains three *t*'s each of which should be sounded: TEN·tuh·tiv.

terra firma. This Latin phrase ("firm land") is a hackneyed expression. If you mean "dry land" or "solid ground," say so.

terrible. Instead of constantly using this overworked intensive, why not drop the thought entirely (few things or events are really *terrible*) or else use *disagreeable, dreaded, dreadful, dire, grim, offensive, loathsome, frightful, regrettable, grave,* or *fearful?* Even these toned-down adjectives probably suggest more *terror* than your statement calls for.

terrific. This word has the same meaning as *terrible* (causing terror or fear) but also is loosely used to mean "splendid," "magnificent," "excellent," or "astounding" (a *terrific* party, at *terrific* speed). Use *terrific* sparingly: it's packed with power.

test out. A wordy phrase from which *out* should be eliminated.

tête-à-tête. This French phrase ("head tu head") means "in privacy," "intimate," "for or between two only." If you use this phrase, say TAYT·uh·TAYT or, more in the French style, TET·ah·TET.

than. If you will think of *than* as a conjunction, it will be easy to remember that a following pronoun should have the same case as its antecedent. Say "Everyone knows more about the situation than *he.*" Say "The supervisors counted on no one more than *him.*"

thanks. A standard but not especially polite word meaning "thank you." *Thanks* is a weary cliché by itself and in such expressions as *thanks be to God, thanks a million, thanks a bunch,* etc. *Thanking you in advance* is a hackneyed term in inferior business letters.

that, which, who. Of these relative pronouns, *that* is used to refer to persons, animals, or things; *which* to animals and things, not persons; and *who* (whom) to persons only. *That* is most properly used in restrictive clauses (those that define and limit what precedes by providing information necessary to full understanding): "A man *that* pays his bills promptly is liked by everyone." *Which, who,* and *whom* are used largely in introducing nonrestrictive (not defining, not limiting) clauses: "This man, *who* pays his bills promptly, is liked by everyone." *That* is often used in illiterate or wordy expressions. For example, *that there* is both wordy and illiterate (*that there* child). *That is to say* is a wordy way to express "I mean" or "namely."

That and *which* (especially *which*) are often used in such a way as to create doubt about an antecedent. Avoid saying, for example, "They are coming if their daughter is well enough, *which* I doubt," because *which* has no definite antecedent. Say, instead, ". . . is well enough. However, I doubt that she will be."

theirselves. This is an illiteracy. Say "themselves."

there is, there are. In rare instances, each of these phrases is needed, but in most constructions they can be omitted without loss. "Three crooks are in this room" says the same thing as (and is a word shorter than) *"There are* three crooks in this room." The easiest way to choose between *is* and *are* following *there* is to turn the sentence around. If what follows is plural (more than one), say "are"; if only one (singular), say "is." ("There *are* oysters in this stew." "There *is* an oyster in this stew.")

these kind. See *kind.*

they. This word (as well as *their, theirs,* and *them*) should have a definite antecedent (something to which it refers) or should not be used. "*They* have good weather in Hawaii" is a vague statement because no one can tell what or whom is meant by *they.* "Hawaii has good weather" makes sense. "In my job, *they* have good training in office techniques" is much clearer if it is revised: "In my job, good training is provided in office techniques."

thick. This word is informal (or slangy) when used to mean (1) friendly, intimate and (2) excessive. Trite or slangy expressions to avoid: *lay it on thick* (overstate or exaggerate), *thick as thieves* (intimate as fellow criminals), *through* *thick and thin* (good and bad times), *a thick fog, thick with smoke, thick with dust, a thick accent,* and *thick-skinned* (insensitive).

thing. This is an all-purpose word used so loosely that it often has no real meaning. For instance, instead of saying "One *thing* I like about him . . ." why not say one "characteristic," "trait," or "distinctive feature?" Because *thing* means "whatever can be thought or believed to have an existence," a good rule to follow is this: *never* say "thing" unless you have some specific entity (object) in mind and then mention the entity itself. This is a *thing* (rule, prescription, item of advice) none of us will ever achieve or do, but it's a *thing* (endeavor, activity, counsel of perfection) we should try to follow.

thingamabob, thingamajig. These are slang terms for a gadget or miscellaneous item the name of which has been forgotten or never known.

think. See *calculate. Think* appears in such trite and tiresome expressions as *think things over, have another think coming, think it through, think up,* (contrive, devise), *think better of, think nothing of, put on your thinking cap, think twice, think aloud,* and *think out. Think to* is a narrowly dialectal term for "remember to" ("I didn't *think to* give Willie his supper.") *Methinks* is an obsolete term. See *I don't think.*

this here. An illiteracy, just as is *that there.*

those kind. See *kind.*

though. See *although.* Only *though* can be used at the end of a sentence, and only *though* can appear in such phrases as *even though* and *as though.*

thusly. This is an illiteracy, one that serves no useful purpose since *thus* does the job needed. If you overuse *thus,* try *therefore, consequently,* or (although wordy) *to some extent.*

ticker. This word is slang when employed to mean either "the heart" ("Jack has a bad *ticker*") or "a watch."

ticket. A slang term for "the proper thing" ("That's just the *ticket* for a weary man"). Use sparingly such trite expressions as *vote the straight ticket* (slate of candidates), *kill a ticket* (dispose of a legal summons), and *that's the ticket* (that's right).

tie. This becomes a slang word when used in *tie one on* (become intoxicated). *Tie* appears in such clichés as *old school tie, tie-in sale* (purchase of two or more items in a connected transaction), *traffic tie-up, tied to his mother's apron strings, tie down* (restrict, hinder, or complete arrangements), *tie the knot* (get married), *tie a tin can on a dog's tail,* and *all tied up* (completely occupied).

tight. This term is slang when used to mean "drunk" or "stingy" (*tight* with his money). *Tight* appears in such slangy or hackneyed expressions as *tightwad* (a miser), *tight-fisted* (stingy), *tight-lipped* (grim, reticent), *tight end* (football jargon), *in a tight spot, a tight fit, a tight feeling in the chest, a tight market, sleep tight, walk a tightrope, tight-knit organization, tight control, a tight schedule, a tight race, sit tight, tight across the shoulders* (chest), and *up tight* (tense).

'til, till, until. The first of these terms is a shortened, variant form of *until*. *'Til* seems needless, is obsolescent even in poetic diction, and should be used rarely, if at all. *Till* and *until* are interchangeable; each normally means "before," "up to," or "when." *Until* is usually preferred over *'til* at the beginning of a statement because of its sound and to prevent confusion. *'Till* is nonstandard.

time. Try to avoid overuse of such trite, informal, or slangy expressions as *working against time, at the same time* (*simultaneously* does the work of four words), *behind the times, for the time being, in no time, high time* (overdue), *in good time* (reasonable time, or "when due"), *keep time on, make time* (slang for ardent pursuit of someone), *from time to time, be on time, since time immemorial, the big time, time and time again, time out of mind, the time was ripe, a sign of the times, the best time of your life, in time of war, my time had come, serve time, a hot time in the old town, a time for everything, ahead of time, at one time, beat someone's time* (slang for prevailing over a rival), *kill time, mark time, pass the time of day,* and *take time by the forelock.*

tiny. See *teeny.*

'tis, 'twas. Each of these terms was once popular but is now considered poetic and archaic. Prefer *it is* and *it was.*

to. See *in*. In addition to its primary meaning of "in the direction of," *to* is used before a verb to indicate an infinitive (*to* walk, *to* eat). In this usage, it may appear in place of the infinitive: "You may eat now if you want *to* [eat]." *To* is unnecessarily added to many verbs that mean "assert": *admit to, certify to, swear to.* The addition of *to* in such instances results in weakening of the verb as well as wordiness. *To* is nonstandard in the sense of *at:* Say "Jack was *at* home," not "*to* home." *To* should be omitted after *where.* Say "Where are you going?" not "Where are you going *to?*" *To-do* is slang for "a stir," "bustle," "a fuss." Among overworked expressions involving *to* are *rotten to the core, starved to death, to that end, torn to shreds, not to my liking, come to* (return to consciousness), *added insult to injury, wet to the skin, to the best of my knowledge, turn to with a will, to and fro,* and *to a T* (here, *T* stands for "tittle" — a small quantity, jot, particle — the expression means "down to the last small detail").

token. A tiresomely used phrase is *by the same token,* in which *token* has a meaning of "sign," "mark," or "symbol." Either *moreover* or *furthermore* will express in *one* word what this trite phrase does in four. *In token of* is also hackneyed, as is *token of esteem.* Possible substitutes for *token: sign, emblem, index, symbol, mark, stamp, image, evidence, proof, memento, augury,* and *indication.*

tomato. You may say tuh·MAY·toh or tuh·MAH·toh, but don't slangily say either when referring to a girl or woman.

too. This word has basic meanings of "also," "as well," and "in addition." When *too* is preceded by *not* (*not too* smart, *not too* hopeful), the meaning of *too* is "very" and, in some instances, contributes to understatement. In a remark such as "It is not *too* likely to rain today," *too* adds little, if anything, and can be deleted. If you think some qualification of the idea of *likely* is needed in this sentence, say "none too" or "not very."

top. Make an effort to cut down on the use of such hackneyed, informal, or slangy expessions as *blow one's top* (lose one's temper), *on top of* (in control, fully informed about), *top off* (finish), *top dog,* (person in authority), *top-drawer* (of high quality), *top-flight* (superior), *topnotch* (excellent), *tops* (topmost, first-rate), *top secret* (highly confidential), *top-hole* and *tip-top* (of highest quality), *on top of the world, over the* *top, the top of the class, take it to the top, top kick* (someone in command), *top-level* (on a high level), and *top priority.*

The word *top* is used so much (*top* post, *top* job, *top* official, *top* player, etc.) that we should put *top* at the bottom and occasionally use words such as *chief, first, foremost, leading, highest, important,* and *principal.*

tore. The past tense of *tear* (pull apart, rend) is *tore;* the past participle is *torn.* Never say "had tore" (say "John *had torn* his coat.") If you get tired of such expressions as *torn down, torn at, torn into, torn off,* and *torn up,* remember that substitutes for *torn* (*tear*) include *rend, rip, split, sever, slit,* and *slash.*

touch. As a verb, this word is slang when used to mean "beg or wheedle a loan." *A touch* is slang for the act of getting a loan. *Touch* appears in overworked, informal, or slangy phrases such as *touch and go* (precarious state of affairs), *touché* (a good point made in discussion or argument), *in close touch, touch off* (start something), *touched my heart, a touch of flu* (or whatever), *the touch of the master, a touch of salt* (or sugar, etc.), *put the touch on, touch it with a ten-foot pole,* and *an easy touch* (a gullible, generous person).

tough. This word is overused as a synonym for "difficult" (a *tough* job). Currently *tough* is being employed in so many different and even bizarre meanings that only the user knows what he means by saying that something or other *is* tough, *looks* tough, or *acts* tough. *A tough* is an informal term for a rowdy person, a ruffian. *Tough deal, a tough man to work for, a tough act to follow, a tough neighborhood, a tough gang,* and *tough luck* are familiar, trite expressions. Among synonyms for *tough* are *durable, firm, hard, inflexible, stalwart, strong, sturdy,* and *tenacious.*

toward, towards. These words for "in the direction of," "approaching," and "with regard to" are interchangeable. Take your pick. However, *toward* is one letter shorter and somewhat easier to pronounce.

trade up. In recent years, this phrase has been widely overused to mean "substituting for something that one has something else that is more elaborate and expensive." People in *trade* (business, commerce, industry) need this phrase. Everyone else can do without it.

transpire. The primary meanings of *transpire* are "to become known" and "to give off vapor through the pores." (The Latin words *trans* and *spirare* mean "breathe out" or "breathe through.") In the meaning of "happen," "come to pass" ("The event *transpired* promptly at noon"), *transpire* is informal and not recommended. Say *happen, occur, eventuate, come about, befall.*

tremendous. This word means "capable of making one tremble," "terrible," "enormous." It is overused as an intensive meaning "wonderful" and "marvelous." When you use *tremendous*, stop to think whether tremors, wonders, or marvels are really involved.

trigger. This word, as a verb, was once confined to *triggering* a gun but is now overused to mean "initiate," "set in motion," and "activate." *Trigger* an occasional sentence by the use of *begin, cause, produce, set off, signal*, and *start* or one of the words used here in explaining current meanings of *trigger*.

trip. A slang term when used to mean a protracted hallucination caused by such drugs as mescaline or LSD. *Trip* is archaic when it refers to dancing nimbly or lightly.

triumphal, triumphant. These words are related, but *triumphal* is usually connected with a planned celebration (a *triumphal* reception). *Triumphant* means "exultant," "victorious" (the *triumphant* basketball team).

trousers. See *pants*.

true. This word is overused (perhaps because it's short and simple) in many phrases where *factual, veracious, actual, real, honest, trustworthy, constant, steady*, and *staunch* might be more precise and surely would be less hackneyed. Have you ever heard, or used, such expressions as *true blue, true feelings, true interest, a true friend, the true meaning, a true copy, a true balance, in true order, a true size, come true, true to life*, and *true love*? And is there any such thing as a *false* fact? Why, then, do we persist in saying "the *true* facts"?

try and. *Try to* avoid saying *try and*, a phrase in widespread but nonstandard use. See *and, come and*.

tune. In the sense of adjusting a television or radio receiver, *tune in* is a standard phrase. The phrase, however, has become a cliché in the sense of "hear," "begin to listen to," or "become sympathetic to." ("That speaker *tuned* me *in* quickly.") *Change one's tune* and *to the tune of* are such firmly established clichés that it will be difficult to *tune out* their appeal.

turn. Among trite or slangy expressions to use sparingly or avoid entirely are *turn a phrase, turns my stomach, turn the corner, turned his head, turn a deaf ear, turn a molehill into a mountain, turn one's hair, turned against him, turn me on, turn of events, at the turn of the century, wait your turn, a turn for the worse* (or better), *an ill turn, at every turn, to a turn, turn in one's grave, not turn a hair, give someone a turn, turn an honest dollar* (until inflation, the phrase was *honest penny*), *turn the other cheek, turn the tables on someone, turn up like a bad penny, turn up one's nose, out of turn, turnabout is fair play, a large turnout, turn tears into laughter, turn one's back* (or face), *turn back the clock*, and *turn in one's chips.*

type. When accompanied by *of*, *type* is standard usage in expressions such as "that *type of* dress." When *of* is omitted, the expression is nonstandard: "that *type* dress." *Type* is a less general word than *kind* and *sort* (both of which, see) and is preferably used when a clearly defined category is involved. In all other instances, prefer *kind* or *sort*. ("He is the *kind* — or *sort*, not *type* — of man we can believe.") Especially avoid such expressions as *high-type person* and *low-type store*. *Type of a* is wordy; omit *a*.

typical. Overused by nearly everyone, *typical* really should be restricted to the meanings of "distinctive," "characteristic," "representative," and "emblematic." *Typical of* is *not* a synonym for *like*. Say "Dr. Flack is *like* most pediatricians," *not* "Dr. Flack is *typical of* most pediatricians."

U, non-U. These are recent, informal phrases, imported from Great Britain. *U* designates "belonging to, appropriate to, language habits and other customs of the so-called upper, or sophisticated, classes." *Non-U* means *not* "belonging to, etc." These vague terms are becoming hackneyed.

ugly. Such phrases as the following, although not "repulsive" and "offensive" (basic meanings of *ugly*), are nonetheless as "objectionable" (another meaning of ugly) as all triteness is: *ugly duckling, an ugly temper, ugly as sin, an ugly frame of mind, ugly crime, ugly customer* (hostile person), and *ugly as a mud fence.*

uh-huh, huh-uh. The former sound (hardly a *word*) is an attempt through spelling to indicate a grunted *yes. Huh-uh* (or *hunh-uh*) somewhat resembles the sound of a grunted *no.*

ultra. This is both an adjective and a prefix meaning "exceeding what is ordinary, common, proper" and "to an extreme or excessive degree." It is a useful word (and word element), but it appears with wearisome frequency in such terms as *ultramodern, ultrafashionable, ultraconservative,* etc. Pronounce the word UHL·truh.

umbrella. Careless speakers transpose the *e* in this word and say uhm·BUHR·ella. The word should be pronounced uhm· BREL·uh.

umpteen. A slang term meaning "a large, indefinite number": "He has *umpteen* friends in that town."

uninterested. See *disinterested.*

unique. In careful speech, *unique* is not qualified by modifiers. If something is *unique,* it is *unique,* period. Avoid saying "rather unique," "most unique," "very unique," etc. *Unique* can, however, be modified by terms that do not actually imply degree, such as *almost unique* and *more nearly unique.* Also, *unique* is overused; occasionally say *exceptional, rare, remarkable, unusual, novel, uncommon, peerless, inimitable, incomparable,* etc.

unless. This word means "except on the condition that." Its use as a synonym for *without* is nonstandard. Say "I will not go *unless* you go with me," not "I will not go *without* you go with me." *Unless and until* is a nonstandard phrase; the terms overlap. Do not say "I will not write *unless and until* you write me." Either word will convey the full meaning intended.

unmindful. If you use this rather cumbersome word, say *unmindful of,* not *unmindful about.* More precise words include *forgetful, careless, oblivious, heedless,* and *neglectful.*

unmoral. See *amoral.*

unpractical. See *impractical.*

until. See *'til.*

up. This small, useful word understandably appears often in everyone's speech. However, *up* is unnecessary in the majority of constructions in which it appears. No need or excuse exists for its presence in such verb phrases as *open up, close up, divide up, add up, hurry up, finish up, settle up, tally up, stack up, drink up, think up, do up,* and a dozen other similar expressions. *Up* is informal and trite in such expressions as *hard up* (without money), *it's up to you, not up to it, up to mischief, up until,* and *what's up? On the up and up* is slang for "honest" and for "improving conditions." Among hackneyed expressions that are informal or slangy may be cited *up and coming, upbeat, up-to-date, ups and downs* (periods of good and bad luck), *up against it, up and around, all up with* (at or approaching the end), and *upchuck* (slang for "vomit.") As a verb, *up* is an impropriety in the sense of "begin or start abruptly." ("Bruno *upped* and ran out of the house.") *Uppish* and *uppity* (arrogant, snobbish) are informal terms fortunately less used now than formerly.

upward. Both *upward* and *upwards of* should not be used in the senses of "almost," "about," or "a bit less than." *Upward* and *upwards of* should be applied only to what is in excess of a stated amount. ("His accident cost him *upwards of* $500"—meaning in excess of that amount.)

urban, urbane. Each of these words is derived from a Latin term referring to a "city," but they have distinct meanings and pronunciations. *Urban* (UHR·bun) means "pertaining to a city," "characteristic of city life." *Urbane* (uhr·BAYN) has a meaning of "reflecting elegance or sophistication," "polished," "suave."

us, we. These are plural personal pronouns in the first person. *Us* is in the objective case, *we* in the nominative. Choose between them according to the function each fulfills in your statement. "*We* taxpayers are entitled to a referendum." "For *us* workers, the outlook is doubtful." After *as* or *than* in a comparison in which the first term is in the objective case, say *us.* ("The clerk gave *them* more than *us.*") But say "Those men are taller than *we*" (because *we* is understood as the subject of the omitted verb *are,* precisely as *us* is the object of the omitted verb "gave" in the preceding sentence.) Also, see *I.*

used to. This is a standard idiom denoting "action customary in the past." ("Jacob *used to* eat more than he should have.") *Used to* is often pronounced in rapid, informal speech as "usta" or "uster." Try to say YOOZD·TO.

usual. For this overworked word occasionally substitute *accustomed, customary, habitual,* or *typical,* none of which is so usual as *usual.*

valet. Once, the only standard pronunciation of this word was VAL·ay. Now also fully acceptable is VAL·it.

venal, venial. These words look alike and sound somewhat alike, but *venal* (VEE·nuhl, VEE·n'l) has a connotation of corruption. *Venial* (VEE·ni·uhl), a term of mild reproach, means "excusable," "pardonable." It may help to keep them straight by remembering that *venal* comes from a Latin term meaning "for sale" *(venalis)* and *venial* from Latin *venia* (forgiveness). Associate *venal* with *penal* and *venial* with *genial.*

verbal. See *oral.*

verbatim. This word, meaning "word for word," "in exactly the same words," is pronounced vur·BAY·tim.

very. This word is used in several informal and not quite standard ways (*very* delayed, *very* forgotten), but the only real objection to *very* is that it is uttered over and over in almost every conceivable instance calling for an intensive. One language expert once told his students never to say or write *very* unless they meant *damn* or *damned* — and then to delete the profanity. The message: use *very* very little or not at all.

via. This overused Latin word meaning "by way of" should be pronounced VAI·uh or VEE·uh. *Via* should not be used in the sense of "by means of," as in this faulty statement: "Aid was rendered the stricken country *via* food, clothing, and medicines."

victory. This word loses a sound in hurried speech. Try to pronounce all three syllables: VIK·tuh·ri or VIK·tuh·ree.

video. Usage has made *video* (VID·ee·oh) a standard term. It refers to the visual portion of a televised broadcast, as distinguished from the sound part, *audio* (AW·dee·oh). In general usage, *video* means "television."

VIP. This informal term (the letters stand for "very impor-

tant person") is hackneyed but undeniably useful. Say each
letter separately.

virtual. See *actual*.

virtually. See *practically*.

vital. This word means "that which is necessary for existence," "essential," "indispensable." *Vital* is both overused
and misused because in few applications is it used to mean
what it really means. It is absurd to say "Helen's presence
at the dance is *vital*" unless it is undeniable that Helen's
absence will cause the dance to be an unqualified failure.
Generally related words with less exaggerated meanings
than *vital* include *needed, wanted, beneficial, helpful, advan-
tageous, desirable, useful, salutary*, and *serviceable*, and, in
the sense of "important," *effective, substantial, weighty,
momentous, consequential, considerable, eminent, prominent, conspicuous*, and *significant*.

vocation. See *avocation*.

wacky. This slang word (also spelled *whacky*) means "silly,"
"crazy." Don't use it, although it derives from a standard
word, *whack* (a blow, a slap).

wad. A slang term for "a large amount" ("a *wad* of clothes,"
"a *wad* of money").

wait. This word, as verb and noun, appears in such hackneyed expressions as *wait on hand and foot, waiting for the
day, wait one's turn, lie in wait, play a waiting game, wait
someone out*, and *on the waiting list*. In the sense of "serve"
or "supply the needs of," *wait on* is a sound idiom, but it is
illiterate when used to mean "await," "wait for." Say "Don't
wait *for* us any longer" *not* "wait on" — unless you are
speaking to servants or attendants. Also idiomatic but overused and informal are *wait out* (delay, or hang on, until a
result is achieved); *wait up* (halt and wait or postpone going
to bed); and *wait tables* (serve food).

walk. This is an essential word in English, but it need not
appear so often in expressions like *walk the plank, walk of
life, walk to glory, walk off with, walk away from, walk out
on, walking on air, a walking encyclopedia, walk on tiptoe,
walking the floor, walkaway* (easy victory), and *walking
papers* (notification of dismissal).

want. In meanings of "fail to have," "be without," and

"desire," *want* is widely and correctly used. It appears in numerous well-known idiomatic phrases such as *want in* and *want out* (both informal) and in *want for* (have need of), *want down, want off, want through, want by,* and *want up. Want for* is nonstandard when used in the meaning of "wish" or "desire." Do not say "I *want for* you to come with me." *Want* is sometimes confused with *wont* (custom, habit) and *won't* (a contraction of "will not"). In careless or rapid speech, *want to* sounds like *wanna.* It shouldn't.

war paint. A somewhat dated slang phrase for "cosmetics" or "finery."

was, were. Do you say "I wish I *was* there" or "I wish I *were* there"? Do you say "If I *was* you" or "If I *were* you"? Whether you say *was* or *were* in such constructions, you have much company. Actually, you should say *were* in both quoted sentences, even though *was* and *were* are alike in that they form the past tense of the verb *be.* It's a question of "mood," the state of mind or the manner in which a statement is made: a fact (*indicative* mood); a request or command (*imperative* mood); a condition or probability (*subjunctive* mood).

The subjunctive mood (here the form *were*) is generally used to express (1) a condition contrary to fact, (2) a supposition, (3) an improbable condition, (4) uncertainty or doubt, (5) necessity, (6) parliamentary motions, and (7) a desire. In "I wish I *were* there" the subjunctive *were* is standard because "I" is *not* there (a condition contrary to fact) and also because the speaker is expressing a desire. One of the same conditions applies to the second quoted sentence. Use *were* (the subjunctive) not *was* (the indicative) in such sentences as these: "Suppose he *were* to arrive now." (Supposition). "He drank ale as if it *were* going to be prohibited forever." (An improbable condition). "Roberta wishes that she *were* going to be invited." (Desire).

Now that these distinctions have been made, you can relax in the sure knowledge that *was* is heard at least as often as *were* in statements such as those cited. But if your aim is to speak as perfectly as you can, remember the distinction between the indicative and subjunctive moods.

wash. This verb appears in numerous correct idiomatic

phrases (*wash off, wash away, wash down*, etc.) and in several expressions that are hackneyed, informal, or slangy: *come out in the wash, wash one's hands of, washed by waves, washed overboard*, and *wash dirty linen in public. Wash* is slang when used to mean "test" or "prove convincing" ("That story won't *wash*"). *Wash out* is slang when it means "to fail" ("The trainee *washed out* of the course"). Synonyms for *wash* include *bathe, clean, launder, mop, scrub*, and *swab*.

way. *Way* appears in so many tired phrases that good speakers find a "way" to avoid it. Some of the following expressions may seem essential, but less trite *ways* can be found to express the meaning of *in a bad way, clear the way, show me the way, the straight and narrow way, on my way, the American way of life, have it your way, if I had my way, by way of, go out of the way, have a way with, pave the way for, see my way clear to, in the family way, lead the way, a long way from home*, and *come a long way*. Except as the name of a committee, *ways and means* is a wordy phrase since "ways" and "means" are interchangeable. The phrase *in any way, shape, or form* is redundant because these terms in most situations are synonymous.

we. See *us*.

weather, whether. Since the former refers to "atmosphere" and the latter is a rather indefinable conjunction, *weather* and *whether* are not confused in meaning. But in speech they often sound alike. Say WETH·uhr (weather) and WHETH·uhr (whether).

weeny, weentsie. These words, blends of *wee* and *tiny*, sound, and are, both coy and juvenile.

well. See *good*. Among slang phrases employing *well* may be mentioned *well-fixed* and *well-heeled* (financially secure, solvent); *well-oiled* (drunk); and *well-yoked, well-tied*, and *well-knotted* (suitably married). Since *well* is joined to several hundred words ranging alphabetically from *well-abolished* to *well-wrought* and *well-yoked*, why not leave *well* alone and never use such clichés as *leave well enough alone*? In other trite words, give *well* a *well-earned rest*. Possible substitutes for *well* include *suitably, appropriately, fortunately, properly, adeptly, skillfully, accurately, efficiently*, and *amply*.

were. See *was.*

whadda, whatcha, whassa. In careless, hurried speech, *what do you* often sounds like *whadda* or *whatcha*, and "what is" comes out as *whassa.* If your hearers understand, all right. But if they don't, or if you wish to acquire a reputation for good speech, slow down and enunciate.

whammy. A slang term meaning a "hex," "jinx," or "spell" ("He put the *whammy* on me").

whangdoodle. Slang for a fanciful creature with unknown and undefined characteristics.

what all. In a question such as "*What all* does he expect of me?" *what all* is considered narrowly dialectal or illiterate. *All* is apparently added for intensifying effect, but its addition is not recommended in either *what all* or *who all* ("*Who all's* there?")

what for. This phrase appears in two nonstandard uses. When it means "punishment" or "reproof" ("The boss gave George *what for* because he was late"), it constitutes an illiteracy. When *what for* is substituted for *why* ("*What* did you do that *for*?"), the expression may be considered either illiterate or just plain wordy.

when, as, and if. See *if and when.*

whence. This word has a built-in meaning of "from." *From whence* is a wordy phrase; use *whence* alone.

where. This word is nonstandard as a conjunction equivalent to *that.* Use *that* instead of *where* in statements such as "I see *where* the Senate is going to recess" and "Jim read *where* his favorite team had lost two straight games." *Where at* ("*Where at* is the house?") is a wordy, illiterate phrase. Omit *at.*

whether. See *if, whether.*

which. See *that.*

while. This word, employed to mean "but" and "although," most often means "at the same time that." Only its use with reference to *time* is well-established, and careful speakers avoid such statements as "*While* he had several motorcycles, he objected to the pollution caused by burning gasoline." For *while*, substitute "although."

who, whom. No situation in English speech and writing causes more difficulty for more persons than choosing be-

tween *who* and *whom* (and *whoever, whomever* when they
are used). Current usage studies indicate that the distinction between these forms is breaking down, partly because
keeping them straight is difficult and partly because many
speakers begin a sentence or clause with *who*, not knowing
how they are going to end the statement. Because most
people consider *whom* less natural than *who*, they sometimes disregard grammatical requirements and use *who*
even when *whom* is clearly indicated.

The grammatical rule is simple: use *who* (or *whoever*) as
the subject of a verb or as a predicate pronoun. Use *whom*
(*whomever*) as the object of a verb or preposition. Here are
some correct illustrations.

1. The question of *who* can go is unimportant. (Here, *who*
is the subject of "can go." The entire clause, "who can go," is
the object of the preposition *of*.)

2. This is the fireman *whom* we saw on top of the building. (Here, *whom* is the object of "saw.")

3. He asked me *who* I thought would be elected. (The
case of a pronoun depends upon its use and should not be
influenced by words that come between it and its antecedent. Check this sentence by omitting *I thought. Who* is then
seen to be the subject of "would be elected.")

4. I danced with the girl *whom* everyone suspected the
committee had chosen Beauty Queen. (Here, check by omitting "everyone suspected.")

When doubtful, substitute *he* or *him* for *who* or *whom* to
arrive at a decision.

1. Who/whom are you voting for? (For who/whom are you
voting? He/him are you voting for? (For he/him are you voting?)

2. This is the kind of public servant who/whom we need.
. . . we need who/whom.
. . . we need he/him.

One final word: unless you are reasonably certain that
whom is required, use *who*. You"ll be right much more than
half the time.

whodunit. A slang term for "mystery story" (who done it).

whole. *As a whole, on the whole, upon the whole,* and *out of whole cloth* (fictitious, without foundation) are trite expressions. *Whole hog* is slang for "everything." *Whole lot* is an informal term meaning "much," "a great amount."

why. As an adverb, conjunction, and noun, *why* is pronounced WHAI. (*Why* did you leave? That is *why* I dislike him.) As an interjection, *why* is pronounced WIGH (rhyming with "high.") "*Why*, he shouldn't have done that."

wide. See *broad.* Watch out for such hackneyed expressions as *wide of the truth, wide of the mark, the whole wide world, far and wide, wide-open town, widespread sickness* (poverty, etc.), and *a wide selection.*

widow, widower. The primary meaning of *widow* is that of a woman whose husband has died and who has not remarried. *Widower* is the male counterpart of *widow.* A *grass widow* is separated, divorced, or lives apart from her husband. (The expression comes from the meaning of "at grass," that is, "roaming loose.") A *golf widow*, (*tennis widow, fishing widow,* etc.) is a woman whose husband leaves her while he goes to play his favorite game. *Widow woman* is an illiteracy.

wiggle. Standard but hackneyed phrases containing *wiggle* are *wiggle out of, wiggle away from, wiggle one's finger,* and *wiggle one's toes. Get a wiggle on* (hurry) is a slang phrase.

will. See *shall.*

wingding. Slang for a lively or lavish party.

wire. Once considered informal when used to mean "a telegram" or "to telegraph," *wire* is now standard usage in these senses. However, don't overuse these hackneyed expressions involving *wire: under the wire* (within limits, deadline), *pull wires* (use connections or associations to advantage), *on the wire* (the telephone), and *lay wires for* (make preparations).

-wise. The practice of attaching this suffix to nouns with the meaning of "with reference to" and "concerning" is widespread and indiscriminate. No one objects to such a sensible word as *clockwise*, but how about *jobwise, attendance-wise, flavorwise, saleswise, economy-wise, politics-wise* and a dozen other terms that you can readily recall (or manufacture)?

Surely some clearer, less jargonish, means can be found to say what is conveyed by "*Taxwise*, your plan is sensible." Among informal, trite, or slangy expressions to avoid are *wise up, a wise move, get wise, wisecrack, wise guy, wisenheimer* (an offensive, arrogant person), *wise-acre* (an overly self-confident person), and *put someone wise.*

with. This otherwise inoffensive word appears in such to-be-avoided clichés as *in with* (on friendly terms, familiar), *with child* (pregnant), *get with it, part with, with all my heart, with a vengeance, with might and main, handle with care, with bated breath, make way with,* and *with the exception of.*

without. This adverb and preposition is nonstandard when used as a conjunction meaning "unless." It is correct to say "We can't live *without* money" (*without* is a preposition here), but it is incorrect to say "We can't live *without* we have money." See *unless.* Don't overuse such hackneyed expressions as *without let or hindrance, without a doubt, without rhyme or reason, make do without, without the law,* and *without a prayer.*

with the result that. Say *so* instead of this phrase.

won't never. This is a nonstandard expression, a *double negative,* which see.

wop. This is an informal, offensive word for "Italian."

work. Slang terms involving *work* (or *works*, the plural of the noun) include *shoot the works* (risk all), *work over* (inflict damage or injury), *the works* (everything), *give one the works,* and *gum up the works.* Trite expressions include *work your way up, work it out, if this works out, hard at work, make short work of, work a change, work into,* and *all worked up* (excited).

worse, worst. The former is the comparative of *bad,* the latter is the superlative. The phrase *if worst comes to worst* is illogical, but that's the way it should be said—provided you wish to use such a hackneyed expression at all. Informal, slangy, or trite expressions to avoid include *worse and worse, in the worst way, get the worst of it,* and *at the worst.* In the sense of "more," *worse* is not fully accepted; nor is *worst* in the sense of "most." Avoid such statements as "I dislike insects *worse* than I do snakes." *Worst kind* and *worst way* are slang for "much" and "very much." "She would like to aid you in the *worst way*" is ambiguous. If you revise the statement to "She would like *the worst way* to aid you," you may have added suspicion of immorality to plain confusion.

would. See *shall*.

wow. As an interjection, *wow* is unobjectionable for informally expressing surprise or pleasure. When it is used as a noun meaning "great success" ("The play was a *wow*"), it becomes slang. *To wow* (move, influence, please) someone is to turn an innocent interjection into a slangy verb.

write-up. This fabricated word has become a standard noun and verb, but the same usage that has elevated it to respectability has reduced it to triteness. Possible substitutes: *report, account, notice, article, review, description, analysis*.

Xmas. You are not likely to say "X·mas" (EX·mus) rather than KRIS·muhs or KRIST·muhs, but it is well to know that this abbreviation is considered informal by all language students and irreverent by some Christians.

X ray, x-ray. This translation from German is now accepted as standard in its roles as noun, verb, and adjective. This is one term pronounced exactly as it looks.

yank. Spelled with a small letter, this word is informal in the sense of "pull," "jerk," "extract." With a capital letter (Yank) it is a shortened form of "Yankee." *Yank* and *Yankee* are probably derived from a Dutch name "Janke," a diminutive of "Jan" (John).

yeah. A tiresomely overused and informal variant of "yes."

yellow. Say YEL·oh, not YEL·uhr. Don't say *yellow* when you mean *cowardly*, unless you wish to be both slangy and trite. An even slangier term for "cowardly" is *yellow-bellied*.

yen. This importation from the Chinese is making its way toward respectability as a noun and verb meaning "a yearning," "a desire," and "to long for," "to want." As of now, *yen* is considered either informal or slangy.

yes-man. An overused informal term for a person who supinely agrees with a superior. Startle your friends and say *sycophant* (SIK·uh·fuhnt).

yet. This is primarily an adverb of time in the sense of "up to the present." For this reason, *yet* in this meaning should be used with a perfect tense, not with the simple past tense. "*Did* you *eat* yet?" is nonstandard; say "*Have* you *eaten* yet?"

yid. This derivation from Yiddish is an offensive, derogatory slang term.

you. When you are speaking directly to a person or group of persons, say *you.* If you wish to refer to a number of people in general and to no one in particular, use pronouns like *one* or *anyone* and general nouns such as *people, persons, citizens,* etc. It may not be rude but it certainly is informal to say to no one specifically "*You* can see the importance of good health" and "When *you* become a Girl Scout, *you* learn much useful information." (This indefinite use of *you* occurs more often in writing than in speaking because one's readers, unlike one's hearers, are rarely present.) Also, try to cut down on those tired "conversation fillers" *you see what I mean?* and *you know what?*

you all. This is an informal expression sometimes meaning only one person, sometimes meaning "all of you." In the latter sense it is unobjectionable, but since the phrase is not fully standard in every meaning, perhaps *all of you* should forget it.

yourself, yourselves. These are reflexive or intensive pronouns (give *yourself* a chance). They are not always interchangeable with *you.* Don't say "My wife plans to write to Mary and *yourself*"; substitute *you* for *yourself.* "I'm hoping that the Smiths and *yourselves* will vote today"; substitute *you* for *yourselves.* Say "*You*—not *yourself*—and your friends are welcome."

zealous. See *jealous.* The term for a zealous person is *zealot.* If you use it, say ZEL·uht. To express the same idea, you could use *fanatic, extremist, monomaniac, faddist,* or *enthusiast.*

zero hour. This word meaning "the time set for an attack" has become a cliché meaning "any critical moment." In this age of rockets and missiles, *H-hour* is likely to replace *zero hour* and itself become trite.

zoology. You say *zoo* the way it's spelled, so that it is only

natural to say ZOO·OL·uh·jee. The preferred pronunciation
is zoh·OL·uh·jee.

zoom. As a term in aeronautics, *zoom* applies only to upward
movement. Through usage, it now refers also to movement
over a level course ("The motorcycle *zoomed* along the high-
way"), but it is nonstandard when applied to downward
movement. Use *swooped* in a sentence such as "The king-
fisher *zoomed down* on its prey."

ZZZ. Can you think of an entry following this one alphabetically? ZZZ is used to represent the sound of a person snor-
ing. If when you speak you "say it right," whatever you say,
your listeners will never go *zzz*.

INDEX

Terms included in this index appear in Parts I and II (pages 1–73).

Items in Part III (pages 75–246) appear in alphabetical order.

73 74   12 11 10 9 8 7 6 5 4 3 2